READY, SET, PRACTICE

READY, SET, PRACTICE: ELEMENTS OF LANDSCAPE ARCHITECTURE PROFESSIONAL PRACTICE

Bruce G. Sharky
School of Landscape Architecture
Louisiana State University

JOHN WILEY & SONS, INC.

New York • Chichester • Toronto • Brisbane • Singapore

This text is printed on acid-free paper.

This publication is designed to provide accurate and
authoritative information in regard to the subject
matter covered. It is sold with the understanding that
the publisher is not engaged in rendering legal, accounting,
or other professional services. If legal advice or other
expert assistance is required, the services of a competent
professional person should be sought.

Library of Congress Cataloging in Publication Data:
Sharky, Bruce G.
    Ready, set, practice : Elements of landscape architecture
professional practice / Bruce G. Sharky.
       p.   cm.
    Includes bibliographical references (p.   ) and index.
    ISBN 0-471-55512-6 (cloth: acid-free paper)
    1. Landscape architecture—Vocational guidance.   I. Title.
SB469.37.S48   1994
712'.3—dc20   94-9041

Printed in the United States of America

10 9

To Nola, my wife and partner in life;
Ken, my friend and partner in business;
Aaron, Rebecca, and Rie, our children
who have made the business of life a joy.

■ CONTENTS

Preface   ix

1. Introduction   1

2. Historical Perspective   6

3. Ethical Perspectives and Professional Conduct   16

4. Forms of Professional Practice   25

5. Professional Continuum   40

6. Marketing Yourself   55

7. Professional Service   75

8. Organizational Perspectives   86

9. Starting a Small Design Firm   98

10. Business Marketing   114

11. Office Records   123

12. Life of a Project   135

13. Legal Issues   152

14. Professional Services Contracts   171

15. Technical Specifications   177

16. Contract Administration   186

17. Concluding Thoughts   206

Appendix I   209

Appendix II   **243**

Bibliography   **251**

Index   **259**

■■■■■ PREFACE

What I Wish for My Students

> That one goes out in a world having understood the value of living true to one's inner spirit—a world that augments one's innate creativity and makes expression of this spirit and creativity the prime goal.
>
> That one has no poverty in life or in the life of the world. That one has an understanding, compassionate heart and a mind that willingly explores both sides of every question. That one develops and relies upon one's own inner wisdom and not dubious pronouncements of outside authorities.
>
> That one develops one's own pathway to connect one's earth life with one's spiritual life. And most of all that one lives in a world without war.[1]
>
> —Anonymous

Landscape architects take great pride in celebrating the diverse nature of their field. It is this diverse nature that attracts people to consider a career in the profession. The opportunity to follow many different and unique paths seems to explain the intensity of commitment, enthusiasm, and always-fresh attitude of seasoned practitioners toward landscape architecture. Few practitioners complain of boredom or of having ended up in a dead-end, repetitious routine. Their formal training seems to have prepared them to accept new challenges. Most private practitioners cultivate a diverse clientele, working on myriad projects in different regions. Public practitioners find opportunities for advancing their interest in a perpetually changing legislative environment that their agencies must address.

Preparing students for a career in landscape architecture has become no easy task. The four-year curriculum, standard twenty years ago, is no longer adequate in terms of addressing both the knowledge and skill requirements of today and the increasingly diverse nature of the profession. The students entering the university today have also changed. Their preparation in the K-through-twelve stream is different from that of their counterparts twenty years ago. The demands of today's standard five-year, first professional undergraduate landscape architecture degree and three-year, first professional master's degree are enormous in terms of subject matter, knowledge, and skill diversity.

Introducing students to the ethical, business, financial, legal, management, contractual, and other nondesign aspects of the profession is currently approached with a single course, or in some cases a two-course sequence, called *professional practice.*

---

[1] This quote was adapted from a handwritten message I encountered on a public bulletin board through a serendipitous happenstance on a visit I made to Santa Fe, New Mexico on September 12, 1986. Although the message was left for someone else, I felt it captured an important message that I wish to share with my students. The quote is prominently placed outside my office door.

Most professional practice courses are stand alone offerings and follow a lecture or seminar format.

A separate professional practice course is taught in most, if not all, accredited landscape architecture programs at North American universities. This is in response to curriculum guidelines promulgated by the Landscape Architecture Accreditation Board. The subject material included in these courses varies widely. That there is no apparent consistency in course content is healthy, although some students may graduate ill-prepared to deal with some aspects of professional practice. Faculty assigned to develop a professional practice course do so according to what they believe are the requirements of the curriculum, taking into consideration the need for preparing students for practice in the real world.

Before writing this book, I contacted each accredited landscape architecture program through a letter survey. The purpose of this survey was to acquire a course description, syllabus, and other course materials for professional practice instruction used by each program. The materials received were used to assess the current course objectives, content, organization, and texts. My goal was to identify a common ground by which a new text on professional practice could be developed. Thirty-four responses were received. A content analysis was made of the course materials received. The results of this analysis revealed that 100-plus different topics were collectively covered as indicated in the course syllabi reviewed. Not all 100 topics were included in all the courses, nor were they given equal emphasis from school to school. Nevertheless, the number of topics indicates the diversity of subjects considered appropriate under the rubric of professional practice.

Additionally, a content analysis was made of the Landscape Architecture Registration Examination (LARE) in preparation for finalizing the topical content for this book. A comparison was made between LARE and the topics found in the course content analysis. A final outline was prepared and became the content structure for this book.

One objective of this book was to meet the needs of faculty teaching a professional practice course. This would be quite a feat, given the diversity of approaches currently followed in most professional practice offerings in North American landscape architecture programs. But I was equally motivated to write this book for another reason. I see a professional practice course as more than an endeavor to teach contracts, business, and specifications. Having been a partner in a landscape architecture practice myself, I found those young people we hired, fresh out of school, to be highly talented and adequately prepared in design. But they came to us poorly prepared to handle other important areas. They had little knowledge and even less awareness of most professional practice issues. Based on my own professional experience, particularly working with entry-level staff, and my current academic endeavors, I became interested in trying to reconcile the gap between a high degree of knowledge and understanding of design issues on the one hand and the largely inadequate level of knowledge and understanding of professional practice matters on the other hand. One obvious solution was to teach a professional practice course. Another solution was to write a book that would enhance the professional literacy of students and recent graduates.

I have also attempted to teach my students to appreciate the unique role ethics and professional conduct play in constituting the foundation of the landscape architecture profession. In developing my own lecture materials I have come to place a heavy emphasis on these virtues. This emphasis is the common thread I weave through the many topics covered in our course on professional practice. This same thread winds through many chapters of this book.

Although my professional experience has been primarily in the United States, I have worked in other countries for periods of up to one year. This work experience has included Canada. In this regard, much of what is covered in this book applies equally to Canada and the United States. Some exceptions might be found in the legal and contracts sections—even though the legal systems of both countries are based on English Common Law.

I have been fortunate to have had fine teachers and colleagues. From each I have come to understand the most fundamental aspects of landscape architecture as well as the more demanding challenges facing the profession. Geraldine Knight Scott, Mai Arbegast, Burt Litton, Garrett Eckbo, Robert Royston, and Robert Twiss inspired me and provided valuable insight during my academic preparations at the University of California at Berkeley.

During a sixteen-year partnership with Kenneth Pendleton at Land Design North in Anchorage, Alaska, I learned first-hand, through on-the-job training, the practical aspects of many of the topics covered in this book. My employment in public and other private offices has also contributed to my understanding of professional practice issues from several different perspectives.

In the process of writing this book I am indebted to many generous people. Professor Clifford Collier, FASLA, provided me with an appreciation for the finer points of ethics and professional attitudes (including the importance of maintaining a good sense of humor). My appreciation goes also to Ace Torre, FASLA, and Design Consortium for allowing me free reign in a picture-taking session of their office in New Orleans. Several colleagues in the School of Landscape Architecture at Louisiana State University, including Professors Neil Odenwald, Van Cox, Sadik Artunc, and Susan Turner, each, in their own way, gave valuable support and provided me with a forum to test ideas for early drafts of material. I must also thank Sandra Moody, the LSU College of Design librarian, who, knowing of my project, recommended numerous helpful references. To Professor Erin Wright of The School of Art, my appreciation for his assistance with several graphic arts elements.

The author gratefully acknowledges the guidance and support given by Dan Sayre, editor for John Wiley & Sons. I also wish to acknowledge those who reviewed early drafts of the manuscript, including Professors D. Rodney Tapp, ASLA, and Cameron R. J. Man, FASLA. I also acknowledge the help of Jeff Edwards, Jeff Elliott, and Steve Aldrich, graduate Landscape Architecture students at LSU, for their assistance during the trying days of finalizing certain difficult chapters. And I am grateful to Mr. Todd Steadman for his commentary, which led to the discussion of the public's perception of the profession presented in Chapter 7.

All the photographs in this book were taken by the author.

For allowing me to work undisturbed at my computer I owe our children, Aaron, Rebecca, and Rie, many weekend outings and attendance at more than a few matinees. And finally, I would like to thank my wife Nola for her encouragement throughout this project. Although nothing was put in writing when she agreed to my taking on this project, now that it is finished I should probably take my turn tending our garden.

BRUCE G. SHARKY, FASLA

Baton Rouge, Louisiana
May 1994

CHAPTER 1

Introduction to Professional Practice

This book is written in the belief that professional practice is one of the most fascinating subjects and certainly one of considerable importance for those preparing for a career in landscape architecture. I am not sure how successful I have been in instilling an interest or a curiosity in the subject in my students, although that is one of my goals for the course. Nevertheless, the course is taught each year.

With this chapter, we are about to open the door into the professional practice world of landscape architecture. Figure 1.1 is a picture of one such door you could very well open during your career. In this case, the door opens into the main office of a prominent landscape architectural firm.[1] During one's professional career there will be many occasions to approach, open, and cross the threshold of doors that mark the passageway to both routine activities and potential opportunities. These might include at least the following:

1. Interviewing a future employer.
2. Interviewing a prospective client for a project.
3. Presenting a proposal to obtain a line of credit from a bank.
4. Seeking a permit or zoning decision from a governmental agency.
5. Obtaining product information for materials or equipment to be specified on a project.
6. Presenting a master plan or design to a client, board, or commission.
7. Going back to school for advanced studies.

The overriding goal of this book is to open these doors by introducing the reader to a diverse range of topics important in preparing for a landscape architecture career. Much of the material covered in this book is given only cursory coverage in most studio-oriented university landscape architecture curricula. If treated as a discrete topic, such as landscape history or landscape ecology, the material may be covered in a lecture course. For the most part, however, much of what is covered in this book is generally left for the student to learn on the job, after graduation.

Although professional practice topics are covered in most accredited university programs, the learning of much of the material occurs during the apprenticeship stage of a professional's early career. As one advances, moving up the ranks from entry level to project landscape architect and then to office management positions, one is given greater responsibility in the business, operation, and management of an office. For most people entering a professional career, they can anticipate advancing up a career ladder. Each rung of the ladder represents a phase of the professional continuum. To advance to a succeeding

[1]Design Consortium, New Orleans, Louisiana.

Figure 1.1 Entrance to a private landscape architectural firm located in a downtown historical district in New Orleans.

rung requires the acquisition of a broader knowledge base and increased capabilities to handle more complex elements of a practice.

As one moves up the ranks in terms of responsibility, a process of continuing education occurs. This process is usually an informal one. The acquisition of new skills and knowledge is accomplished through practical experience, although some find the time to attend short courses or evening classes. As one assumes greater responsibility in an office, the learning curve shifts from primarily project production (planning and design) to personnel and office managment. As a manager, the landscape architect becomes more involved in contracts, specifications, business, and marketing. Much of the success of an office or agency is dependent on the capabilities of middle and upper management to learn and to acquire competency in these areas.

Successful landscape architectural professionals build on the knowledge and skills learned in school by acquiring additional expertise and skills after graduation. This process enables them to accept greater responsibility in the work they do, and eventually to assume a leadership role in the organization.

Figure 1.2 depicts an important relationship in landscape architecture. Leaders in the field of landscape architecture have acquired knowledge and specialized skills over time in

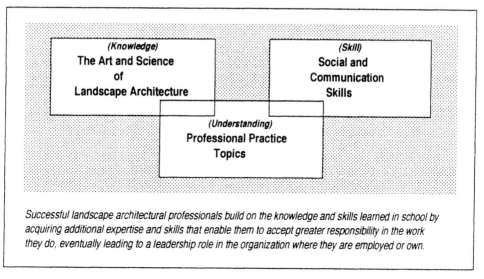

| (Knowledge)
**The Art and Science
of
Landscape Architecture** | (Skill)
**Social and
Communication
Skills** |

(Understanding)
Professional Practice
Topics

Successful landscape architectural professionals build on the knowledge and skills learned in school by acquiring additional expertise and skills that enable them to accept greater responsibility in the work they do, eventually leading to a leadership role in the organization where they are employed or own.

Figure 1.2   The balance of knowledge and skills.

their careers, enabling them to advance from follower to director in the organizations in which they practice. They have learned that to excel and become effective in achieving their professional goals they must balance the art and science of landscape architecture with social and communication skills, as well as master the body of knowledge under the general heading of professional practice. The mastering of all three areas provides the means for these individuals to effect creative works of longstanding value.

Chapter 1 provides an overview of the book's purpose and content. Chapter 2 provides a historical perspective of the landscape architectural profession. Emphasis is given to explaining the characteristics of the profession that make the practice of landscape architecture in North America unique in several ways. Ethics and a professional code of conduct have together elevated the standards of performance of those practicing landscape architecture. Ethics has also played an important role in forging the direction the profession has taken in the United States and is covered in Chapter 3. Chapters 4 and 5 describe the diversity of landscape architectural practice, and Chapter 6 provides guidance in finding employment. Chapter 7 explains the service nature of the profession while Chapters 8 through 11 focus on the process of starting a small firm, and the organization and marketing of a private practice. Chapter 12 describes the life of a project, from the inception of a design idea through work drawings, contracts, and construction. Chapters 13 and 14 review the legal issues and contracts involved in professional practice. Chapter 15 reviews technical specifications and the relationship between drawings and specifications. The chapters on legal issues are complemented by Chapter 16, on contract administration. This is the phase of a project where the landscape design is transformed from paper to reality.

The concluding chapter is offered as an epilogue. It contains a collection of thoughts on how to respond to aspects of the profession that do not neatly fall under any particular main topic heading. They are, nevertheless, ideas the author wishes to share in anticipating a long, professionally and personally rewarding career for his readers.

At the end of most chapters appears a section titled "In-Basket." The concept of the In-Basket is to present practical situations that represent real-life challenges encountered in

TABLE 1.1 Guide to Important Landscape Architecture Professional Practice Terms

1. Change order
2. Hold harmless clause
3. Mechanic's lien
4. Punch list
5. Standards of care
6. Performance bond
7. Sole proprietorship
8. Surety bonds
9. Cost plus contract
10. Statute of limitations
11. As-built drawings
12. Bid bond
13. Davis-Bacon wages
14. Certified payroll
15. Application for payment
16. Tort laws
17. Multiplier fee basis
18. Code of ethics
19. Contract administration
20. Notice to proceed
21. Substantial completion
22. Basic services
23. Stop work order
24. Third-party damages
25. Errors and omissions insurance
26. Materials lien
27. Bid instructions
28. Preliminary estimate of costs
29. Bidding and negotiations
30. Request for proposal (RFP)
31. Practice act
32. Liability insurance
33. Third-party claim
34. Submittal review request
35. "Or equal" clause
36. Liquidated damages
37. Construction easement
38. Public practice
39. A/E contract
40. Accounts receivable
41. Design development
42. Post construction evaluation
43. Supplemental services
44. Performance specifications
45. Contract documents
46. The Occupational Safety and Health Administration (OSHA)
47. Judicial jurisdiction
48. Observation
49. Substitution
50. Shop drawings
51. Occupany permit
52. Balance sheet
53. Marketing niche
54. Personal daily journal
55. Time sheet
56. Warranty period
57. Sub-consultant contract
58. Landscape ordinance
59. American Disability Act
60. Equal opportunity employer
61. Joint venture
62. Chapter S corporation
63. Prime consultant
64. Standard Forms 254 and 255
65. Proprietary specifications
66. Instructions to bidders
67. Lowest responsible bidder
68. Council of Landscape Architectural Registration Boards (CLARB)
69. Key man insurance
70. ASLA, AIA, and ASCE
71. Arbitration
72. Indemnify
73. Accrual basis
74. Procurement laws
75. Direct expenses

the profession. In formulating a response to each situation, the reader will draw from the chapter reading, finding a "hands-on" application of the material. The maximum benefit can be gained from formulating a fully worked out response or variety of responses if the In-Basket situations are discussed in groups of two or three individuals.

The material included in this book is essential to the practice of landscape architecture. Table 1.1 lists the key points covered in the book. This table can be used as a study guide in preparing for examinations. The more thoroughly you master professional practice subjects, the better your chance to move up the ranks from entry-level staff to middle and upper management, and eventually to become a business partner or agency director.

Figure 1.3   Grant Park, Chicago. A legacy of the City Beautiful Movement and the work of landscape architect Edward Bennett.

The leaders in the profession are those who have sufficiently grasped and developed a command of these terms and the material covered in this book. As leaders, they understand that to be an effective landscape architect, they must have an understanding of client and user needs, balanced with a working knowledge of human relations, business finances, people and project management, legal matters, and marketing subjects. The art and science aspects of landscape architecture are what attract most people to the field. The degree to which you can achieve financial and professional goals as well as make a contribution to your community is dependent on your skill in handling professional practice subjects.

CHAPTER 2

Historical Perspective: Toward Establishing the Profession

1. Introduction
2. Historical Perspective
3. Practice in the United States Compared with Rest of the World

1. INTRODUCTION

Landscape architects practicing their profession today would barely recognize the profession as practiced by their nineteenth-century forebears. Changes have come in education and training, development of skills and expertise, nature of practice, clientele, and professional values and attitudes. The profession started out as a few horticulturally oriented individuals, pretty much self-taught in design and who performed, more or less, in the role of labor foreman. Today, landscape architects are a well-trained, distinct group of planning and design professionals. Since Frederick Law Olmsted coined the term *landscape architecture,* the profession has evolved into an influential factor in the planning and design of the built environment and in the management of the natural environment.

These changes have come about as the body of knowledge, training, and skills have evolved. Intervention on the part of the U.S. government has also had an influence on the profession. Important government influences have included the park movement, environmental legislation, and various mission objectives of federal agencies, such as multiple use and sustainable management. Through these and other government agenda the profession has flourished with landscape architects becoming important players in assisting government to better manage the land and water resources of the nation. A number of individuals practicing the profession have made their mark and had their influence on the evolution of the profession. Their influence has not only shaped how the profession is practiced but has also led the profession to embrace certain attitudes that have further defined it. These attitudes have included, most notably, the acceptance of social consciousness in the thinking and work of landscape architects as well as a strong empathy for the environment.

Tracing the evolution of the profession is a fascinating journey that will be taken in an abbreviated manner in this chapter. It is not within the scope of this book to provide a detailed or exhaustive account of this journey, for it is done elsewhere (Figure 2.1) in the available literature.[1] The highlights of landscape architecture history, although abbreviated,

---

[1] See, for example, Laurie, *An Introduction to Landscape Architecture;* Newton, *Design of the Land;* Tobey, *A History of Landscape Architecture*; and Tishler, *American Landscape Architecture.*

Figure 2.1   Collection of books on landscape architecture on display at the ASLA Bookstore.

provide an overview of the major themes and contexts that have influenced the practice of landscape architecture in North America. The goal here is to understand the key personalities and events that together have shaped the practice of landscape architecture in the United States, producing a unique profession that is particularly relevant for the twenty-first century.

2. HISTORICAL PERSPECTIVE: FROM BABYLON TO THE END OF THE TWENTIETH CENTURY

Although the profession and the term *landscape architecture* are relatively modern, people have been practicing both the art and the science of landscape architecture for thousands of years. However, early practitioners were not necessarily associated with any distinct profession. An early precedent where landscape architectural principles were employed are the Hanging Gardens of Babylon. Principles of design similar to those considered by landscape architects were used in the design of public spaces and private gardens through the ages to Renaissance Europe. The design and installation of these early built landscapes were accomplished, for the most part, by an array of individuals and trades employed in a manner very different from today. Since there was no distinct landscape architecture profession during these earlier years, works deemed today as falling under the purview of landscape design were usually designed and executed under the direction of the owner or by someone who had the interest and the necessary experience or training relevant to the project. The person or persons overseeing the design and the installation probably would not have had any specialized design or horticultural training but would have been selected on the basis of leadership skills—their ability to manage people and their familiarity with the logistics of obtaining and handling land-scape and other materials—and/or selected from the more highly educated ranks of the day. The selection of the designers of the early gardens and public spaces was made with little apparent regard as to whether they had specialized training in landscape design.

From the Renaissance period until the nineteenth century, many of the notable works studied in landscape architecture history courses today would have been designed by the client or commissioned to someone trained in architecture, engineering, or perhaps art. During this period, the garden evolved into an art form, no longer relegated only to meeting the practicalities of food production. The science of horticulture also flourished, and became an important body of knowledge for those specializing in the craft of landscape design.

Post-Revolutionary United States

The influence of the Italian gardens spread to England during the Industrial Revolution. The Romantic movement took hold in the eighteenth and nineteenth centuries, establishing a landscape design tradition that continues in England and many parts of Europe even today. Both the Renaissance and the Romantic styles found fertile ground in the United States beginning with George Washington at Mount Vernon and Thomas Jefferson at Monticello. Washington, a competent surveyor, agriculturist, and horticulturist, laid out the grounds of his Virginia residences. Washington made use of the Romantic style, installing broad panels of lawn accentuated with simple plantings of trees and shrubs. He used plantings to define and articulate space as well as to enhance views to the surrounding countryside. Jefferson's remodeling of the gardens of his residence and his plans at the University of Virginia are an early indicator of America's emerging taste for the Romantic English style.[2] Washington and Jefferson are each considered to have been responsible for both the design and general oversight of the installations. The client, the designer, and the contractor were one and the same person. The labor force generally available to Washington and Jefferson on their property holdings more than likely installed the landscape plantings and associated elements under a foreman following their instructions.

Andre Parmentier, a Belgian who had established a nursery in Brooklyn, New York in 1824, designed some of the first completely new landscapes in the United States. In 1828 he described his style as a melding of the romantic and the picturesque, which he said was an attempt to oppose the formalism prevalent in most of the United States at the time.[3] He worked on several estates located along the Hudson River in New York practicing in a manner similar to what is called *design-build* today.

Andrew Jackson Downing further advanced the application of the picturesque in the United States. He argued in favor of the beauty of naturalistic landscapes. He believed the aesthetic and moral values of these landscapes were important to the young and industrializing nation. His appeal was to the middle-class, which was emerging in leaps and bounds due to the newly acquired wealth brought about by a rapidly developing economy. Downing's theories were well articulated in his popular book, *Treatise on the Theory and Practice of Landscape Gardening Adapted to North America,* published in

[2]Tobey, *A History of Landscape Architecture*, pp. 149–150.
[3]Laurie, *An Introduction to Landscape Architecture*, p. 37.

1841. In it Downing presented the view that landscape gardening was an art. Downing was a horticulturist with a farming background. His installed works of landscape drew heavily on these two areas. Downing, like Parmentier, obtained commissions primarily from private clients where he was hired to first design and then oversee the installation of the landscape. He was engaged in the capacity of a foreman, following the design-build model.

In nineteenth-century America, the theories of landscape design were in large part developed in response to a concern for public health and the unhealthy conditions becoming increasing prevalent in the Eastern cities. Those pioneering in what was to become the landscape architecture profession had a concern for morality associated with the idea that "nature itself is the source of moral inspiration."[4] Also during this time came the development of the Romantic movement, which came to influence theories of landscape design "based on informality, naturalism, and the picturesque."[5] The public park movement also emerged during this period and with it developed the informal idiom of curvilinear drives and paths, irregular-shaped lakes, informal landscape plantings, and rustic furnishings. Park planning and design emerged as distinct areas of specialization with the growth of park systems in cities throughout the United States. Park planning and design became an increasingly important, specialized area of practice for those offering their services as landscape architects.

The Influences of Olmsted and Others

The man who would become a leader of the post–Civil War period in landscape architecture was Frederick Law Olmsted. Olmsted's approach to the practice of the field greatly influenced the process and nature of professional practice of landscape architecture in the United States. According to his design philosophy, Olmsted, like Downing, saw landscapes as a cure for social ills of the emerging urban population density. Olmsted was interested in the integration of large, parklike open spaces into cities, believing the American people had become displaced as the country rapidly industrialized. Every city, he believed, should have a park at its heart. He believed physical health depended upon an antidote to urban decline. He was able to apply his theory when he and Calvert Vaux designed Central Park in New York City in 1858. It was while designing Central Park that Olmsted coined the term *landscape architecture.*

Olmsted believed the term *landscape gardening* limited the focus to the garden. He felt a more comprehensive term was needed that would encompass "mountain, sky, and garden," which better represented concerns he and other like-minded designers expressed in their designs.[6] As the demand for his services increased, Olmsted established his firm, which grew in stature and influence with many important works implemented throughout the United States.

Olmsted expressed great interest in the landscape architect's ability to improve the quality of community and urban life, and he introduced environmental conservation ethics to the profession. In 1865, he was able to petition for the preservation of the region that has since come to be known as Yosemite National Park. Olmsted was instrumental in estab-

[4]Laurie, op. cit, p. 65.
[5]Laurie, op. cit, p. 65.
[6]Tobey, op. cit, pp. 37–38.

lishing an important legacy by contributing to the development of the National Park Service, which was established in 1916.

Jens Jensen, an immigrant to the Midwest from Denmark in 1884, was the first landscape architect to establish the philosophy that beauty was everywhere. He maintained that there was no longer a need to look to Europe for inspiration. He was an early proponent of regional expression, arguing for an approach that sought inspiration from the region in which one would be designing. Jensen's work is marked by the use of native, indigenous plant species. His philosophy was characterized by an appreciation for nature and looking toward the power and the teachings of the land. Jensen's theories have been recently "rediscovered" as interest in conservation and regionalism have become popular.

In 1899 came the establishment of the American Society of Landscape Architects (ASLA). In the next year, 1900, the first formal educational program in landscape architecture was begun at Harvard University. By 1910, the professional society had grown from its original 11 founding members to 68. One decade later, the profession had nearly doubled, despite the fact that many landscape architects left the profession to establish the even newer profession of city planning. In 1993, the membership of ASLA was over 10,000 with an estimated 30,000 practitioners in the United States.

The Changing Nature of Landscape Architectural Practice

It is important to note that the nature of practice has not always been, as it is today, dominated by the private design consulting firm. The change in how landscape architects practice came about sometime near the end of the nineteenth century. This change saw the landscape architect shift from principally the role of a foreman or person hired to oversee the execution of designs (perhaps landscape designs of their creation or that of their clients) to that of today as a principal in a firm or a professional employee hired on a consulting basis to prepare design plans. Certainly the Olmsted office was in the forefront as the change occurred. The landscape architect as a design or planning consultant was a mode of practice that came to dominate the profession after World War II. More recently, however, design-build has become an increasingly important form of professional practice. The reemergence of the design-build model can be explained in part as the result of changing client preferences and economic influences as well as the personal preferences of landscape architects themselves. In some regions of the country the design-build model has come to dominate, for example, in the rural midwestern and the southern states.

Women in Landscape Architecture

Women have played an important part in the establishment of the landscape architecture profession since the very early days. Beatrix Jones Farrand was a landscape architect practicing at the turn of the twentieth century. She is credited with a substantial volume of outstanding and important landscape work, including the design of the gardens at Dumbarton Oaks (Figure 2.2), and the planning and design of the campuses at Princeton University and Cal Tech. She, along with Olmsted, Hubbard, and others, was a founding member of the American Society of Landscape Architects in 1899.

Figure 2.2 View from garden gates at Dumbarton Oaks, Washington, D.C. by Beatrix Farrand.

The Twentieth Century and the Modern Movement

The movement toward modernism and abstraction began during the Depression years. Thomas Church is associated with the early application of this new movement along with several other landscape architects employed with the Works Progress Administration (WPA) and other public works projects. Church incorporated Mediterranean styles with simple abstract shapes. His creations popularized the concept of creating strong relationships between indoor and outdoor spaces. He developed gardens designed to accommodate outdoor living activities, thus making the gardens a primary living space rather than simply extensions of the indoors.

Following World War II, Garrett Eckbo championed the idea that landscape architects had a social responsibility. Eckbo, Church, Geraldine Knight Scott and others who worked for the WPA during the Depression years and those working for the U.S. Forest Service and other government agencies since the turn of the century established an important tradition of public and social service. This tradition is a unique aspect of landscape architecture in the United States. Eckbo also advanced the importance of regionalism, principles of ecology, and a multidisciplinary approach through his professional practice and as an educator. His peers included James Rose and Dan Kiley. The three led a movement in landscape architecture that paralleled a similar movement in architecture—that of rejecting the Beaux Arts traditions. Rose felt new projects should relate to a specific place or culture rather than imposing concepts and elements from the past. Kiley approached a new project by first simplifying the elements and issues. He believed a practical and rational solution would result, and that it would have a strong functional foundation.

The work and writings of Lawrence Halprin represent a shift in the thinking of landscape architecture. Halprin was an influential force in the socially changing 1960s in California. Halprin sought, through a design process of collective creativity, to accommodate people through designs based on ecological principles and forms found in nature (Figure 2.3). He, perhaps more than any previous landscape architect, represents the best assimilation of all the various factors that were then defining what has become unique to American landscape architecture.

Design with Nature and Environmental Stewardship

Ian McHarg was another personality to have a major influence on shaping the landscape architecture profession in the United States. In the 1970s, McHarg, then chair of the Landscape Architecture and Regional Planning program at the University of Pennsylvania, developed a curriculum unique to landscape architecture education. McHarg advanced an approach to design that based land planning decision making on natural and social scientific factors. His elaborate but effective system of overlaying landscape attributes in a series of transparent, colored maps eventually evolved and became an important contributing factor in the development of the geographical information system approach to large-scale site and regional planning. McHarg's theories of using natural factors for determining land-use suitability were popularized in his book *Design with Nature,* first published in 1969.

The practice of landscape architecture in the United States can be characterized as having the qualities of a multidisciplinary approach, an environmental ethic, a spirit of regionalism, a consideration for people and an understanding of their behavioral preferences, and a unique aesthetic sense. The long-standing tradition of landscape architects practicing regional and city planning has made its imprint on the profession. Landscape architects in the United States are trained and have experience working with complex site design problems involving mixed-land-use developments and projects located in difficult physical site

Figure 2.3 Levi Plaza, San Francisco, by Lawrence Halprin.

conditions. In working with these challenging project types, landscape architects in the United States have developed and honed skills that make them ideally suited to the rapidly emerging global economy. The scale and complexities of working globally require a breadth of knowledge and experience that place landscape architects trained in the United States squarely in the forefront. The historical precedents that influenced the evolution of the profession in the United States coupled with the profession's lead in finding applications to computer and other new technologies has placed U.S. practitioners in a strategic position amongst their peers throughout the world.

3. PRACTICE IN THE UNITED STATES COMPARED WITH THE REST OF THE WORLD

A Profession Based on a Planning and Not a Gardening Tradition

The practice of landscape architecture in the United States has several important characteristics that distinguish practitioners in the United States from those in most other parts of the world. In many countries, landscape architecture emanates from a gardening tradition, which relies heavily on horticultural knowledge, particularly as applied to working with private and public gardens. Thus, landscape architects are hired in many parts of the world for their practical horticultural knowledge as well as their expertise in garden design. If one could generalize, landscape architectural training in Europe, at the university level, places an emphasis on horticulture, landscape construction, and detail design.

Other approaches in landscape architecture education exist in the European university. In addition to programs that place an emphasis on horticulture, there are curricula that seem to be an engineering hybrid. Several university-level landscape architecture programs in Germany and Austria meld civil engineering with horticulture, ecology, and landscape construction. In addition to horticulture and engineering, some landscape architectural training emphasizes the natural sciences—ecology, geography, and soil science.

Design and the design process have been the prevalent tradition of landscape architectural education and practice in the United States for some time. This tradition has a historical context. The early work of Frederick Law Olmsted, such as the design of Central Park, and similar examples by others, provided opportunities for those practicing in the late 1800s and early 1900s to be involved in establishing the expertise and credentials of the profession. Historical opportunities (such as the park movement, the coincidental establishment of the National Environmental Policy Act, and the publication of McHarg's *Design with Nature*), governmental influences (the establishment of agencies engaged in park development, resource management, and regulation), as well as the enactment of conservation-minded legislation (such as the Wilderness Act, and the Wild and Scenic Rivers Act), and educational influences (the establishment of university degree-earning programs in landscape architecture) have left their mark on the landscape architecture profession in the United States.

The U.S. model for academic preparation in landscape architecture is becoming increasingly prevalent as the phenomenon of globalization takes place and as faculty and practitioners from the United States work in other countries. Likewise, students from overseas that come to the United States to complete their university education and training are influenced by the U.S. model.

To summarize, the profession in the United States (and in Canada) has evolved from the formative years, beginning with Frederick Law Olmsted, to its present form in a way that

Figure 2.4   Residential community using ecological planning principles to locate and site roads and home sites, Portola Valley Ranch, California.

has established a profession uniquely qualified to solve design problems considering natural and cultural systems (Figure 2.4). Table 2.1, summarizes the framework of influences that have forged the development of the landscape architectural profession in the United States.

TABLE 2.1   Developmental Influences of the Landscape Architecture Profession in the United States

1. Historical Precedents

- Design viewed as a vehicle for relieving social ills of rapid urbanization brought about by the industrial revolution.
- Landscape architects plan and design nonresidential projects, large scale, regional, and urban in nature.
- Landscape architects in the forefront in the design of new towns, communities, and park and open systems.
- Lanscape architects plan and design public places of high visibility such as university campuses, urban plazas, and parkways such as in Smokey Mountains.
- The establishment of the National Environmental Policy Act (1970) and the publication of McHarg's *Design with Nature* with the subsequent incorporation of environmental and regional planning knowledge and technical skills in landscape architecture education.

2. Government-influenced Opportunities

- The hiring of landscape architects as managers and professionals in governmental service.
- Creation of jobs or consultation work for landscape architects as a result of federal and subsequently state and local legislation.

TABLE 2.1   *(Continued)*

* Knowledge and skills in master planning of open space and large-scaled park lands of government-owned lands. Landscape architects have utilized these skills and knowledge in carrying out of important legislation such as the Wild and Scenic Rivers Act, the Wilderness Act, National Environmental Policy Act, the National Coastal Zone Management Act, Wetlands Preservation, and others.

3. Educational Influences

* Professional status and prestige to the profession with the establishment of an academic program in landscape architecture early in the formative years of the profession.
* Research and scholarly work of faculty in landsacpe architectural programs influenced by university promotion and tenure policies.
* Influence of those entering the profession through the MLA's first professional degree program; designed to meet the needs of those entering the field as a career change.
* Introduction of behavioral studies, cognitive analysis, and new technology (including remote sensing geographic information systems, image processing, and computer applications).

CHAPTER 3

Ethical Perspectives
and Professional Conduct

1. Introduction
2. Landscape Architecture—a Profession Not a Trade
3. What it Means to Be a Professional
4. Basis of Professional Behavior—Moral Philosophy
5. ASLA Code of Professional Conduct
6. In-Basket

1. INTRODUCTION

Understanding what it means to be a professional and practice in a professional manner are important concepts for individuals to grasp as they accept the role and responsibility of being a landscape architect. Ethics and professional conduct are the basis for establishing standards for professional behavior and for accepting responsibility. By accepting and implementing ethical standards and adhering to a code of professional conduct, the individual will have a firm basis to practice landscape architecture in a professional and responsible manner.

While ethics forms and shapes the conduct of landscape architects, factors that influence the execution of their work maybe driven by other considerations, such as function, aesthetics, and economics. Ethics and the establishment of standards of professional conduct have had a strong influence on the profession of landscape architecture. This influence has been particularly evident in the strong sense of responsibility landscape architects have held as they aspire to solve societal issues and in their stated role as stewards of the environment. When performing a service as an employee or for a client, the landscape architect will consider factors outside the realm of the project objectives and requirements. A landscape architect will consider not only the needs, wants, and desires of the client or user but will also develop design solutions that lead to safeguarding the environment as well as achieving some societal benefit. Consideration of society and the environment are ethically derived commitments. In the case of landscape architects, these commitments are codified in the American Society of Landscape Architects (ASLA) Code of Conduct.

2. LANDSCAPE ARCHITECTURE—A PROFESSION, NOT A TRADE

Landscape architects frequently describe their work in terms of one activity: design. Design in association with strong linkages with the land, plant materials, the environment, and the arts form strong visual images that define the profession. Other elements associated with landscape architecture are also important in understanding the nature of the profession. Landscape architects work with plants and the soil, and they consider climate and water systems that support plant growth and maintenance. They work within entire ecological systems. In planning and designing projects for their clients, the landscape architect must have an understanding of how to create and organize space and patterns of movement through space—circulation. Landscape architects must also have an understanding of the dimension of time and its implications of change, such as the growth and life cycles of plants. Further, understanding and applying design principles in the context of time and space require a unique combination of expertise not found in other design professions. Since change is such an important aspect in their work, particularly the changes that are inevitable working with natural elements, landscape architects have assumed the added responsibility of caring for and nurturing the environmental and societal elements in which they work. In working with elements having a time dimension, landscape architects, acting in a responsible manner, must consider the dynamic and changing aspects of their designs. They must consider the ramifications of their design decisions in the future. This consideration of the future and the need to make responsible decisions in the present have influenced the profession to answer the call for responsible action on the part of its practitioners.

Although landscape architecture may be considered an occupation, the professional aspects of this occupation distinguish it from trade or blue-collar vocations. The characteristics that take landscape architecture out of the trade realm are not always sharply delineated but do serve as a starting point. Let us examine the elements that together distinguish landscape architecture as a profession.

Education and Theory

The formal training of landscape architects at the university level prepares students for a professional career in landscape architecture. Through their formal education, students acquire specialized knowledge and mastery of theories applicable to the effective practice of the profession. Practitioners maintain minimum competency through professional practice internship, preparation for the professional license examination, and continuing education and professional development.

Relationship to the Client

The relationship between the client and the landscape architect is unique from the standpoint of responsibility. The landscape architect has the implicit responsibility of looking out for the project needs and safeguarding the interests of the client. This is formalized in professional service contracts but is more often described by the codes of conduct promulgated by the professional organization's members.

Code of Ethics and Professional Conduct

Individuals who become members of the American Society of Landscape Architects agree to accept and follow a code of conduct and ethics codified by the organization. Both the code of ethics and code of professional conduct describe acceptable standards of behavior.

Figure 3.1   Landscape architect carefully preparing a detail for a set of construction drawings.

Professional Precepts

Landscape architects, through their formal training and membership in ASLA, establish a commitment to several society goals. These goals include a commitment to stewardship of environmental resources, the enhancement of the quality of life in the built landscape, safeguarding the welfare of society, and the advancement of the body of knowledge of landscape architecture.

Standards of Care

Landscape architects understand the importance of exercising a high degree of care in applying their skill and knowledge in performing services to a client or employer (Figure 3.1). Landscape architects who uphold high standards of care in the performance of their work also serve to safeguard the health, safety, and welfare of the public.

3. WHAT IT MEANS TO BE A PROFESSIONAL

What does it mean to be a professional? The word professional suggests a certain behavior of a distinct group of individuals having a unique combination of formal education, training, knowledge, and skill. In addition to having education, training, and knowledge, to be recognized as a professional one must follow high standards of professional conduct and adhere to a code of ethics. In addition, individuals in the design professions maintain a special relationship with clients and others they work for. This relationship places the professional in a position of maintaining the interests of the client. One's motivations in providing professional services are not wholly for self-serving objectives but rather are derived from one's commitment to the client's interests.

The dictionary[1] defines *profession* as "an occupation or vocation requiring training in the liberal arts or sciences and advanced study in a specialized field." The definition goes on to specify a profession as a community of similarly trained and educated individuals qualified for one specific occupation or field. The dictionary, although a useful starting place, does not provide a complete or adequate understanding of a profession, as relates to landscape architecture. To be truly professional, as the word has come to be understood in the age of specialization, the need for high standards in working within a litigious and regulation-filled design services environment demands a greater emphasis.

Being a professional requires more than having specific knowledge and skills. Obtaining a formal education is certainly a primary requirement; however, other attributes contribute toward distinguishing landscape architecture as a profession as opposed to a vocation or trade. These include adherence to a code of conduct and belief in conducting one's self in an ethical manner. A professional also can be defined by his or her relationship with clients and by a unique set of societal goals and values that guides one's actions and decisions.

Formal Education:

The formal education of a landscape architect in North America has evolved over many years since the establishment of the first university landscape architecture curriculum at Harvard University in 1900. Presently two types of degrees in landscape architecture are offered: accredited and nonaccredited. The accredited degree is the preferred one from the standpoint of many employers and most state registration boards. Accredited degrees are offered at the bachelor or master's levels. The body charged with determining if a degree-granting program in landscape architecture is accredited is under the purview of the Landscape Architecture Accreditation Board (LAAB). Accreditation and the LAAB are discussed in Chapter 5.

Continuing education is important for maintaining one's professional status. Although not universally adopted at this time, many states, in overseeing the licensing of landscape architects, require licensees to provide proof of obtaining continuing education. An individual's license can be revoked should this requirement for continuing education not be met. ASLA is currently considering continuing education as a requirement for maintaining membership. ASLA offers several different venues of educational opportunities to its membership. These opportunities include programs offered through the Annual Meetings, the Continuing Education Program, and regionally held educational seminars. University programs also sponsor continuing education in specialized areas of the profession.

Likewise, the U.S. Forest Service and other government agencies recognize the importance and benefits of providing opportunities for continuing education for its professional

---

[1] *Webster's New World Dictionary of the American Language.* Cleveland and New York; World Publishing Company, 1954.

Figure 3.2   U.S. Forest Service professional staff reviewing preliminary recreation planning document for accuracy and completeness.

staff (Figure 3.2). Participating in continuing education can, in some cases, be a condition for advancement up the career ladder in the Forest Service and other organizations in the public and private sectors.

Relationship with Clients

The relationship of the landscape architect to his or her client is a unique one. The landscape architect is obliged to insure the interests of the client are protected in any decision or action made. When working under contract, the landscape architect is serving the needs and requirements of the client, acting as an agent of the client, not on his or her own behalf. The relationship is similar to that of an executor to an estate. As an executor, one is committed to achieving the interest of the estate, carrying out the wishes of the estate by utilizing one's best judgment, and applying one's knowledge and skill to the best advantage of the estate.

Societal Imperative

Landscape architects are committed to several societal imperatives. This commitment is another unique aspect of the profession. Landscape architects are committed to improving the condition of the community and society while maintaining the intrinsic values of environmental resources. This same commitment embraces a broad responsibility in venerating and/or protecting cultural and historical values of a region or a nation. Landscape architects also consider themselves stewards of the environment. These commitments find expression in their work. In the design process, landscape architects will aspire to incorporate societal considerations in their work. This will often mean considering social, cultural, and environmental goals that are generally outside the usual limits of a project or design services contract.

Landscape architects have been trained to look outside the physical boundaries of a project while considering the needs and requirements of the client. Context, then, is given important consideration by landscape architects during the design process. The consideration of social and environmental context ensures that a project is a good neighbor and will enhance community values and needs.

Professional Conduct and Codes of Ethics

A code of professional conduct promulgated by the American Society of Landscape Architects, a professional organization, expresses in general terms the standards of conduct expected of all its members. A code of conduct is written to establish a basis of mutual respect and understanding among the members. Further, a code may be dedicated to achieving some broader set of objectives that represent the basic societal values held by the membership, such as advancing the body of knowledge of the profession, improving the quality of life for all persons, or acting to safeguard the environment.

4. BASIS OF PROFESSIONAL BEHAVIOR

The factors that mold an individual's personal ethics are one's moral education and childhood development. Parental guidance, religious education, and experience dealing with others contribute toward the development of an individual's personal morals. Standards of correct behavior, normative right and wrong, and other philosophical, ethical, and moral maxims are developed by each person throughout his or her formative, teen, and young adult years of growth.

Moral philosophy can vary significantly among individuals. These philosophies are influenced by personal development, relative degrees of altruism, and self-interest. Upon joining a professional group, individuals are expected to conform their basis of moral behavior to the ethical code of the group. In effect, the ethics of the professional group are imposed upon the ethics of the individual member. This is done though a mentor process as well as by the promulgation of written codes of professional conduct and ethics.[2]

Most professional groups, such as the American Society of Landscape Architects, establish and promulgate codes of ethics to reduce the variation in the ethical conduct of individual members.[3] Such codes are designed to guide practitioners to act not only in the interest of the profession but also to ethically serve their clients and the general public. A group's code of ethics suggests standards of behavior that relate to the interest of the group to improve its standing in the eyes of the public its members wish to serve.

Legislative bodies are able to restrain citizens from certain socially harmful or unethical acts with imprisonment, fines, or other forms of reprisal. Professional groups, however, do not have these means of punishment to guide the ethical conduct of their members. Threat

---

[2]Beauchamp and Bowie, *Ethical Theory and Business.*
[3]Beets, "Personal Morals and Professsional Ethics: A Review and an Empirical Examination of Public Accounting."

of sanctions, peer pressure, loss of membership, or limited support of the organization's services is generally all that is available to enforce ethical conduct standards for professional groups. Therefore, professional organizations often appeal to their members' sense of professionalism. They request adherence to established codes on a voluntary basis, encouraging the exercise of self-discipline above and beyond personal morals and legal requirements. Professional codes of ethics are designed to benefit professions and their members, their clients, and the general public. This is supported in the case where the professional organization—such as ASLA—states that the profession exists to serve the public.

Professional codes of ethics can be effective in guiding the actions of the practitioners. When a practitioner is faced with a decision having ethical implications, he or she can look to their organization's codes of conduct to determine the group's recommended action. An effective code should provide a profession with a degree of stability and consistency in ethical decision making.

Adherence to a common set of rules serves to bond members of a professional organization. This bond implies an ethical community that further strengthens a group's sense of self-esteem and value. Codes of conduct and ethical standards may also help define for the profession its value to society. Additionally, members may achieve satisfaction from being part of an organization whose members, holding similar moral standards and values, allow them to comfortably work and compete among their peers. For the most part, members of a professional organization are willing to abide by the codes of conduct and ethical standards of the organization in the belief that the rules benefit the profession and society as well as the individual member.

5. ASLA CODE OF PROFESSIONAL CONDUCT

The American Society of Landscape Architects has adopted, through its Board of Trustees, both a code and a set of guidelines for professional conduct. The code expresses in general terms certain responsibilities to society and the environment as well as the level of professional conduct expected of its members. In adopting the code, the ASLA Board of Trustees gives no guarantee of the moral actions on the part of its general membership. Adherence to the code depends on the integrity and commitment of each individual member to act in a responsible, straightforward manner with clients and other professionals.[4]

The tone set for the codes is established in the preamble to the ASLA Code of Professional Conduct. This objective indicates that members of ASLA, by adopting and following the codes of conduct, will establish a bond based on mutual respect and a dedication to improving the quality of life for all persons. Adherence to the codes and guidelines is implicit to membership in ASLA. Although there is no legal basis for enforcing members to abide by the codes and guidelines, failing to do so could result in loss of membership.

Code of Professional Conduct

Table 3.1 outlines the Code of Professional Conduct promulgated by ASLA. The codes express a responsibility of ASLA members toward furthering certain social and environmental imperatives as well as their responsibilities toward clients and employers. These

[4]American Society of Landscape Architects, *Membership Handbook,* Washington, D.C., 1992.

TABLE 3.1   ASLA Code of Professional Conduct

I. The member shall exert every effort toward the preservation and protection of our natural resources and toward understanding the interaction of the economic and social systems with these resources.

II. The member has a social and environmental responsibility to reconcile the public's needs and the natural environment with minimal disruption to the natural syustem.

III. The member shall further the welfare of and advance the profession by constantly striving to provide the highest level of professional services, avoiding even the appearance of improper professional conduct.

IV. The member shall serve the client or employer with integrity, understanding, knowledge, and creative ability, and shall respond morally to social, political, economic, and technological influences.

V. The member shall encourage educational research and the development and dissemination of useful technical information relating to planning, design, and construction of the physical environment.

codes reinforce the commitment of ASLA members toward the stewardship and conservation of natural, constructed, and human resources. The intent of this stewardship role is to obligate the members to create works and provide services that useful, aesthetic, safe, and enjoyable purposes.[5]

Guidelines for Professional Conduct

Table 3.2 outlines the ASLA Guidelines for Professional Conduct. These guidelines delineate acceptable professional conduct between members and their clients and employers and other professionals. The guidelines also serve to exemplify the integrity with which members are expected to conduct themselves.

TABLE 3.2   ASLA GUIDELINES FOR PROFESSIONAL CONDUCT

I. A member shall make full disclosure to the client or employer of any financial interest which even remotely bears upon the services or project.

II. A member shall truthfully and clearly inform the client or employer of personal qualifications and capabilities to perform services.

III. A member shall not make exaggerated, misleading, deceptive or false statements, or claims to the public about personal professional qualifications, experience or performance.

IV. A member shall not give, lend or promise anything of value to any public official in order to influence the official's judgment or actions in the letting of contracts.

V. A member shall be free of any constraint from fellow members to participate in a price or competitive bidding selection when such method is selected by a client, but the member is encouraged to advocate to the client the public benefit to be derived from selection processes that establish as their primary consideration in the selection of landscape architects the ability and competence of the landscape architect to provide the required services.

VI. A member shall recognize the contribution of others engaged in the planning, design and construction of the physical environment and shall not knowingly make false statements about their professional work nor maliciously injure or attempt to injure the prospects, practice or employment position of those so engaged.

[5]Ibid., contained in the ASLA Definition of Landscape Architecture.

6. IN-BASKET

1. A principal in the firm in which you have been recently hired has been reviewing your resume and past work in other firms. She has asked you to include several of your projects in the new firm's brochure, one of which received recognition in the local ASLA chapter's annual awards program. Under what conditions would it be acceptable for your projects to be included in this brochure if at all?

2. A prospective client has contacted you to discuss a future project to be designed and constructed on property partially located on protected wetlands. The client has financial restraints that require that the property be developed to yield the maximum profit. Discuss an approach that will enable you to consider your client's needs and still adhere to ASLA's code of conduct regarding land stewardship.

3. A client of long standing has asked you to assist in developing a process of selecting a consultant to develop a master plan for a large tract of land. You wish to accommodate this client but at the same time would like to be considered for the project. Develop an approach that would allow you to do both while avoiding the appearance of improper conduct.

4. Your boss, the superintendent of parks of a small town, has asked you to prepare a design services request for proposal. One of the selection criteria he wants to include is consultant fees. You know consultant fees will be an important consideration by the selection board, for the city must stretch the limited funds available for park development. How would you approach your task, keeping in mind the ASLA guidelines for conduct regarding fees in a competitive bidding process?

CHAPTER 4

Forms of Professional Practice

1. Introduction and Areas of Practice
2. Landscape Architecture: A Service Profession
3. A Profession among Many in the Design Community
4. Areas of Professional Practice
5. In-Basket

1. INTRODUCTION AND AREAS OF PRACTICE

A Unique Career

Landscape architecture offers a unique career opportunity for those preparing for the twenty-first century. The profession is particularly suited to those who are interested in design and are concerned with the environment and the quality of life in our cities and outdoor surroundings. Many persons are first attracted to the profession due to their interest in plants and residential garden design. From this early introduction, an evolution takes place during a student's formal landscape architecture education. Students are presented with new aspects of the profession and learn of its diverse nature. With each new turn another vista opens into a new facet of the profession. Students set new career goals, perhaps turning from becoming designers of gardens to becoming designers of parks and zoos, planners of tourism centers and resorts, designers of urban spaces, managers of public lands, or administrators regulating environmental programs.

A Career with Diversity

Landscape architecture is one of several professions, including architecture, interior design, and engineering, that considers design to be its primary activity. Creating designs, the act of designing outdoor spaces with the expectation that what is designed will eventually be built, is commonly held by those in the profession as the main focus of landscape architecture. However, not all landscape architects design, although much of their university education is focused on developing design and graphic communication skills (Figure 4.1). The profession has undergone significant change in terms of knowledge and skill requirements. Those now preparing to enter the profession must acquire diverse knowledge and skills to be competitive in finding good employment. Many landscape architects apply their formal educational training in areas such as:

- planning functions for public agencies and large corporations
- government regulatory or management activities

Figure 4.1 University programs in landscape architecture are in academic units such as colleges of environmental design, horticulture, and natural resources.

- product sales such as irrigation, plant materials, or outdoor lighting
- business or marketing
- university teaching

Diverse positions landscape architects may hold include:

- administrator with nonprofit groups such as the Nature Conservancy or the Boy Scouts
- professional staff with a private consulting firm or government agency of environmental specialists preparing environmental impact reports or hazardous waste plans
- manager of an arboretum or botanical garden
- editor of a magazine.

There are many other individuals who, having first earned a landscape architecture degree, have gone on to find employment in a plethora of seemingly unrelated fields. Many of these people have achieved prominence and professional satisfaction in nontraditional areas of landscape architectural practice. Diversity of practice may have as much to do with career changes as available employment options.

Most university landscape architecture programs having an active recruitment agenda promote a physical design or an environmental planning image to attract prospective students. A typical description of the profession contained in college catalogues or brochures might be worded similarly to the following passage:

The profession of landscape architecture combines art, natural sciences, and social and cultural disciplines with a strong design and technology base. Those in the profession create and shape the places where people live, work and play. Landscape architecture is one of many professions involved in the planning and design of the built environment, both new places as well as previously built places of historical, cultural, or environmental value.

Landscape architects often work with teams of scientists, foresters, wetland biologists, horticulture specialists, and other disciplines in a diverse range of project types. Landscape architects have played an important role in the creation and master planning of the system of national parks not only in the United States but in many countries in Latin America, Africa, Southeast Asia, and elsewhere. They have also been involved in the design of new communities and in the redevelopment of older sections of existing cities. Landscape architects also have helped plan for the conservation or enhancement of historic places and natural areas. Landscape architects can be found in positions of upper governmental administration as managers of public lands such as national forests or regional open space and trail systems, as well as in the private sector as principals of landscape architectural and multidisciplinary firms.

Each new area of professional involvement may require enhancement of one's formal landscape architectural education. Acquiring specialized knowledge and skills may also come directly from work experience. Supplementing what is learned on the job, obtaining new skills and acquisition of new knowledge is gained through advanced study in graduate school, attendance of short courses, or other formal and informal continuing education programs. Continuing education is an important aspect of maintaining professional proficiency and relevance as one progresses in one's career.

2. LANDSCAPE ARCHITECTURE: A SERVICE PROFESSION

In providing design services, one works with ideas that are transferred onto paper or communicated verbally. The design ideas are usually specific solutions or recommendations that solve a client's project requirements. Landscape architects are hired to apply their specialized knowledge, skills, and experience to meet the needs of clients and employers. Landscape architects create designs and plans in the form of physical products—such as drawings, written specifications, and reports—or in the form of verbal communication as in an office or on-site consultation meeting. These products are referred to as *instruments of service,* and are physical extensions of professional services. Professional services are what a client seeks when hiring a landscape architect. The client is seeking recommendations of what to do to meet certain objectives or to solve specific problems. It is the interaction and communication between client and landscape architect that forms the central core of professional services. How the results of these services are communicated and transferred to the client becomes the physical manifestation of professional services. The type of services provided together with their tangible products depend on client needs, the nature of the project, environmental and cultural attributes at the project location, and legal or governmental requirements (Figure 4.2).

The kinds of problems landscape architects solve vary greatly. Problem solving, in a design sense, has to do with recommending a course of action together with materials to be installed in a specific way, for instance, prescribing modifications of outdoor spaces and natural or disturbed areas in order to:

Figure 4.2 A water-based day-use area located on U.S. Forest Service lands designed to serve an urban population.

- provide for prescribed uses or activities
- enhance the physical quality of outdoor places for human use and appreciation
- remediate natural areas or systems in the environment made dysfunctional through previous human actions.

The products of landscape architects are often thought of in terms of the plans and designs they prepare. However, the designs are prepared on paper-like products and are considered instruments of practice. They are used by the landscape architect to guide the realization of the plans and the construction of the designs. The designs rendered in graphic and written form represent the physical qualities, dimensions, and materials that embody the client's program or goals.

Client Satisfaction

To remain in someone's employment or to continue a profitable practice, a landscape architect should be committed to the concept of user or client satisfaction. When the services of landscape architects are sought, there is the expectation that they will follow a process that will yield a product superior in quality to anything the client could produce.

Taking the narrow view of the landscape architect as the "artist" is not appropriate in the majority of client–landscape architect situations. Landscape architects, in preparing designs or developing master plans, are not doing so for their own satisfaction. Their efforts are for another's use, enjoyment, or satisfaction. However, personal satisfaction, gained from a job well done, is certainly a necessary outcome in performing a service. Individuals must be satisfied that they are doing the best, most appropriate work feasible within their capability and within the circumstances of the specific project situation. Satisfying others' needs and requirements is clearly an attitude with which each practitioner must be comfortable.

There are rare practitioners whose work is of such exceptional quality that they continue to attract clients regardless of whether or not they place value on client satisfaction. But for most landscape architects, user and client satisfaction is deemed an important goal and most landscape architects attempt to perform their work so that personal or professional satisfaction is balanced with satisfying the needs and desires of the client and the employer.

Products and Solutions

There are both tangible and intangible results produced by landscape architects engaged in service to clients and employees. The products of the landscape architect's work are ideas, planning recommendations, and design solutions. Design solutions consist of a prescribed set of recommendations presented in drawn, written, model, or verbal form. They may also be presented in video, computer-generated images, and other forms of photographic electronic media. These products are used to guide the construction and installation of built works. They may also be used to guide in the management of land and water resources.

3. A PROFESSION AMONG MANY IN THE DESIGN COMMUNITY

Landscape architects often collaborate with one or more professionals from other disciplines such as architecture and civil engineering (Figure 4.3). A single project, such as the reclamation of a river segment to meet outdoor recreation needs in a downtown area, may require the services of landscape architects, civil engineers, environmental scientists, artists, city planners, water quality engineers, lawyers, sociologists, geologists, and economists. Such professional collaborations are stimulating and can be a very rewarding aspect of one's career as a landscape architect.

There are areas of design work where overlap exists between disciplines. A landscape architect may cross over into the realm civil engineering in the areas of:

- site grading
- road alignment and parking lot layout
- subdivision layout
- mineral extraction site restoration plans

Conversely, architects often compete for certain types of work for which landscape architects are equally capable and may traditionally perform service. Architects, like landscape architects, will provide design services for the following types of projects:

- urban plazas
- park and school playgrounds

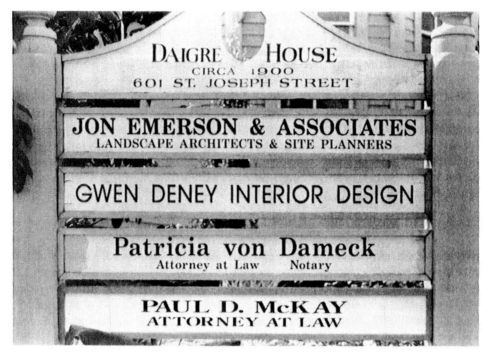

Figure 4.3   Landscape architects often work on projects as part of a team composed of many disciplines, such as other design professionals, lawyers, and artists.

- site master planning
- visitor education and interpretative systems
- environmental graphics such as signage

The professional services of today's landscape architects also involve work in the natural environment. This work includes development of management strategies to be applied where it may be necessary to accommodate man's activities while making wise use of the natural environment. The work of landscape architects here is to apply knowledge and techniques derived from the natural sciences to achieve hoped-for results. For example, a landscape architect might be employed to develop remediation solutions for restoring lands disturbed by activities such as hard rock mining or hazardous waste disposal.

The work of many of today's landscape architects also has stretched the profession in the area of historical preservation. Historical preservation involves work on historic sites, gardens, buildings, and cultural places or events. This area of service has a strong research component where the landscape architect might work in a formally structured, systematic manner similar to an anthropologist. A landscape architect working on a historic site will follow a process researching facts to uncover the layers of building site conditions over time. Understanding the component elements of the historical layers and their significance to past cultures or events singularly characterizes this growing area of practice. Preparing designs and developing management strategies are often a part of the restoration of the cultural or historical significance of the studied site and its significant features.

Eco-tourism has emerged as an important economic activity in many parts of the world. Increasingly, travelers are interested in learning more about the historical and cultural attributes of a region. They are particularly interested in experiencing the vernacular manifestations of a region's people and history within an environmental context. For example, many foreign visitors coming to the United States for the first time come with the national parks on their itinerary rather than Disney World. They come prepared to visit the hinterlands. They travel to Appalachia, the West, and Southwest with the desire to see the "real people" and examples of cultural remnants they read about in *Tom Sawyer* and *The Last of the Mohicans*. Eco-tourism is a phenomenon of widespread importance throughout the world. Landscape architects find work associated with eco-tourism increasing as the profession responds to the changing economic trends of the fast-approaching twenty-first century.

The landscape architecture profession differs in several important ways from other careers in the professional design community. These differences can be explained in terms of formal educational preparations, and curriculum and accreditation standards. The profession's precepts and values also play an important role in forming and shaping its character. The disciplines from which the profession draws its knowledge base include the performing and visual arts and the natural and environmental sciences. There are also strong ties with the social and cultural sciences. Very much like engineering, landscape architecture is considered an applied science. Landscape architects are currently increasing their use of computers and other technologies in executing service.

Landscape architecture has a small population relative to other design professions. Table 4.1 provides a snapshot of the relative number of practitioners in the allied design professions.

4. AREAS OF PROFESSIONAL PRACTICE

People educated and trained in landscape architecture find work with a variety of employers. The diversity of opportunities sorts out into four major categories termed *areas of professional practice:*

- public
- private
- academic
- non-traditional

Generally, educational training at the university level does not make distinctions between the four areas. In several instances, a distinction might be made where a program, by virtue of its unique geographic location or the broad context of the larger mission of a university, might place an emphasis on one of the four areas. In these cases, the degree of emphasis depends on faculty interests, funded research opportunities, or regional setting social con-

TABLE 4.1   Estimated Numbers of Practitioners in the Design Fields

Profession	Estimated No. of Practitioners
• Landscape Architecture	25,000–35,000
• Architecture	100,000–150,000
• Engineering	250,000–300,000
• Planning	50,000–60,000

text. For example, a program located in a rural setting in close proximity to extensive federally owned lands might emphasize public service as an appropriate response in preparing students for future employment. Another program, located in the midst of a highly urbanized region, would most likely place emphasis on preparing students for employment with private firms specializing in urban design and city redevelopment planning issues. All programs are greatly influenced by their geographical, cultural, and historical context as well as their regional context.

Private practice appears to receive the greatest emphasis in most professional programs, however. This emphasis on private practice occurs not so much by design as it does by a variety of influences such as the greater visibility of the work of private practitioners over that of their public service and academic counterparts. Most students selecting landscape architecture as a major learn of the profession by the visible works of private practitioners. Private practitioners seem to write more about their profession than their government-employed colleagues. Also, writers and contributors in popular magazines (garden and home magazines such as *Sunset* and *Southern Living*) focus more attention on private practitioners' work. Works of landscape architects employed by state and federal agencies are not widely recognized by the lay public. The efforts and programs of government agencies give recognition to the agency rather than to a professional individual. In landscape architecture programs, course and studio work tend to stress private projects, such as business parks and residential communities, although public projects, such as parks or educational campuses, might also be assigned as studio projects for the students to work on.

Likewise, most university-level professional practice courses tend to place greatest emphasis on private practice. The knowledge and skills taught in these courses draw from a literature that caters to private enterprise. This same knowledge and skill base is applicable to all professionals, regardless of employment category, although those teaching these courses may draw from private sector experience.

Coursework will include not only design but other subject areas such as landscape construction, history, graphics, and plant materials. Managerial and administrative skills, legal issues and questions of ethics, project management and documentation are also equally important areas taught in varying degrees of intensity and depth in most accredited, professional degree programs.

Four Areas of Practice Reviewed

Public Practice   Landscape architects working in public practice are employed as staff or managers in federal, state, or local agencies. Their duties and responsibilities directly relate to the mission of the agency that employs them. An agency's mission relates directly to an administrative response to an executive order or legislative action called an *enabling act* or *law*. The creation of an agency or government program is often the result of a legal mandate, requiring the establishment of a new agency or program. Compliance will often result in the hiring of new professional staff.

This staff will frequently have specialized skills and experience related to the intent of the law or executive directive. The passage of certain types of appropriation bills, primarily public works bills, at the federal and state level can place new demands for landscape architectural staff to be hired at those levels as well as in regional and local governmental agencies receiving money from the federal or state programs. Appropriation bills may be passed with two objectives: for providing new money to improve economic conditions; or for the design and construction of new public works programs, such as

Figure 4.4   Landscape architects are employed by a variety of federal, state, and local government agencies designing parks and recreation facilities, managing resources on public lands, and working as professional staff for city and county planning and zoning departments.

public recreation development or transportation improvements. Both types of legislation create new positions for landscape architects as well as other professionals in the public and private sectors.

The specifics of an agency's mission may be modified or further defined by an annual budget or the wording contained in an appropriations bill. Given the legal and legislative nature of defining the roles and responsibilities of an agency, the role and responsibility of agency staff tends to create a stable working environment. This environment frequently creates a hierarchy of specialists, a unique characteristic of public practice.

Public practitioners who remain employed with an agency for a length of time tend to perform administrative and management functions. In an administrative and management role, public landscape architects will oversee the work of less experienced or less senior staff. Although this might lead to a misperception on the part of nonpublic practitioners, public landscape architects are indeed employed to provide design and planning functions, with job descriptions similar to their counterparts working in the private sector (Figure 4.4).

There are many job titles for public practitioners aside from landscape architect:

- recreation specialist
- planner (campus, park, etc.)
- city planner
- interpretive specialist

- grants coordinator
- zoning officer
- program director/ manager

The specialized knowledge and skills of landscape architects are used by public agencies for a variety of positions. For instance, landscape architects are employed by the U.S. Forest Service, the National Park Service and the U.S. Fish and Wildlife Service for visitor service functions. A landscape architect may be hired as a park naturalist or wildlife refuge interpreter to meet with the public as part of a visitor education program. This function may not, on the surface, appear to utilize the design training of an individual directly but does capitalize on the communication skills of landscape architects.

Landscape architects employed by government agencies perform a variety of functions related to the mission and legislative authority of the agency. Agency authority falls under three broad headings:

- administrative
- regulatory
- operations and management

Landscape architects may be employed as managers or staff with a job description that has multiple responsibilities that include the following:

- program policy and planning
- project programming and budgeting
- site selection and reconnaissance
- interagency/governmental coordination
- regulatory function
- planning and design
- program and project review
- management (agency program, personnel, and project)
- administrative and regulatory implementation
- facility maintenance
- public service–user interface
- program operations

The process for government hiring involves various steps formalized by personnel hiring guidelines. A typical government process includes many steps such as (1) submitting a detailed application form, (2) review of the applications by a personnel board or committee, (3) preparation of a ranked listing or roll of applicants meeting the job description criteria, (4) contacting candidates for an interview, and finally (5) making an offer and hiring a candidate.

Public practice offers a very exciting and fulfilling career for landscape architects. Many landscape architects working for government agencies have been involved with programs representing the cutting edge of the profession. In the early days of the twentieth century, park planning and management on the national scale afforded many landscape architects in government positions the opportunity to explore new areas of large-scale planning and design, an opportunity not available to their private-sector counterparts. Planning activities often lead to design and implementation of real projects. Many government landscape architects are involved in the design of these projects. Once a project is on-line, the landscape architects may participate in resource management assignments.

The 1930s and 1940s provided landscape architects working for government agencies new professional opportunities in public housing and community planning. More recently, with the passage of the National Environmental Protection Act (1970) and other environmentally related legislation, landscape architects have become leaders in the development of environmental impact assessment and visual resource management activities. Currently, government employed landscape architects find themselves in the forefront of developing planning and design teams that are charged with preparing wetland management plans, programs for special ecological zones, and historic site restoration plans, or in managing geographical information. Landscape architects working in public practice tend to become highly skilled and make many important advances in their areas of specialization.

Private Practice To say that landscape architects in the private sector are primarily motivated to work for profit while landscape architects in government work only to serve others is a simplistic overgeneralization. Although the nature of each of these two forms of practice is distinct, the decision of selecting one over the other cannot be so easily explained as profit or service motivated.

Landscape architects who choose to work in the private sector may do so initially for opportunistic reasons as well as because of influences from faculty during their university preparations. But the process of obtaining employment in the private sector is much more straightforward than for a government agency. The red tape sometimes involved in making a hiring decision in a government agency can have a deterring effect on some people.

The employee selection process in private practice is generally less formalized or rigid than it is in the government and academic sectors. Hiring in smaller and midsized firms involves fewer steps for the most part. A slightly more regimented hiring process could be expected for larger firms having multiregional offices. The process of hiring simply means advertising a position, reviewing letters or applications, selecting the most promising applicants, reviewing portfolios of work, interviewing, then making a decision and negotiating an employment offer.

While government landscape architects tend to specialize, private practitioners usually do not. The mission-driven nature of government agencies is replaced in the private sector by private firms specializing in working with particular client groups or project types. Although some private offices may target a variety of clients or project types, individuals working in a private firm often must perform a variety of functions as schedules, workloads, and project needs change (Figure 4.5).

A few examples of the activities that landscape architects in private practice perform include:

- management and administrative tasks
- business development and marketing
- client, prime consultant, and sub consultant coordination
- design and planning

Figure 4.5   Private landscape architecture firms tend to be small; the average size is fewer than two employees.

- client and user interaction
- construction administration
- preparation and presentation of documentation to agency staff, boards, and commissions for government permits, and plan review

There are a variety of private practice employment opportunities for landscape architects. In years past, most landscape architects worked for other landscape architects in small or medium-sized offices. More recently, however, landscape architects have found employment in other private practice situations, including:

- A/E offices, such as architectural or multidisciplinary engineering firms
- land development
- design-build
- green industry employers, including contractors, nurseries, irrigation and lighting companies, and product suppliers
- industrial corporations
- theme park, resort, and tourism-related enterprises

Academic Practice   With forty-seven universities offering accredited bachelor degrees and twenty-five universities offering master's degree programs in landscape architecture, the profession is well represented in the academic world (Figure 4.6). There are opportunities for landscape architects interested in education to pursue an academic career. This path might include a full-time academic or part-time adjunct appointment in a landscape program. Landscape architects are also employed part-time or full-time on an adjunct appointment with a nonlandscape program or an architecture or horticulture program. There are many landscape architects involved in teaching. Their activities extend beyond accredited degree programs to include a number of other academically related employment situations, such as:

- continuing education and evening school programs
- university cooperative extension education and research
- community college courses, including two-year degrees
- support courses in university architecture, natural sciences, and other design and non-design programs
- community and state vocational education programs

Landscape architects in academic practice are involved not only in teaching but in an exciting variety of other activities. Many are hired on a teaching appointment basis but may also be hired to conduct research, public education programs, and community service. Often, academic appointments carry multiple responsibilities such as teaching and research or teaching and administration. An active record of teaching, research, and community service is generally expected of most faculty wishing to advance through the ranks to full professor and obtain tenure. In some cases, a faculty member wishing to maintain an active professional practice can substitute professional practice for research

Figure 4.6 An academic career offers a variety of opportunities for creative expression and professional development for landscape architects.

and scholarly activities, although in most universities emphasis is placed on research over professional practice.

As a result of this emphasis, most landscape architects in the academic sector teach and conduct research. Those who desire to further the profession's knowledge base may direct their nonteaching efforts toward research and scholarly activities. Those faculty whose interest remains in design can maintain their interest through consultation and private practice. Both avenues are appropriate and important because a faculty member equally engaged in both research and practice offers benefits both in the classroom and in establishing the expertise of the program as a whole. A research-based and consultant- based faculty maintains the relevance and practicality of a program, which further strengthens a student's practical and theoretical base.

Non-traditional Forms of Practice The skills and knowledge of landscape architecture find application and relevancy in a variety of applications in the modern world. This became evident as the landscape architecture profession became more influential in dealing with environmental and quality-of-life issues. The mix of academic preparation in the arts and natural sciences gave the profession relevance to work in broad ranges of areas including resource management, complex land planning, visitor interpretation and education, eco-tourism, remediation and restoration specialties, and computer applications and other technical application skills.

The expanding employment options for landscape architects can be classified under three headings: (1) institutional or nonprofit organizations, (2) construction industry, and (3) emerging forms or specialty areas of practice. Some examples of each include the following:

Institutional, Nonprofit, and Service Organizations

- youth and community organizations: Boy Scouts, YMCA
- special-interest groups: Sierra Club, Nature Conservancy, downtown development organizations
- semigovernmental institutions: World Bank, American International Development, United Nations, Tennessee Valley Authority
- professional organizations: American Society of Landscape Architects

Construction and Green Industry

- construction: building constructors, design/build, project management.
- green industry: nursery, product and equipment sales and service.
- landscape maintenance.

Emerging Forms and Specialty Areas of Practice

- specialty consultation: historic landscape restoration, golf course architecture, zoological planning and design, rural landscape planning, river front planning, environmental graphics
- plant materials: speciality in native plants, xeriscape, erosion control, land reclamation, indoor plants
- resource management: coastal zone planning, wetlands management and restoration, river recreation planning

- technology: computer applications, aerial photography, remote sensing
- other: environmental education, interpretative planning, environmental artist or musician, author and editor, technical products specifier (tennis facilities, athletic fields and marinas)

The breadth of academic preparation coupled with the diverse nature of the profession make those trained as landscape architects ideally suited for an ever- expanding range of professional applications. The diverse range of applications for landscape architecture knowledge and skills has given rise to an expanding range of employment opportunities for landscape architects trained in the United States and throughout the world.

5. IN-BASKET

1. List the areas of expertise a landscape architect would bring to work on a multidisciplinary team for the U.S. Forest Service planning a new visitor interpretative area within forest lands recently set aside and managed to protect an endangered wildlife species.

2. What areas of investigation would a university faculty member research that would benefit landscape architects working on projects involving the redesign of older parks located in the inner-city?

3. Discuss your preferences for seeking employment with either a public agency or private firm. Why would you prefer one over the other? What do you perceive as the short-term and long-term advantages of your chosen field given your career goals as you see them now?

4. If your goal is to work in a design-build firm, what elective courses would you take while in school to better prepare you for this career decision?

5. If your goal is to work for an internationally-based private firm, what preparations would you make while in school to increase your chances of securing employment with such a firm?

CHAPTER 5

Professional Continuum

1. Career as a Process of Growth and Change
2. Phases of a Professional Career Continuum
4. Professional Organizations
5. Licensure and Professional Registration
6. In-Basket

1. CAREER AS A PROCESS OF GROWTH AND CHANGE

Landscape architecture is a profession. It is also a career. The word *career* suggests a continuum, a process involving growth and change over time. A career, then, is not something static. Upon completing the prescribed formal education for landscape architecture, a dynamic process begins with an internship to gain practical experience followed by licensure and continuing with professional development and maturation.

The process of professional development does not follow a rigid path and has not been institutionalized. You can steer your own course over the remainder of your professional life. A career can take many different paths, each leading to a variety of destinations. The process is steered by the professional goals and personal aspirations you establish for yourself. The course you take will be tailored to meet both your professional and personal needs. To a large extent, your career path will be determined by opportunities or circumstances that present themselves at a time when you might be considering a change in employment. You can create opportunities or at least nurture them through a process of goal setting. Upon first preparing (formal education) and then entering the career (internship), you will be embarking on a continuum of professional development. With each step, beginning with school, to the entry-level job, to succeeding positions, you will advance in capability and competence. As you increase your professional capabilities, your base of knowledge and experience will broaden. Each step builds on the last, expanding your expertise as well as your sense of personal value.

Your personal goals and aspirations may lead you to other endeavors, perhaps in other areas within landscape architecture or quite possibly in another field altogether. These changes may involve accepting greater responsibility in administration, management, and leadership, or a change in professional focus, from physical design to environmental planning and regulation, or toward becoming an educator with distinguished research interests. These changes in professional focus and responsibility have as much to do with innate skill and talent as they do with an individual's motivation for advancing professionally and developing new interests.

The process of change in landscape architecture starts with the commencement of one's formal education. Here the focus is on expanding one's awareness of the world and how we live in it. During the formal education process, students will acquire new knowledge and develop an understanding of the world and important issues they will be concerned with in the future. With this new knowledge, students will be in a position to apply their skills to the problems they will face as professionals.

Once a landscape architecture degree is earned, the learning process shifts from a classroom and design studio environment to the real-world, practical environment of the first paying job. It is in this new learning environment that recent graduates begin apprenticeship. As apprentices, the ex-students work with experienced professionals learning how to apply the knowledge gained in the university to real-life problems as well as broadening their knowledge, perspective, and understanding of professional activities.

After the apprenticeship period is completed, the next step is taking and passing a state landscape architecture license examination. When licensure is achieved, the learning process shifts to new areas. The young professional's emphasis turns toward professional development, which is a process of professional growth and career development. Through this process the professional advances to become a seasoned practitioner. As one practices the profession, new knowledge is gained. Professional skills and capabilities become more effective as they are performed. One may eventually establish an area of specialization or expertise. The choice of expertise depends on each individual's intrinsic abilities, goals, and interests (Figure 5.1).

The professional development process continues with many intermediate steps. As you acquire greater competency you may move from a staff role primarily involved with production into a managerial role. A manager's role usually involves administra-

Figure 5.1   Seasoned practitioner inspecting recently completed fishing pavilion designed to meet new access standards.

tive activities as well as managing projects and the work of others in the office. Eventually, in the continuum of a career, practitioners in management take on administrative, legal, and business responsibilities. Administration includes setting the course of a business or formulating policies of a government or semigovernmental agency. Ultimately, one's involvement in the profession makes room for other endeavors such as community service, education, and a greater involvement in professional and community service organizations.

2. PHASES OF A PROFESSIONAL CAREER CONTINUUM

A career in landscape architecture progresses through many stages (Figure 5.2). Each stage (or phase is described in detail in the following sections to help you understand the profession of landscape architecture as a continuum.

Preparation Phase

Academic Preparation   Once the decision is made to declare landscape architecture as a major, a student would normally seek advice and receive counseling from a department faculty member or chair. The new student would be placed at an appropriate level in the program and be provided with an academic plan of courses required to earn a degree (Figure 5.3). The assumption here is that the degree sought is what is called the "first professional degree." A first professional degree could be either the BLA (Bachelor of Landscape Architecture) or MLA (Master of Landscape Architecture). The BLA is the appro-

Preparation
- Academic preparation: enter at Bachelor's or Master's level
- Internship or apprenticeship
- Entry level

Professional Practice
- Licensure
- Advanced academic studies: specialization, refinement, new skills
- Mid-level: project management, functional area manager
- Community service
- Management: area manager, owner
- Continuing education

Shift in Emphasis: Altruistic Stage
- Professional organization
- Profession change
- Giving back to profession through teaching, mentoring, public service

Figure 5.2   Landscape architecture professional continuum.

Figure 5.3   There are approximately sixty university degree-granting landscape architecture programs in North America where students can earn either a BLA or an MLA.

priate degree for a student who has not yet earned a college degree. Developed in the last two decades, the MLA is a degree offered to meet the needs of university graduates who have practiced in a profession other than landscape architecture. The MLA first professional degree option has become popular for those coming from careers unrelated to design.

The time required for a landscape architect (holding a BLA degree) to earn an MLA is two years. For those studying landscape architecture for the first time and enrolled in an MLA first professional degree, the minimum time requirement is three years. There are masters programs of one- and two-year duration that non-landscape architects may consider; however, these non-accredited degrees usually require much longer terms of apprenticeship before the graduate is eligible to take the landscape architecture registration examination.

Two types of professional programs in landscape architecture are available: accredited and nonaccredited. Accreditation is a process involving the evaluation of a program, its faculty, curriculum, facilities, and alumni. Whether or not a program is accredited affects the length of time a graduate is required to apprentice before taking a state's professional landscape architectural licensing examination and before receiving national certification via the Landscape Architectural Registration Examination. It is generally accepted that having a degree from an accredited landscape architecture program is preferable and is ultimately worth more in terms of salary and competitive advantage for employment.

Professional Practice Phase

Entry Level Position or Apprenticeship Upon earning their first professional degree in landscape architecture, most graduates strive to find employment and gain professional experience. Generally they seek employment with two types of employers: public agency or private office.[1]

Practical experience may begin with an entry-level position such as draftsman or landscape assistant. Given job market conditions or their own interests and skills, graduates may seek employment in some other field that has a need for the knowledge and skills of a landscape architecture graduate, such as a planning agency of a local government, or an agency or consulting firm involved with environmental assessment or remediation. Other employment alternatives might include working with a multidisciplinary A/E firm, as a research assistant for a not-for-profit group such as the Nature Conservancy, or as staff or editor for a magazine such as *Southern Living*. Entry-level positions are appropriate for an apprenticeship. The entry position generally matches the skill level and knowledge of graduates wishing to build and expand their formal academic education. Responsibility at this level allows the student with primarily classroom experience to adequately handle the practical needs of working with real clients and projects while under the professional guidance of a seasoned practitioner.

Professional License Forty-five states and the provinces of British Columbia and Ontario require individuals to obtain a license to practice landscape architecture. The licensing process was established to protect the health, safety, and welfare of the public. Applicants must pass a test to receive a license. The test ensures that the applicant demonstrates a minimum competency of knowledge and skill to practice landscape architecture in the state. Moreover, each state has its own set of criteria that one must fulfill prior to taking the licensing examination. Academic preparation, either a bachelor's or master's degree from an accredited program and a one- or two-year apprenticeship work-

---

[1]Not everyone who graduates immediately runs out to find a job. Some graduates set some time aside to travel or perhaps go on to graduate school to pursue advanced study in a related field.

ing under a licensed landscape architect, are the usual preexamination requirements. Upon obtaining a license, those working for a firm or agency can expect to receive greater responsibility or perhaps an increase in pay. Others may begin establishing their own private practice.

Advanced Academic Studies   A relatively small percentage of students with Bachelor of Landscape Architecture degrees pursue an advanced degree. This is partly true because few employers of landscape architects make an advanced degree a condition of employment or advancement. Individuals wishing to pursue an academic career, however, must certainly seek advanced degrees such as a master's degree in landscape architecture, geography, environmental studies, or other related areas in the natural and behavioral sciences. Some will go on to earn a doctoral degree to move up the academic promotional ladder, to further their research interests, or to satisfy their own intellectual needs.

For some, seeking an advanced degree, going back to school means expanding their knowledge of a particular aspect of the profession they find interesting, or which they believe will enhance their professional credentials and earning power. For others, it provides an opportunity to investigate entirely new areas and advances in the field. And for those who have decided on a teaching career, the master's degree in landscape architecture or a related field is the universally accepted minimum standard for a tenure-track, academic appointment.

Mid-level: Project Management   As your skills and capabilities increase, you will generally be given more responsibility. When you become a seasoned professional reaching the point of capably handling work assignments with little or no direction, you may then be given the responsibility of managing one or more projects. Depending on the size of the office and its workload, individuals can advance from entry-level to project designer then project management positions.

The project manager will often have from two to five years of professional experience. There might be anywhere from one to a great many project managers depending on the size of the office. Upon reaching the level of project manager, a landscape architect will be skilled in all aspects of project production, including planning, design, and execution of construction implementation documents. Most project managers will also work directly with the client. Interaction with the client might include initial communication and negotiations with the possible exception of contractual and financial negotiations, which are generally the responsibility of the office administrators, the owners, the principals, or the agency administrator.

The duties of the project manager are to schedule and manage the production of all required work for specific projects assigned to them. Usually project managers are given the responsibility for handling client contacts, coordinating project-related activities with other consultants or responsible agencies, and managing the efforts of support staff as well as working on the projects in a production capacity themselves.

Management and Administration: Agency Managers or Private Firm Owners
People with strong entrepreneurial or leadership drives or with a desire for ownership will eventually reach a stage in their professional career when they will want their own firm or aspire to be a principle of an existing firm. For those well along in their careers as public and academic practitioners, becoming an administrator in an organization satisfies a leadership need analogous to their counterparts in the private sector.

The key responsibility of a manager or owner is to develop the policy and direction of the organization. In government, this often requires that the manager identify specific procedures, actions, programs, and goals that together carry out the intent of the agency s mission or statutory obligations. A manager in a private-sector organization is responsible for establishing policies, procedures, and the overall direction of the company involving all aspects of a business, including financial, marketing, personnel management, general administration of projects, and business operations.

For some in management and administration, their involvement in design and the execution of services is limited to overseeing projects and quality control of the professional staff's executed work. These managers delegate work to others. Not all managers and administrators delegate; rather, they manage the office so that they maintain an active role in the design, production, or execution of work. Likewise, owners may be quite involved in the day-to-day activities of the office. They are able to do this by hiring others to manage the business and administrative affairs of the office. This model is more likely to occur in the private sector than elsewhere, although some public administrators are able to maintain a hands-on presence.

Seasoned Practitioner Phase

Service and Altruistic Endeavors   Many who stay in the profession and continue to be actively engaged in and committed to what they are doing as landscape architects often reach a plateau where they may want to continue to making valuable contributions to the profession while seeking other outlets of creativity. This plateau affords a panoramic perspective filled with opportunities that may lead them in new directions utilizing their knowledge, skill, and experience. The desire to give back something to the profession or society through public service, teaching, or mentoring is common among seasoned practitioners in landscape architecture. The decision to become active on community boards and public commissions gives the seasoned practitioner an opportunity to make a contribution to society on a voluntary or salary basis. Some may choose to make a contribution by becoming involved in education as a teacher or program chair. Joining the academic ranks as a full- or part-time instructor provides a rewarding avenue in which to share one's knowledge and professional experience with students.

Others have turned their attention to politics and service to professional societies such as the American Society of Landscape Architects. Although few in number, several landscape architects have successfully run for public office. Others have become active in ASLA as state chapter and national officers.

Still others may decide to change careers completely, which might involve going back to school or completing specialized training. Or, the landscape architecture professional might simply cross over into a related area such as joining a corporation that produces and supplies green industry products, becoming involved in sales for a similar industry, working for a provider of liability insurance, or moving from the private to the public sector as an administrator.

In a nutshell, a career in landscape architecture is an evolution from student to practitioner, to manager and administrator, and finally to greater involvement as a mentor or participant in altruistic activities. As you continue in the profession you will extend your knowledge base and acquire new skills in management and administration. In the final stages of the professional continuum, many seasoned practitioners give back to society through education, service, and philanthropic endeavors.

4. PROFESSIONAL ORGANIZATIONS

The American Society of Landscape Architects (ASLA)

The American Society of Landscape Architects was established in 1899. Originally incorporated under the laws in the State Commonwealth of Massachusetts, the Society has become the profession's national organization with over 10,000 members. ASLA is legally chartered as a not-for-profit education organization. The Society's national headquarters is located in Washington, D.C. and employs a staff of about thirty-five.

The mission of the Society "is the advancement of the art and science of landscape architecture by leading and informing the public, by serving its members, and by leading the profession in achieving quality in the natural and built environment."[2] The basic objectives of the Society are embodied in the Long Range Plan adopted by the Board of Trustees in 1987. The objectives can be translated into the priority activities of ASLA, summarized as follows:[3]

- **Public Information and Service**

Among the most important of the Society's objectives is greater public awareness of the impact of landscape architecture and the role played by landscape architects.

- **Public Policy**

Maintenance and implementation of an ambitious public policy agenda also stands at the forefront of ASLA objectives. Issues addressed include acid rain, wetland preservation, water resource managment, appropriate harvesting of natural resources, and the entire range of important ecological issues.

- **Education and Professional Development**

Through the Council of Education (COE), the Landscape Architectural Accreditation Board (LAAB), assures both the public and the profession that landscape architecture programs maintain the highest possible level of educational preparation to advance practitioners' level of competency (Figure 5.4).

- **Information Resources**

Communication is critical not only to professional education, but to all of the challenges facing landscape architects. As a result, a major objective of the Society is to harness all available media—print, electronic, audio-visual, and database systems—to ensure landscape architects stay at least one step ahead of rapidly emerging trends and developments.

- **Chapter Services**

ASLA's forty-six chapters are the national organization's lifeline to the profession and have led to the Society's new focus on providing responsive, innovative programs to chapter members.

[2]American Society of Landscape Architects, *1993 Members Handbook.*
[3]Ibid.

Figure 5.4 The American Society of Landscape Architects (ASLA) offers many services assisting its members to advance in their careers as well as providing information to the public. ASLA publishes the *Landscape Architecture Magazine* as well as many specialized documents, textbooks, and newsletters.

- **Membership Opportunity**

  Literally thousands of ASLA members are actively involved in advancing the profession at the local, chapter, and national levels. This opportunity for participation in the life of the Society has been an important membership benefit since ASLA's founding in 1899 (Figure 5.5).

- **Management and Administration**

  In developing the Long Range Plan, the leaders of the Society were mindful that success was possible only if the finances of the Society were well managed and if ASLA's headquarters were staffed by a core of competent professionals. The twin focus continues to receive high priority.

The Society is governed by an Executive Committee and a forty-seven member Board of Trustees representing forty-six individual state chapters plus a student representative. Each chapter has a leadership body elected by chapter members. Most chapters have a president, president elect, secretary, and treasurer. These officers together with the chapter trustee (who represents the chapter and sits on the National Board of Trustees) constitute the chapter executive committee or board. Each chapter sets its own agenda of chapter activities, and has a budget with sources that include membership dues and other fund-raising activities.

Many of the activities and programs of ASLA are carried out by the voluntary contributions of its members through more than forty standing committees and task forces. There

Figure 5.5 During the annual meeting of the American Society of Landscape Architects approximately 2,000 or more members gather to participate in educational sessions, workshops, and products shows. A design award program offers landscape architects the opportunity to gain recognition for exemplary work.

are other opportunities to serve the Society and to be a contributor in furthering its goals. A number of individuals are appointed to serve as liaisons to national organizations of design, environmental, and other interests and disciplines related to the profession of landscape architecture.

Membership in the Society falls into four professional categories.

- **Members**

Landscape architects whose ability, attainments, aims, and character are judged to promote the purpose of the Society and who, through an appropriate combination of academic and/or professional experience, meet the qualifications established in the bylaws. Full membership is limited to landscape architects who reside in the United States, its possessions, or bordering countries, and to landscape architects who are citizens of the United States and are residing or working abroad. Only full members may attach "ASLA" after their name in correspondence or on letterhead and other official or professional printed matter.

- **Fellows**

Members with a minimum of ten years' standing as full members with ASLA, may be elected as fellows in recognition of their outstanding contributions to the profession by excellence in executed works of landscape architecture, in professional school instruction, in professional writing, or in direct service to the Society. In order to be considered for fellow status one must be nominated by ones' chapter or by the Council of Fellows. Only a fellow may attach "FASLA" after his name in correspondence or on letterhead and other official or professional printed matter.

- **Associates**

Landscape architects who have earned a degree in landscape architecture and have worked a minimum length of time may apply and be accepted as an associate member. Associate members may not attach "ASLA" after their name in any correspondence or for any purpose.

- **Foreign Associates**

Landscape architects who are not residents of the United States, its possessions, or countries bordering the United States, but whose ability, attainments, aims, and character are judged consistent with the purpose of the Society.

5. LICENSURE AND PROFESSIONAL REGISTRATION

Background

Landscape architects, like architects and engineers, are licensed under state statutes within the state in which they practice. Forty-five states have licensing or registration laws for individuals who practice or call themselves landscape architects. The licensing of landscape architects began in 1954 in California and Louisiana. Neither the federal nor local governments have licensing laws. The licensing of landscape architects and other design professionals is soley under the purview of state governments.

States license professionals for one primary purpose: to protect the health, safety, and welfare of the public. When it is determined that the services provided by a profession may adversely affect the health, safety, and welfare of the public and the general public does not have the capacity to determine if a practitioner is competent to properly perform the services, the state may require licensing of that profession. Individuals must have a license to practice landscape architecture in each state in which they wish to practice. Each state, through its laws and statutes, performs the following:

- defines the profession
- specifies the qualifications required to practice the profession.
- outlines the administrative procedures required for licensure.

There are two types of licensing laws for landscape architects. The first is a *title law* wherein only those who have satisfied the requirements for licensure in the state having a title act may call themselves landscape architects. The second licensing law is called a *practice act*. A practice act enumerates the services that constitute the practice of landscape architecture. Only individuals licensed to practice the profession may perform those services.

Generally, a state will establish a board to carry out the administrative and regulatory functions of a licensing statute. In some cases, these responsibilities are assigned to an existing board. Landscape architects are regulated in some states by their own board or by existing boards such as a horticulture commission or an an architecture and engineering licensing board. The members of these boards are appointed by the governor or state legislative committee. Boards usually include a mix of members including representative practitioners and lay persons (also called *public members*). Where several professions are regulated by a single board, membership includes representation from each profession plus one or more public members.

The licensing boards are totally independent from similar boards in other states. Each establishes its own definitions, criteria, and requirements. Each has the option of developing and administering its own examination for testing minimum performance and knowledge competency. In the case of landscape architectural boards, they have organized under the national umbrella organization called the Council of Landscape Architectural Boards (CLARB). CLARB was formed initially to exchange information and to develop a standardized examination to be given to applicants who meet the criteria to take it. CLARB bylaws state the objectives of this board:

> [T]o promote high standards of landscape architectural practice; to foster the enactment of uniform laws pertaining to the practice of landscape architecture; to equalize and improve the standards for examination of applicants for state registration; to compile, maintain and transmit professional records to Member Boards for registered landscape architects who meet the standards of this Council.[4]

CLARB is totally independent of the American Society of Landscape Architects, and is not a national licensing body. Rather, it is an association of state regulatory boards established to assist individual boards to fulfill their charges more effectively. One of the important services of CLARB is the design, preparation, and grading of the Landscape Architect Registration Examination (LARE). The LARE was developed in cooperation with all of the CLARB members. The examination provides the basis for both initial state licensure and reciprocal registration. Individuals who have obtained a landscape architectural license may apply for CLARB certification. CLARB certification documents an individual's education, experience, and licensure history. With these documents, an individual can obtain the recommendation from CLARB for member state boards to grant reciprocal registration to the CLARB certificate holder without the requirement of further examination.

Each state registration board has its own application procedures and requirements for candidates to qualify to take the LARE examination. These requirements include education and professional experience. The requirements usually are that the applicant be a graduate from an accredited first professional degree program and have worked one or more years (depending on the state) under a licensed landscape architect. Additional qualifications may be required; the applicant should contact the appropriate board in the state where licensing is being sought.

LARE Examination

The various parts of the LARE examination contain multiple choice, written, and graphic responses to questions. The LARE examination contains seven test sections. Other sec-

[4]Council of Landscape Architectural Registration Boards, *Understanding the LARE* (Landscape Architecture Registration Examination), Fairfax, VA, 1992.

tions may be added by the individual state boards. The applicant will be notified of the number and categories of sections. The LARE examination tests for knowledge, skills, and abilities. The design of test questions is based on specific tasks and knowledge areas deemed necessary to perform landscape architectural services without endangering the health, safety, and welfare of the public. The test sections currently included in the LARE examination are shown in Figure 5.6.[5]

The tests administered by the individual state licensing boards are graded all at once in one location by a team of graders under the direction of CLARB. The graphic and written responses are evaluated by a team of trained graders. The process for establishing passing scores is not based on a predetermined percentage of points. The passing score for each section will vary from year to year depending on the difficulty of the questions of each section. The exams are evaluated in the following areas:

- grammar, legibility, completeness sufficient to assign a score
- following of rules and directions.
- program requirements that incorporate all elements into the solution, how size and shape of elements fit the program, specified relationships of program elements accommodated
- design logic, including effectiveness of the solution, solution response to site and pertinent off-site elements, opportunities, and constraints
- technical aspects, such as adequacy of size and shape of program elements, satisfactory addressing of safety issues, observation of legal constraints such as zoning and building codes

A candidate must earn a passing grade on all sections included in the examination. A candidate may retake sections of the exam as many times as necessary in order to achieve a passing score.

Depending on the requirements of each state, once the candidate has passed all sections of the exam he or she is eligible to be licensed in the state the exam was taken. Some states may have additional requirements to be met after the exam is successfully passed. These requirements might include an interview.

Once licensed, the candidate's yearly fees must be kept current in order for the license to remain valid. Some states require licensees to meet certain minimum continuing education requirements each year. Procedures for documenting and verifying continuing education activities vary from state to state as do the number of continuing education credit hours required annually. There is no limit to the number of states in which one can be licensed. Licensure or some form of registration may also be required for a landscape architect to practice in certain other countries. It is the responsibility of each practitioner to inquire and verify the legal requirements any government or jurisdiction may have to regulate the practice of landscape architecture. This type of research should also include government permits and ordinances, as well as tax laws.

---

[5]Council of Landscape Architectural Registration Boards, *Understanding the LARE* (Landscape Architecture Registration Examination), p. 25).

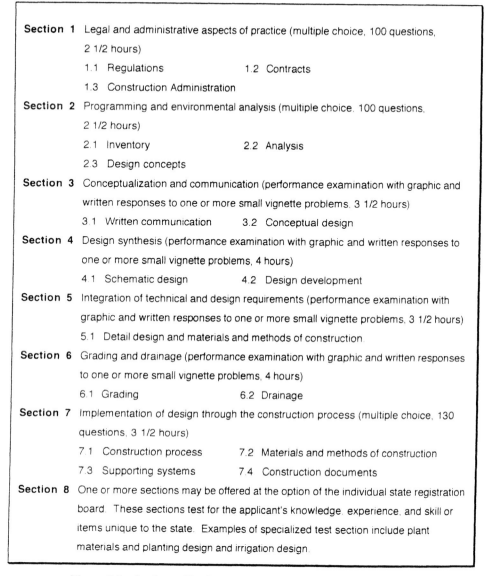

Section 1 Legal and administrative aspects of practice (multiple choice, 100 questions,
2 1/2 hours)

1.1 Regulations   1.2 Contracts

1.3 Construction Administration

Section 2 Programming and environmental analysis (multiple choice. 100 questions,
2 1/2 hours)

2.1 Inventory   2.2 Analysis

2.3 Design concepts

Section 3 Conceptualization and communication (performance examination with graphic and
written responses to one or more small vignette problems. 3 1/2 hours)

3.1 Written communication   3.2 Conceptual design

Section 4 Design synthesis (performance examination with graphic and written responses to
one or more small vignette problems, 4 hours)

4.1 Schematic design   4.2 Design development

Section 5 Integration of technical and design requirements (performance examination with
graphic and written responses to one or more small vignette problems, 3 1/2 hours)

5.1 Detail design and materials and methods of construction.

Section 6 Grading and drainage (performance examination with graphic and written responses
to one or more small vignette problems, 4 hours)

6.1 Grading   6.2 Drainage

Section 7 Implementation of design through the construction process (multiple choice, 130
questions, 3 1/2 hours)

7.1 Construction process   7.2 Materials and methods of construction

7.3 Supporting systems   7.4 Construction documents

Section 8 One or more sections may be offered at the option of the individual state registration
board. These sections test for the applicant's knowledge. experience, and skill or
items unique to the state. Examples of specialized test section include plant
materials and planting design and irrigation design.

Figure 5.6   Sections of landscape architects' registration examination.

6. IN-BASKET

1. Would you agree that someone who is an experienced carpenter is no less a professional than a landscape architect? Describe what attributes distinguish a professional.

2. Assessing your abilities and professional interests, describe the type of projects you think you will be doing in five years and in ten years. Consider what type of office you will be working in, what you will be doing, and your responsibilities.

3. Assuming you are financially prepared to attend graduate school, would you consider

returning to earn a master's degree in landscape architecture or a related field? Describe how earning an advanced degree might help you in furthering your career goals.

4. Imagine you are a principal in a private firm or hold a management position with a public agency. What contributions do you see yourself making in your community and in what type of organization could you see yourself serving on as a member of its governing board in order to provide a public service?

■■■■■■ **CHAPTER 6**

Marketing Yourself

1. Introduction
2. Some Initial Thoughts
3. The Employment Search Process
4. Marketing Concept in the Job Search
5. Determining Job Market Opportunities
6. Solicited and Unsolicited Approaches
7. Ten Steps in Preparing for the Job Search
8. Terms of Employment
9. Tips for Starting Out
10. In-Basket

1. INTRODUCTION

Understanding and being able to satisfy the needs of potential employers is the key to being competitive and successful in the job market. In this chapter, the approach taken to prepare for the successful job search will be the market-oriented approach.[1] Marketing is an integral function of any business. To apply this concept to the job search, one should consider and prepare a market-oriented strategy for finding employment. A market-oriented strategy consists of systematically identifying unfulfilled needs and wants of employers. The successful application of a marketing approach to the job search process will include determining and targeting the employers you can best serve, considering your own skills, strengths, experience, knowledge, and professional goals, and then seeking out potential employers where there is a good match (Figure 6.1).

2. SOME INITIAL THOUGHTS

Within 15 to 20 seconds after shaking hands, the employer's decision to hire or not is close to being made. This can be demoralizing thought, considering all the effort that goes into preparing for an interview. Employers still rely on first impressions, the gut reactions to body language and eye contact, in their decision-making hiring process. All the preparations that go into producing a resume and portfolio do not have anything like the impact of the handshake, the initial, brief verbal exchange, and your appearance. One's attitude is crucial both at the first meeting and throughout the interview process. A positive attitude contributes to the chemistry or vibrations in formulating first impressions. The importance

---

[1] Kotler, *Marketing Management.*

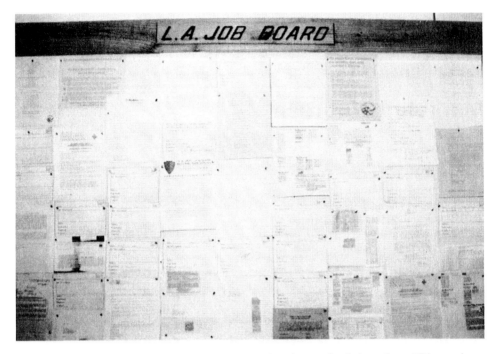

Figure 6.1   Many schools provide employment search assistance for their students. This may be as simple as posting employment notices on a bulletin board, or offering a course in portfolio preparation and job search techniques.

of dress and grooming cannot be overlooked. When the interview is over, you don't want the interviewer to remember you by the color of your dress, shirt, or tie. Rather, you want the lasting impression to be one of an overall professional image.

Securing a good job can be an elusive enterprise. Careful planning and preparation are required to be successful in the job market. It is recommended to approach the job search with clear goals in mind. You should have a clear, visual image of the kind of job and employment conditions you want. Knowing what you are looking for makes it easier to evaluate employment options. Finding quality employment opportunities takes considerable more effort.

The ideal job does not in all probability exist. Therefore, being clear about professional goals makes it easier to decide which jobs to pursue and which not to pursue. A good position is one in which:

- There is opportunity for advancement.
- The employer is interested in advancing the profession and committed to continuing employee education.
- The employer has a concern for employees' welfare in terms of adequate pay and benefits.

3. THE EMPLOYMENT SEARCH PROCESS

Conducting an effective job search requires a process as involved as any used in design. An attractive job prospect provides good opportunities for professional growth, and adequate salary and benefits. These kinds of employment opportunities do not come about by accident. Rather, they are obtained through careful planning and the execution of a well-thought-through program. Table 6.1 presents the major components of effective job search.

No one looking for a job can hope to find a good position simply by being a good designer, although being a good designer and having technical competence are certainly desirable qualities. The search must take into consideration beforehand the "Job Description" that employers prepare for each job position category. Each job description consists of a list of the responsibilities, skills, and qualifications most desired for each position.

TABLE 6.1   An Effective Employment Search Process

1. Identify personal goals and strengths.

Assess your strengths and your career and personal interests, identifying:
   a. Career goals in terms of where you want to be in:
      • Near term: 1-3 years
      • Long-term: 3-8 years
   b. Career needs in terms of employment experience and education needed in order to obtain long-term career goals.

2. Gather good information.

Research and find facts related to understanding employment trends:
   a. Follow business and economic sections in newspapers and other printed media.
   b. Follow governmental programs particularly involving capital improvement, and interest rates.

Research and gather information to understand prospective employers in terms of:
   a. Their personal needs, and skill requirements.
   b. The type of work, clients, and projects.

3. Develop an employer database of potential employers.

Match your knowledge, skill, experience, and qualifications with prospective employers you plan to target.
   a. Type of employer (public, private, academic, other)
   b. Type of work (staff technical support, mid- and upper-level professional staff, management, other)

4. Design self-marketing products.

Determine the message you want to convey and the vehicles to market yourself:
   a. Portfolio
   b. Resume
   c. Letters and other written materials
   d. References
   e. Other techniques including video, computer floppy disk, etc.

5. Develop contacts, leads, and interviews.

Strategy for two situations:
   a. Responding to employment ads: Prepare and organize portfolio, resume, and any written correspondes to meet the specifics of the qualification requirements and job description.
   b. Unsolicited contact: Contacts with prospective employers initiated by the person looking for employment utilizing the following approaches:
      1. Setting up interviews
         • Written correspondence
         • Telephone
      2. Interview
      3. Follow-up correspondence
         • Thank-you letter
         • Acknowledge offer of acceptance

Competition is also important in the search for employment. The competition for employment can be fierce, for both recent graduates or seasoned practitioners. The job market follows cycles. There are times when job seekers can expect several job offers with very little effort. Other times, employment opportunities are not so plentiful, requiring a long, wearisome search. Qualified professionals who understand the staffing needs and have the necessary skills required by prospective employers can, if they utilize a marketing strategy, be successful in the job hunt. Sound application of marketing strategies can improve your success in the job market regardless of regional or national economic conditions.

4. MARKETING CONCEPT IN THE JOB SEARCH

The process of finding a job should be approached with at least as much thought as one employs for a complex design project. The preparations required for a successful job search are no less demanding, perhaps requiring as much inventiveness and creativity as any urban design or site planning project. If you approach it in a conscientious, well-planned manner, you can expect to increase your chances of finding and landing a good position with an excellent employer. The business of finding a job should be approached as a marketing activity. Instead of marketing a product, you are marketing yourself. You are the product, the very somebody a prospective employer needs. Upon embarking on a job hunt, consider this very simple question-answer sequence:

Question: Why would someone hire you?
Answer: Because they need you.

Yes, it is just that simple. You are hired because you are needed. You are chosen for the job because you have the right combination of knowledge, skills, and experience that match the specific personnel requirements of a prospective employer. In addition, you will probably find that you are hired because you are in the *right place at the right time*.

Your particular knowledge, technical skills, abilities, experience, and people skills—as a package—should match the knowledge, skills, abilities, experience, and people skills *needs* of the employer. In other words:

$$\text{Employee Experience} = \text{Employer Needs}$$

or

$$\text{Your knowledge, skills, and experience} = \text{Employer's knowledge, skills,}$$
$$\text{and experience requirements}$$

When an employer is considering hiring, that employer has a set of *selection criteria* to evaluate prospective employees. The criteria might include:

- general and technical knowledge
- communication skills—written, graphic, and verbal
- technical skills and organizational abilities
- relevant work experience
- professional, and personal motivation

- interpersonal skills
- professional organization involvement
- extracurricular interests, hobbies, and community involvement

The selection criteria define the type of employee that best meets the current or projected workload of an employer. Not all employers are necessarily looking for the same qualities or have the same needs. The type of work, the clientele, the particular set of services offered, and the chemistry of the existing office personnel influence a decision to employ someone as much as does their experience and qualifications.

To find quality employment you must plan, prepare, and carefully execute a marketing program of yourself. A person's marketing program should be designed to respond to a set of specific selection criteria. What will land you a job with one employer may not even get you an interview from others. You should know the needs and requirements of each prospective employer or agency and tailor your marketing materials (portfolio, resume, supporting materials) accordingly. The chances of selling a broom to the owner of a shag rug are slim. The likelihood of selling a vacuum cleaner to the owner of a shag rug is much better.

Avoid the shotgun approach to finding a job, for it is problematic at best. Sending a resume along with a preprinted "To Whom it May Concern" cover letter to 500 prospective employers generally reaps poor results. Marketing is as much an art as a science and is as much the result of inspiration as it is from perspiration.

What are employers really looking for when reading your letters and resumes, or when talking with you across the table during an interview? Generally an employer evaluates prospective employees using a combination of considerations, including at least the following:

- **Knowledge:**

  Knowledge and understanding of technical information as well as diversity of interests and a good grasp of general nontechnical knowledge

- **Skills:**

  Range of pertinent skills needed for the projects at hand

- **Experience:**

  Work experience with a diversity of project types

- **Compatibility:**

  Interpersonal skills, candidate's ability to fit in with existing personnel

- **Gut reaction:**

  Intuitive (favorable or unfavorable) sense of whether it is going to work out, considering personality, capability, and potential

The considerations above require little explanation except for "gut reaction." The attributes of one person that trigger a gut reaction by another person have a lot to do with human nature. Whether someone has a good feeling about another, likes the other person (for whatever reason), believes the other person is being truthful and can be trusted, are conclusions that humans make every day about one another. These are human quality assessments made within a short time period, during the first meeting. Human beings communicate with one another in many ways, including verbal language and body language. Based on these forms of communication, together with available pertinent information, people react and make decisions.

Most relationships between people in business, as in personal life, are successful when people trust one another and feel some common basis for carrying on their relations. Human responses to others, if positive, also create a sense of community and of caring. People caring about others contributes to the sense of community in an office where employees enjoy and look forward to coming work each day. Successful business leaders understand the importance of a caring environment and reward those who contribute in building this sense of community and trust in the workplace. In selecting new employees, these leaders are looking for people who fit into the existing office community and who they believe will contribute positively toward the health of this community as well as to the professional capabilities of the office.

One should approach job hunting with the same market focus used by manufacturing giants such as Proctor & Gamble, Ford Motor Company and Coca-Cola. Much of the success of these companies has been the result of quality products but is also due to successful marketing efforts. These companies design and market their products by understanding and targeting specific publics. Someone looking for good employment must have the same mind-set as these companies. Consider who you are, what your skills are, and how and for whom these skills would be most attractive and beneficial.

The next step is to package the product (your knowledge skills, experience, and abilities) so that the intended market (potential employers) will want to buy (hire) the product (you). In other words, develop a combination of materials including:

- resume
- portfolio
- work samples
- letters of interest or introduction

These materials should communicate your:

- education and training
- skills
- experience
- personal and professional interests
- professional goals

Then attempt to match these with potential employers or show how your professional preparation and experience fit the employer's job description. The key to finding and landing a great job lies in gathering the right information about the prospective employers, including the type of work they do, their clientele, and unique characteristics of the region they serve. Additionally, information gathering should include current economic conditions, particularly short- and long-term trends in the region where you are seeking to work.

5. DETERMINING JOB MARKET OPPORTUNITIES

Even in times when the job market is weak, there are firms hiring. At the national and global levels, there are forces[2] at play that directly relate to demand of landscape architectural services. While there may be firms laying people off, others firms may be in a hiring mode. These firms continue to secure new contracts in difficult economic times through having developed and applied an effective marketing strategy. Offices considering hiring additional staff may either have a backlog of work or be gearing up for what they believe will be some very busy times in the near future.

What are the sources for assessing the job market? There are several sources that provide important clues of current and future economic conditions. The newspapers provide clues on economic forces and government programs affecting the job market of the present and near future. The deliberations of the U.S. Congress considering a major expenditure for capital projects portends jobs and work. For example, the U.S. Congress periodically considers programs allocating billions of dollars for capital improvement projects. The money becomes available in the form of an appropriations bill. Many federal appropriation bills fund federal projects and also have sums allocated to fund projects at the state and local government level. The projects can be for roads, sewers, bridges, parks, transit facilities, and a whole range of other projects. These expenditure programs often create work for design professionals such as A/E firms (engineers, architects, and landscape architects) under professional services contracts.

During periods when interest rates on borrowing money drop, job creation and A/E service contracts increase. With lower interest rates it can be anticipated that real estate construction will increase; which also creates more jobs and contracts for landscape architects. The lion's share of home buying in the recent past has been primarily by people who already own their own home but wish to increase their standard of living. If interest rates are low, home buying will increase and the buyers will include first-time home owners. Home ownership is still a primary goal of most Americans and home ownership by individuals, couples, and single-parent families is expected to increase. Likewise, as the activities of the home building industry increase, hiring of landscape architects will usually also increase.

Landscape architects seeking employment today should neither limit their search to nor anticipate finding positions with traditional employers. Although traditional employers hiring landscape architects can be counted on to some extent, the growth areas for employment from now until the end of the century will be with nontraditional employers. Job seekers can also expect to find increasing employment opportunities in new regions outside the United States. The jobs that will be most plentiful and probably have the best range of starting salaries will be in five sectors:

- engineering firms or multidisciplinary A-E firms
- government agencies
- construction firms, including design-build
- green industry: nurseries, growers, landscape contracting and maintenance
- international employers and clients

---

[2]Forces affecting the job market—for landscape architects—include national growth, employment, and production picture; strength of the dollar and the foreign trade deficit; interest rates (particularly the rates offered by the Federal Reserve); new construction activity; and federal programs designed to affect the economy (such as a jobs bill or other government spending program designed to create jobs).

Landscape architectural firms involved in the real estate development industry (new housing and redevelopment) and serving these five sectors can anticipate demand of their services. With increased demand for landscape architectural services, recent graduates can expect to find employment at entry-level positions.

Students with some relevant work experience will always find the going easier when job hunting than students without previous work experience. Employers, when evaluating a student's resume, place value on a variety of work experience including:

- work in a nursery
- work with a landscape or building contractor
- work in a professional office—private or public (engineering, architecture, or landscape architecture)
- work with a maintenance contractor, including private gardening work during school and summers

6. SOLICITED AND UNSOLICITED APPROACHES

The two primary avenues for obtaining employment include solicited and unsolicited approaches. The solicited approach is when one is responding to an advertised position, whereas the unsolicited approach involves strategies for finding potential employers and in some way convincing them that they need to hire you. Both approaches require advance preparations, including resume and portfolio, letters and other forms of written communication, and telephone or personal contacts.

Solicited Approach

In the solicited case, where an employer is looking to fill a position, much of the advance preparations of the job hunter should focus on the position announcement and job description. The skills and experience the employer is looking for will be outlined in the job announcement or job description. The employer will usually provide a written job description if requested. The prospective employee should read over carefully both items (job announcement and job description) and prepare a resume, portfolio, and other materials that show experience and the ability to fulfill the job description and qualifications desired.

Unsolicited Approach

The unsolicited approach requires the person seeking employment to offer his or her services to prospective clients not necessarily engaged in seeking help or in filling a position. In this case, a job description or position announcement is not available; one in effect is trying to create a position by making one's qualifications or experience attractive enough to create some interest in targeted employers. Using ingenuity and marketing talents, a job seeker identifies potential employers, prepares resume and portfolio materials, then makes personal contacts that will hopefully ignite a perspective employer's interest.

This approach requires the job seeker to know the prospective firms or agencies well enough to understand their potential needs. Through research, the job seeker will find out about prospective employers' clientele, the services offered, and the skills they find potentially attractive. For example, if you are adept at computer applications and know of targeted employers wanting to gain computer capabilities, offering these skills might create sufficient interest to, in a sense, create a new position in the office and get you hired.

7. TEN STEPS IN PREPARING FOR THE JOB SEARCH

1. Describe the type of firm or agency in which you would like to be employed.

Targeting is an important concept when job hunting. Targeting requires you to make choices and be selective about the type of employer you feel most qualified to work for. When targeting is considered, you will recognize that certain employers would best meet your career objectives while providing a good match of skills and experience.

2. Describe the kind of projects you would like to be working on.

A corollary concept to targeting is recognizing that firms and agencies tend to specialize in certain types of work. Before setting out into the employment market, it is best to identify the type of work, projects, and clients that best meet your interests and skills.

Broad categories of work types include:
- project design and planning
- administration and management
- regulatory functions
- resource and environmental management
- education and research.

Broad categories of clients include:
- private developers, entrepreneurs, or corporations serving local regional, multiregional, or international clients
- private individuals or families
- public agencies serving populations or communities representing local, regional, state and federal levels
- public agencies having administrative, regulatory or planning authority for prescribed environmental or land-based units or resources

3. Select a city, region, or country where you would like to work.

Even though you may be willing to relocate where the best employment exists, selecting a target geographic area is a good strategy in the job search. By selecting a geographic area, you can more efficiently gather information useful in preparing your portfolio and resume materials. Identifying a region simplifies and gives focus to the fact-finding phase of employment-seeking preparations. Useful information unique to the targeted region might include:
- economic factors and trends
- environmental considerations
- materials and industry construction standards
- legal and regulatory affairs
- client and project type opportunities

4. Research targeted firms or agencies.

Learn about their work by researching:
- Published sources: Study professional and trade magazines (such as *Landscape Architecture Magazine*), ASLA professional design awards program, published agency pamphlets, and mission statements.
- Network sources: Glean information from conversations with people familiar with targeted employers. Other network sources include alumni, social, and professional colleagues.

5. Develop a distinct image for your resume package.

This package includes a resume and correspondence used in your job search, such as a letter of application, a transmittal letter, and a follow-up thank-you. Most resumes are one page with the exception of academic resumes and special-purpose application situations where prospective employers ask for more complete information. A resume should be tailored to the employment position for which you are applying. Include any qualifications related to the position sought. Make sure to use words and nomenclature described in the specific job announcement when responding.

There are several types of resumes including:
- Functional or skills resume: This is effective for students or recent graduates who have little or no applicable work history. This type of resume stresses education and skills (Figure 6.2).
- Chronological resume: This type of resume is used when the applicant has an applicable employment history and track record of accomplishments. Work history is briefly described in reverse chronological order with the most recent position listed first.
- Targeted resume: This type of resume is constructed to address the specific information requested by the employer or is developed using the information researched by the applicant of the targeted employers. The information contained in these resumes stresses skills, unique or exemplary accomplishments (such as design awards), specialized or advanced education, publications, management and administrative history, and professional society activities (Figure 6.3).

6. Develop a distinctive portfolio package that tells a story.

The professional portfolio is a very important marketing and evaluating tool in the design professions. It is used by the employer for evaluating the skill and competency of prospective employees. It is used by the applicant to demonstrate applicable experience, skill proficiency, and abilities.

The portfolio should be capable of meeting a variety of situations encountered in the job search. Essentially, it is a marketing tool, marketing your experience, strengths, and skills. In order to be an effective tool, it is best that it be designed to be flexible so that the materials contained in the portfolio can be rearranged, depending on your understanding of the needs of the employer and the job description.

Before presenting your portfolio or running through its contents, it is best to have a clear idea beforehand what drawings you will show, their order, and why they are being

Resume

Libby C. Farrand

956 Lowe Cove • Baton Rouge, LA 70888 • 504/761.4343

Objective: To obtain an entry-level position with small landscape architecture firm utilizing my design, CAD graphics. and writing skills. I work well in groups or independently.

Education: Louisiana State University, Baton Rouge, LA, May 1994.
Degree: Bachelor of Landscape Architecture. GPA 3.5.

Skills: **Human Relations:**
Retail sales in outdoor specialty store working with customers in selecting equipment such as backpacking, skiing, water sports, and technicl outerwear. Server at family restaurant and customer service at large super market

Computer:
Macintosh: Word, Excel, Mac Architrion, Pagemaker.
IBM: AutoCAD and Microstation (complete senior design project done on computer)

Design and Construction:
Graduate of 5-year design-oriented program. Studio design projects involving site planning, regional planning, urban design, research park. mixed land use. Construction: grading, retention/detention pond design, wood structures. irrigation.

Experience: Retail Sales: > Customer Service (I 1/2 years) outdoor specialty store.
> Server: 6 months at Shoney's family restaurant. LA.
Landscape: > Summer work on landscape installation crews in New Orleans. with Le Norte Design, landscape and development company.
Other: > Customer service: 1 1/2 years with Garden District Nursery.
> Newspaper delivery: 5 years with the Morning Sun Times.
First Aid: > Certified in Louisiana, EMT Level One.

Interests: Outdoor sports including canoeing, hiking. mountain biking. rollerblading. and skiing. Physical fitness sports including aerobics and running.

Personal: DOB 12/14/70 Nonsmoker, drug free. father is high school science teacher. Mother is middle school foreign language teacher. Family enjoys outdoor recreation.

References & Portfolio Available Upon Request

Figure 6.2 Resume of a recent graduate suitable for an entry level position following a skills resume format.

W. Russell Dillingham
687 Azalea Cove • Baton Rouge. LA 70999 • 504/764.6996

Objective:	To obtain a project management position with multidiscipline urban design firm utilizing my five year's urban design, CAD graphics, and contract administration experience.

Education: Louisiana State University, Baton Rouge, LA, May 1988.
Degree: Bachelor of Landscape Architecture. GPA 3.4.

Skills:
Human Relations:
Work well in multiple discipline teams. Good verbal skills.
Participated as Boy's Club soccer coach 2 years, team made all-city 1992.
Board member of Downtown Redevelopment Taskforce, Baton Rouge.

Computer:
Macintosh: Word, Excel, Mac Architrion, Pagemaker.
IBM: AutoCAD and Microstation (complete senior design project done on computer)

Design and Construction:
CBD design feasibility planning, urban design, research office park, mixed land use.
Construction Documents: Full responsibility for putting several downtown urban design
bid packages together. Some contract administration experience.

Experience: Retail Sales: > Customer Service (I 1/2 years) LA Wholesale Nursery.

Landscape/ > CJB Urban Design and Development, Entry level 1988-90.
Professional: > Urban Systems. Inc. project designer, CAD operator 1990-92.
> City of New Orleans, urban designer, riverfront park 1992-93.
> Gates Partnership, project manager, urban design 1993-current
responsible for $2.5 million urban city park rehabilitation project.

Registration: Louisiana 1234 - Landscape Architecture

Interests: Travel and study of urban design projects. Outdoor sports including
canoeing and hiking. Physical fitness sports including swimming and running.

Personal: DOB 12/14/68 Nonsmoker, drug free. Married.
Willing to travel and relocate. Moderate command of Spanish language.

References & Portfolio Available Upon Request

Figure 6.3 Resume of a job seeker with five years experience following a targeted resume format.

presented (what points you want to make about your qualifications). Consider what you intend to say, before the interview, about the materials by way of explanation or elaboration.

Be selective; put your best work forward. Often students try to use the portfolio to demonstrate their development by beginning with projects from their early years leading chronologically to the present. This is interesting but not necessarily effective in terms of demonstrating your qualifications and what you have to offer to your prospective employer.

Show what reflects your best work, your best skills, your strengths, and areas in which you excel. Also show work that meets the job description—the skills and demonstrated experience the prospective employer is looking for.

7. Make initial employer contacts.

Make initial contact by telephone or by letter. The initial contact should attempt to briefly introduce yourself, indicate you are looking for a job, and that you are specifically interested in working for the firm or agency you are calling. The letter should be short and to the point. Don't beat around the bush; ask for the job! Say simply and in a straightforward manner that you are available and want to work.

If there *are no positions* open, still request to make a visit just to introduce yourself, leave a resume, and have a chance to become familiar with the office. This way, although no positions are open, you might accomplish the following:

- Generate sufficient interest and make a positive impression that will carry over into the future when a position does become available.
- Determine whether the firm or office is what you anticipated and, if so, if you would be interested in working there at a later date.
- Find out if your office host is aware of any other position openings that you might want to pursue. Offices are often plugged into the network of employment opportunities that exist in a city or region.

If there *is a position opening*, start out by referencing where you read or heard about the position announcement or show your knowledge and interest in the specific firm or employer. In the initial contact you should attempt to do the following:

- Establish a date and time for an interview appointment.
- Learn about the person or persons who are conducting the interview including their positions in the office.
- Find out what you should specifically do to prepare for the interview; determine what materials and information you should bring to the interview regarding your qualifications.
- Ask for precise directions in cases where you are not familiar with the location of the office.
- Find out what the dress code of the office is so as to prepare accordingly.

8. Make preinterview preparations.

Make sure your application, resume, and portfolio qualifications match with the employer's needs. Know how to get to the interview location and arrive at least five if not ten minutes early. Being on time is crucial to getting a job. No excuses.

Also recognize the importance of thorough and advanced preparations. With adequate preparation comes confidence. Confidence is key to having a successful interview.

9. Prepare for the interview.

There are several purposes for having an interview, including the employer's opportunity to clarify or obtain additional information about you, the person behind the written resume. The interview also helps the prospective employer evaluate your interpersonal skills, and assess your weaknesses and strengths.

Job interview topics might be structured to determine:

- your personality and interpersonal skills, particularly your ability to get along with others
- your qualifications as they relate to the requirements of the position
- your knowledge of the employer's needs
- your interest in the job and your availability

10. Follow-up with a letter or telephone call.

Be quick to say thank you both verbally after the interview and through a follow-up letter or call. Convey your appreciation for having the interview. If you are interested in the position, make clear your interest in being hired. Close the letter with a statement that requires an action on the part of the employer. An action ending might be simply to ask if they would let you know when a decision will be made or if they need any additional information about you, and that you would like the opportunity to provide it.

8. TERMS OF EMPLOYMENT

With so much effort and attention focused on getting a job, little thought is given sometimes to what questions to ask once a job offer is made. Questions like "What is the salary?" is an obvious first question, but there are a range of terms or conditions of employment that need to be considered and thought about before accepting a job offer. Find out as much as possible about the terms of employment before making a decision to accept or reject a job offer. Often, many of the terms or conditions of employment offered by one employer far outweigh those of another employer.

Job Description

The job description outlines the function of work or why the job position exists. It answers the question of "What is it that I am going to be doing, what will be my responsibilities, what will I be expected to do?" It may also list the skills or training desired for the job as well as any specialized experience or knowledge.

Along with the job description may be a job title. A job title indicates where you fit in the office structure, the chain of command and what title your position will carry if you are identified in any correspondence or listed in a proposal.

Common job titles include:

- **Principal:** Partner or owner in a private firm or chief administrative officer in a government agency.
- **Associate:** A term that sometimes suggests an ownership position in a private firm but generally connotes a senior, leadership status. An associate position may have administrative responsibilities that go beyond just managing a project. A regional office of a firm or agency having multiple offices might be managed by an associate-level professional.
- **Project Manager or Job Captain:** A senior-level position reserved for someone licensed and with sufficient experience to manage one or more projects at a time.
- **Assistant:** May be a position held by an entry-level employee just graduated from school or someone with limited, relevant professional experience. In larger offices, the assistant level is someone with at least one or two years' experience.

Salary

Salary is based on education, qualifications, skills, and experience. Specialized skills and experience can enhance a person's salary prospects. Salaries are influenced by conditions of supply and demand. In regions where the availability of qualified professionals is high or regions deemed desirable to live and work in, salaries often are lower than where the opposite conditions exist.

Salaries for government agencies' employees are less influenced by supply and demand forces. Instead, government salaries are established by commissions or personnel policy review boards. Salary levels are prescribed for each job description and are based on the education, qualifications, and work experience required.

Raises

There are several important questions related to salary and raises that a new employee should learn the answers to at the outset. The office's policies on raises should be reviewed particularly as to when they are given, how much they are likely to be, and how are they decided. Consideration for employee raises may be made on an annual basis, based on longevity and performance. Other criteria might include the requirement of obtaining a license or various types of certification, and continuing education credit. Getting a raise may be something as simple as just asking for a raise. Most employers have a policy and follow a procedure before giving raises.

Raises may also come with improved firm profitability. Some private firms determine individual employees' raises on a profit contribution basis, that is, by measuring each employee's contribution to the firm's profitability. Legal codes and procedures dictate salary and raise considerations for most governmental personnel. Although profitability and other entrepreneurial criteria may not figure in government personnel regulations, longevity, work experience, educational advancement, and qualification enhancement are important considerations for determining raises for government agency employees.

Benefits

Benefits offered by a firm or agency have become increasingly important in recent years. For example, with rising medical costs, an attractive medical benefits package may be the overriding basis for choosing to work for one firm over another. Benefits include:

- medical, dental and life insurance
- leave and vacation, and paid holidays
- child care and maternity leave
- profit sharing, pensions, and retirement
- reimbursement for professional dues and education expenses
- financial support for employees' activities in professional organizations
- reimbursement for moving and job relocation expenses
- personnel vehicle parking, commuter transportation costs

Often, an employee may not be eligible immediately for certain benefits. A three-, six-, or twelve-month waiting period may be required before receiving certain benefits. Certain portions of a company's benefit package, such as profit-sharing plans, may not go into effect until after six months or 1,000 hours have been worked. Some benefits, such as profit sharing and retirement, usually have a vested interest clause. This clause provides a scheduled percentage of ownership in the benefit program. Each percentage increment is based on an employee's length of time with the organization, one year providing the lowest percentage of employee ownership and ten the common minimum period for an employee to be fully vested with 100 percent ownership. Fully vested ownership in a profit-sharing or retirement benefit program would allow the employee to take away the entire amount in the employee's account if the employee is terminated or resigns.

In the case of medical insurance, payment of premiums may be shared by the employee and employer or fully paid by one or the other depending on the policy of the organization. Where the employer pays for the medical premiums, the coverage may be more extensive and premiums lower due to the leverage enjoyed by the employer than the coverage and premiums that could be obtained under an individual policy purchased by the employee.

Office Hours, Overtime, and Flextime

The 40-hour work week is commonly held by most people to be the work-week standard in the United States. This is certainly true in the public and white-collar service sectors, in industries dominated by unions, and in most blue-collar trades.

In the private sector of the design industry, a 60-hour-plus work week seems more the standard. Not all offices encourage longer working hours; however, for those offices that do promote longer hours the basis for doing so varies. Regardless of the reason for 40-hour-plus work weeks, one should find out beforehand office policies regarding work-week hours and the handling of overtime.

Clarify if office policy provides for overtime payment, particularly for salaried employees. In case overtime pay does not apply to salaried employees, you should assess the adequacy of your salary considering the additional hours you might have to work. Most offices do not pay overtime for salaried employees while others pay straight time with no premium such as the time and a half paid in many nondesign service industries.

Review or Trial Period

The common practice in private offices is to offer a position with a three-to-six-month trial period. The purpose of making a job offer with a stipulated trial period is to give both parties an opportunity to assess if the employee's qualifications adequately meet the job requirements and to determine if the chemistry between the new employee and existing office staff will make for a good combination. Also at the end of this trial period, several components of a company's benefit package, such as profit sharing and retirement plans, may go into effect should a permanent position be offered.

Many government agencies have something similar to a trial period, called a *review period*. Offering a permanent position with a proviso of a review period enables agency management to terminate a new employee more easily given government personnel regulations and policies. Often a pay raise and upgrade in job position accompanies a decision to keep an employee on a permanent basis.

The trial or review period is very often to the advantage of an employee. It allows the employee time to determine if the position and people are right for his or her qualifications and career expectations. At the end of the trial period the employee often has the opportunity to renegotiate some of the terms of employment, such as salary and job responsibility. Often, an employee will take a position at a lesser salary and with not as much responsibility as hoped for just to get a foot in the door. Assuming both parties want a permanent position to result after the review period, both employee and employer can renegotiate employment terms.

Your Immediate Supervisor

Knowing who you will be working under is a fair question to ask at some point between accepting a position and commencing work. Often, the person conducting the interview (particularly in smaller organizations), or involved in some way during the interview process, will be the person that the new employee will report to. It is reasonable for the position candidate to meet the person he or she will be working for or reporting to and to spend some time with that person before accepting the position. In fairness to both parties, the employee and the employee's supervisor should assess the chemistry between them to determine if the relationship has a good chance for success.

Types of Projects and Responsibilities

The prospective employee should have a clear understanding of the type of projects and attendant responsibilities involved in a job before accepting a position. The employee has certain expectations about the kind of projects and responsibilities that will be assigned. Likewise, the employer has similar expectations about the qualifications and interest of the employee to fulfill the job assignments and needs of the firm or organization. The job requirements should be clearly described and mutually understood before a job offer is made by the employer and accepted by the employee. Should there be a misunderstanding at the outset of the trial or review period, hard feelings can quickly escalate to the extreme disappointment of both parties. Eventually this could lead to termination—by the employer or by the employee.

9. TIPS FOR STARTING OUT

Advancing or finding personal or professional reward in one's field does not come by accident. A personally rewarding professional life is a result of planning and purposeful preparations. As in most aspects of life, there are no guarantees in the design professions. But there are several actions you can take and attitudes you can embrace that will improve your chances for professional success and personal rewards. A professionally and personally rewarding life involves actions that encompass constantly changing targets. While there are no sure recipes for success, you can consider following certain principles that, if adapted to current economic and professional development trends, should increase your chances for a successful professional career and personally rewarding life.

Achieving the Competitive Advantage

Competitive advantage is a marketing term that should be understood well before a student enters the employment market. It means you prepare and make planned, purposeful decisions that will enhance your resume, making you more desirable to potential employers than competing job seekers. Well before graduation, choices and decisions should be made to improve your competitive advantage over other potential entry-level candidates.

As a working goal, you should build your resume, seeking employment that will enhance it, improve your marketability, and ultimately develop a competitive advantage. Building your resume can begin while in school. This is done through work experience (summer and part time during the school year) and by expanding your qualifications with a diversity of elective and specialized courses. This should increase your desirability and competitiveness in preparation for graduation. Once you graduate and obtain your first "real job," you should continue to prepare and make choices that will enhance your competitive advantage in the job market.

Improving your competitive advantage in the job market can be done in the following ways:

- Take courses through continuing education programs to expand or provide depth to your professional knowledge and skills.
- Obtain an advanced degree in the same field, or in an allied field such as planning or engineering, or make a lateral move into another field (such as environmental studies, business, or law).
- Become an active member in community and professional organizations. This will not only expand your professional growth but will allow you to make a contribution to your community and profession. It will also expand your network base, and increase your contacts. Involvement in community life can eventually open up new professional opportunities and will provide support (in the form of solid references) as you advance or change employment.

Variety in Early Job Experience

Consider two to three different employment experiences in the first two to three years after graduation. This can give depth and range to your professional qualifications portfolio. Job hopping may be frowned upon in some professions but not in the design fields, at least in the first few years. It is expected that stability will come as one becomes a seasoned practitioner advancing from entry levels to positions having more technical and management responsibility.

In obtaining a range of experiences, consider a variety of employers from both the public and private sectors of professional practice. Also try to obtain experience working with a variety of project types. One or two years of government employment should be considered in the mix even if the ultimate goal is to work in the private sector. Regardless of whether you plan to make private practice or government service your career choice, both employment types should be sought in the formative years of a career. If government service is your career goal, it would serve well to be knowledgeable and have first-hand experience working in the private sector to learn the design and production procedures. On the other hand, if the private sector is the career track sought, knowledge of government process would be helpful later when you are a consultant working on a government contract.

Extra Ingredients: Creativity and Intelligence

In times of high unemployment, it is extremely difficult to arouse the attention of employers to consider yet another job applicant. Standard advice for getting a job in a soft job market goes by the wayside. In a highly competitive job market, taking risks, being creative, and being smart are the ingredients for attracting serious attention and consideration. These ingredients will not replace an employer's need for solid technical skills and experience, but will separate the job seeker from the crowd.

Going the extra mile in your preparations can make the difference in attracting an employer's attention. Find innovative techniques to demonstrate your skills. Experiment with the use and capabilities of various communication technologies. Select one or more, and develop an application that will communicate your specialized skills and capabilities. Some of the technologies that have application in marketing an individual to potential employers include:

- video programs of your work
- photocopiers in preparing colored images from slides or other media
- floppy disks prepared with multimedia software programs

Persistence without being a nuisance can also pay off in cases where you have strong reasons to believe real opportunities exist. Applying your marketing skills, making thorough preparations, and using good judgment are the extra ingredients that can result in finding a desirable position Be selective, know what position you want relative to meeting your career goals. Then seek out employers who offer opportunities that match your career goals and pursue these employers with a well-coordinated marketing effort.

10. IN-BASKET

1. List what you could do over the next year to improve your marketability and enhance your chances of finding quality employment considering the competitive advantages concept.

2. Provide a step-by-step procedure for the creation of a self-marketing strategy.

3. Make specific suggestions for preparing your resume, letters of correspondence, and portfolio that will get an employer's attention.

4. Look through the newspaper and news and business magazines from the last month and identify specific sources that illustrate economic trends and governmental laws and programs that will influence employment opportunities over the next year.

5. Prepare two lists of questions: one of a job seeker (you) and a second of a prospective employer. Write the answers as if preparing for a job interview. Also put together a list of how you would dress and what materials you would bring to the interview.

6. Consider you are being interviewed for a position you want very much but have reason to believe that the salary being offered is too low for you to live on. Prepare a script outlining how you would negotiate your salary and conditions of employment by accepting a lower salary initially but establishing a process that would result in a higher salary within a specified time period.

CHAPTER 7

Professional Service

1. What Is a Landscape Architect?
2. Design Takes a Back Seat
3. Landscape Architecture Is a Service Profession
4. Areas of Professional Activity
5. Skills of the Effective Landscape Architect
6. In-Basket

1. WHAT IS A LANDSCAPE ARCHITECT?

Todd Steadman, a landscape architect and former garden editor of *Southern Living Magazine*, conducted an interesting study several years ago. Using a video recorder to document people's answers to his questions, Steadman interviewed shoppers in a half-dozen landscape architectural sites throughout the country to ask what they thought a landscape architect was. The responses were often embarrassed looks on their faces or blank stares, or half-hearted guesses that completely missed the mark.

Few of Steadman's respondents gave answers that would pass as satisfactory to a landscape architect. For a seasoned landscape architect viewing the video, the answers were at first blush comical. Although Steadman's random interviews were not scientifically constructed, it was a very telling exercise nonetheless. He found that, for the most part, the public has a very limited awareness of the existence of the profession, much less of what a landscape architect does (Figure 7.1).

If the average person on the street has little or no knowledge about the profession of landscape architecture, it should be no surprise that students studying landscape architecture have a limited understanding about it as well. The average student's understanding of the functions performed by landscape architects can be described in one word: *design*. Therefore, it is not surprising that the activity of design is the foremost attraction that motivates most students who enroll in a landscape architecture program (Figure 7.2).

2. DESIGN TAKES A BACK SEAT

In attempting to paint a more realistic picture about what landscape architects do, two points must be made:

- Landscape architects are required to do more than just design.
- Practitioners devote a decreasing percentage of their time designing as they advance in their career.

Figure 7.1 A Saturday outing along a popular waterfront pedestrian and bicycle trail by a satisfied public with little knowledge that it was designed with the involvement of a landscape architect.

Figure 7.2 Students receiving a critique for a one-week urban design charette at the final presentation of their work.

76

As individuals advance in their career, they find that project administration and personnel management responsibilities increase. Less time is spent designing. More time is spent managing people, communicating with clients, and administering the legal and financial aspects of a practice. Eventually for most practitioners, design will take a back seat to other areas of professional activity. Time spent designing diminishes as the demand for services expands to meet the specific needs of a client or employer. Other activities take up more of a professional's time when involvement in the life of the project expands to include additional areas of responsibility such as project and personnel management, contract negotiations, marketing, and business and financial planning.

3. LANDSCAPE ARCHITECTURE IS A SERVICE PROFESSION

Like architects or engineers, landscape architects perform services for others—their clients or their employers. They do not produce goods in advance to be stored in a warehouse and later sold. Rather, they produce ideas specific to a site or a particular set of program elements. Their designs, recommendations, and ideas are tailored to meet requirements of site-specific conditions or user needs.

For many students in the formative stages of their career, the responsibilities they see for themselves as landscape architects are parallel to their view of a painter's responsibilities. The notion that a painter is dedicated to the canvas is romanticized by many landscape architecture students. This dedication focuses on the journey of coming to terms with the media, the exploration of ideas, and the communication of these ideas as a unique expression of individualistic design concepts.

The services of a landscape architect, however, go far beyond the personal exploration of an artist, although exploration is an important aspect in the development of professional values, aspirations, and goals. The preparations that typically go into the training of a landscape architect are based on:

- a specialized university curriculum
- the acquisition of a general and specialized body of knowledge
- a mastery of technical skills
- professional experience

While the profession has many specialized areas of knowledge and skills, the tenets of the profession emphasize the importance of a sound understanding of design as a process. The formal education of landscape architects further emphasizes the incorporation of social, economic, and ecological considerations into the design process (Figure 7.3).

4. AREAS OF PROFESSIONAL ACTIVITY

Landscape architects apply knowledge from many other disciplines—including the arts, humanities, and social and natural sciences—in creating their design solutions and solving problems of clients and employers. Equally diverse is the range of services landscape architects perform. These include:

- consultation
- planning and research

Figure 7.3 Faculty leading a group of junior high school students on a nature walk introducing them to the application of ecological principles to landscape design (a service program offered by a landscape architecture program to community schools).

- design
- implementation

A landscape architect could be hired to perform any of these functions singly or in combination. What service or combination of services are appropriate depends on the needs and requirements of the client. In some cases, the range of services is determined by government regulations and site-specific circumstances, such as preexisting conditions in a historical district or an area designated as wetlands.

Consultation

A person who provides consultation services is often referred to in the design industry as a *consultant*. A consultant offers ideas, recommendations, advice, and technical expertise in exchange for a fee. Sometimes people refer to someone as a consultant as if consulting was a distinct discipline, which it is not. Nevertheless, the term is commonly used in the design and building industry, where landscape architects are lumped together with other professional consultants such as architects, engineers, financial advisors, visitor interpretative specialists, biologists, and hazardous waste specialists. It is increasingly common for these consultants working together to combine their expertise on projects.

Consultation is the activity of providing advice in the form of information, procedural recommendations, or ideas. In exchange for a consultant's services, a client will remunerate the consultant by paying a fee. Fees are negotiated between a client and the consultant prior to commencing work. The dollar amount of a fee is based on a specific, defined scope of work.

A consultant provides advice that can be general, as in recommending alternate uses for a piece of property, or can be very specific, as in making seeding recommendations for controlling surface soil erosion of a graded roadway slope. Consultant recommendations can be provided orally, by letter, or in report form. The recommendations can also be given over a period of time, such as in recommending specific design improvements for a home owners' association or for a board of directors of a country club golf course.

Types of consultation activities include research, investigative activities, expert opinion, technical advice or recommendations, analysis and evaluation, budgeting and capital improvements, or project feasibility planning. Examples where consultation services by landscape architects are employed include the following:

- recommending plant materials for specific site conditions or projects
- writing technical specifications for landscape materials
- preparing a landscape maintenance program for a project site
- providing expert witness testimony
- preparing budgeting and capital improvement recommendations
- conducting feasibility planning for a proposed project

Planning and Research

Landscape architects provide other types of nondesign services for an employer or for a client. These nondesign services are broadly described as planning and research. Landscape architects provide these services in conjunction with others such as design, or as their primary service to a client.

Landscape architects employed to provide planning services will conduct research, perform feasibility evaluations, or prepare comprehensive plans for clients or public agencies. The activity of planning generally consists of a series of steps, each step laying the ground work for subsequent steps in a process of investigation, discovery, and recommendations. This process follows a predetermined strategy for arriving at a set of recommendations. Table 7.1 outlines a typical planning process consisting of six phases that are executed sequentially.

Planning involves research, or a process of fact finding. It may also involve inventorying existing or historical conditions. The activity of research often requires some level of analysis or evaluation of information collected. The analysis in turn may require the development of decision-making criteria to be used to sort out and place relative values on the data collected. These criteria are then applied in a systematic way to arrive at conclusions or recommendations. Research may also involve other forms of decision-making analysis such as:

TABLE 7.1   Phases of a Planning Process

Phase I	Research, inventory, and programming
Phase II	Analysis of Phase I findings
Phase III	Preliminary recommendations and/or alternatives
Phase IV	Selection of optimum alternative and recommendations
Phase V	Draft report/plan and recommendations
Phase VI	Final report/plan and recommendations

- comparative analysis of comparable or competing programs
- cost/benefit analysis
- election of alternatives or the best alternative
- summary recommendations together with short- and long-term implementation, funding, and legislative measures or strategies

Examples where planning and research are the primary area of service for landscape architects include the following:

- preparing a design feasibility report of street beautification improvements for a downtown redevelopment district
- preparing a plan with recommendations for the restoration of a historic landscape project
- preparing a report together with cost analysis and step-by-step procedures for the rehabilitation of a wetland area
- conducting the research, carrying out site inventory and evaluation, and preparing design guidelines for improvements of an existing installation such as an expanding community college campus
- preparing a master plan and implementation guidelines for a park, trails, and an open space plan for a city, county, or state agency

Design

The broad range of activities that fall under the category of design has as its common denominator the activities of *problem definition* and *problem solving*. Problem definition leads the designer to understand the nature of a problem, and its component parts and the critical relationships among them.[1] Problem solving is a decision-making process that uses what is learned or understood about the problem to formulate a plausible solution. Both problem definition (understanding) and problem solving generally are carried out to maximize economic, aesthetic, social, and environmental considerations. These considerations may be translated into project goals such as:

- energy or economic efficiency
- sustainability
- low maintenance cost
- enhancement of visual quality
- historical integrity
- responsiveness to society
- conformity to governmental requirements

Designers, whether landscape architects, architects, or graphics artists, are employed to solve problems. Through an exploratory process they define a problem in terms of its component parts and the relationships among them. This process then proceeds to developing some type of organizational framework. The framework suggests a viable solution to the

---

[1]The word *problem* is used here to mean a *project*, in terms of planning or site-design.

problem as defined by the landscape architect in a context defined by site-specific conditions as well as nonsite considerations. The nature of the problem varies depending on the client's expectations and requirements, the user's needs and desires, the project site, and the environmental, political, social, and governmental context. Design is a cultural phenomenon dictated by technology, social structures, and behavioral patterns of the region or society where the design is to be located.

A landscape architect is generally involved in the design of outdoor places, for a specified use or for a cluster of activities. The activities make up the project program. Landscape architects design for specific users, considering user needs balanced with and sensitive to a defined environment, including the cultural and historical context of the region.

Landscape architects typically talk about their designs in terms of *concepts*. Concepts are the operating ideas that provide meaning and explain the theoretical basis of particular design ideas. A design concept can also be explained as the organizing framework or rationale out of which the physical manifestation of the solution emanates. The resulting physical manifestation of the design concept is presented by the designer as the answer to a specific set of problems, needs, or functional requirements of the client, user, and site.

Where do these concepts or ideas originate? One popular belief is that ideas are intuitive inventions. Design solutions are also thought to emanate from a rational process of discovery. Most university courses in design stress the notion that process is an important generator of concepts and ideas. Acquiring general knowledge, gaining an understanding of physically and culturally derived systems, and knowing and understanding environmental elements and processes can assist one in arriving at appropriate—if not justifiable—design concepts and solutions.

Design is a cultural phenomenon.[2] The creation of designs is the result of an interactive process among various elements that consist of (1) a body of knowledge, (2) available and appropriate technology, (3) the cultural milieu of the project location and of the designer, and (4) the professional tenets held by the designer. As a process, design utilizes these four elements in varying degrees of importance, to arrive at new permutations, combinations, and syntheses of physical or prescriptive solutions that make up the design solution or *proposal*.

Landscape architects solve problems by organizing and forming spaces and creating physical forms. In the case of a community park, the landscape architect designs the spatial sequence of program elements together with their physical forms, positioning the elements in a functional and aesthetically pleasing arrangement. The design might also be in the form of a set of prescriptive operations such as written recommendations for soil preparation, seeding, and planting to revegetate a cut slope in a landfill with highly erosive soils.

Implementation

As technology, demographics, and the market change, so too will the practice of landscape architects. The emergence of the market-driven economy in the 1980s has given greater

---

[2]White, *The Concept of Cultural Systems*. The concept of cultural systems with culture seen as a distinct order of phenomena and in recognition of the systematic character of cultural phenomena in actuality. Culture is understood as the structure and behavior of such systems.

Figure 7.4 Those who enjoy the construction process can find career alternatives to satisfy this interest by joining a design-build firm or by developing an expertise in construction administration working for a design firm or government agency.

importance to the concept of service in satisfying customer needs and desires. The concept of service in an economy that is rapidly changing and becoming more global will influence the practice of landscape architecture as we end this century and enter the next.[3] The notion of the landscape architect as a consultant designing projects and representing the client's interest in the field while others construct their designs is shifting to a more hands-on concept. The landscape architect as an implementor as well as a designer of projects is becoming an increasingly important career option. The design-build form of practice previously discouraged by the American Society of Landscape Architects is becoming one of the most viable opportunities for practice in many regions of the United States, as well as in the global arena.

Several emerging and growing areas of service engaging landscape architects include:

- construction contract administration
- materials selection and procurement coordination
- construction installation (design-build)
- postconstruction maintenance or maintenance programming

The hands-on nature of these forms of practice is appealing and has become increasingly popular for many entering the field (Figure 7.4).

[3]Cetron and Davies, *The Gardening of America.*

5. SKILLS OF THE EFFECTIVE LANDSCAPE ARCHITECT

To perform well, a landscape architect must be well-rounded in abilities, skills, and knowledge of the profession. In Table 7.2, the skills considered basic for performing at a credible level are matched with the basic professional service activities of consultation, planning, design, and implementation. In practice, all the skills are required for each service area, depending on the specific requirements of a particular project and the needs of the client.

The American Society of Landscape Architects has sponsored various surveys to present a "snapshot" of the profession from various points of view. Leading landscape architects attending the ASLA-sponsored Bridge Conference[4] in 1989 were surveyed to compare topics of importance in landscape architecture education relative to what is viewed as important in practice. The survey asked participants to rank in order of importance sixteen topics covered during their own landscape education and used in their practice today. The findings of the survey are presented in Table 7.3.

To summarize, practitioners perceived written communication as being a valued skill for students to master in school but placed more emphasis on graphic communication in practice. They cited oral communication as an important skill both in school and in practice. They ranked site analysis and design of highest importance in school but less so further on in one's career. Construction, environmental science, and ethics maintained an important position both in school and out. Interesting were the low values given to the humanities, and natural and social sciences. Knowledge of political systems and processes, although not ranked high on the list, did increase in importance after graduation in the eyes of the practitioners.

Academic, public, and private practitioners have placed increasing emphasis on the importance of written and verbal communication. The membership of the Council of Educators in Landscape Architecture (CELA) and the American Society of Landscape Architects have discussed and reaffirmed the importance of and the need for developing communication skills in order to become an effective practitioner. Several university programs have incorporated writing into their curriculum. Writing skills are seen not only as a

TABLE 7.2   Skill Requirements of a Landscape Architect

	Consultation	Planning	Design	Implementation
Verbal Communication	•	•	•	•
Written communication	•	•	•	•
Technical knowledge	•	•	•	•
Interpersonal, social	•	•	•	•
Graphic communication		•	•	
Organization and management		•	•	
Problem solving	•	•	•	•
Knowledge of laws, government regulations, and procedures	•	•	•	•
Leadership	•	•	•	•

[4]A survey was conducted during the August 1989 ASLA Bridge Conference, asking participants to rate the importance of a number of topics during their own landscape architecture education and later in practice after they had graduated.

TABLE 7.3 **Importance Ranking of Primary Topics In Landscape Architecture Education**

Topic	Importance in School	Importance in Practice
Site analysis and design	1	3
Oral communication	2	2
Construction, grading, drainage	3	4
Design theory	4	7
Written communication	5	1
Environmental science	6	8
Graphics	7	9
Professional ethics	8	5
Plant materials	9	11
Computer applications	10	12
LA history	11	16
Business practices	12	6
Natural sciences	13	12
Humanities	14	14
Social sciences	15	14
Political systems & processes	16	10

requirement for effective communication but also as an important problem-solving and design-generating tool.

The purpose here is not to dwell on the importance of written communication for the profession. Rather, it is to emphasize the importance and need for students of landscape architecture to work toward building a holistic knowledge base and range of skills while in school. To survive in the business sector, among competing disciplines in government and in the highly competitive global market, landscape architects must be prepared with an adequate knowledge base and an effective working understanding of important and emerging environmental issues and political and social considerations. Additionally, landscape architects must have a full range of technical skills and be able to adapt to emerging technologies while maintaining flexibility in order to effectively compete in the marketplace of the future.

6. IN-BASKET

1. Look up *landscape architect, landscape designer,* and *landscape contractor* in the *Yellow Pages*. Tabulate the number of listings under each category and calculate the percentage of companies by category. Compare the number of landscape contractors that offer design services with the number of landscape architectural firms.

2. Make an appointment with a landscape architectural office. The purpose of the visit is to determine what percentage of a principal's time is devoted to working on design as compared with someone who has worked in the office for three to five years and with someone else who is at an entry-level position.

   a. Determine the amount of time spent by each person in other activities, such as business and administration, marketing, project management, and site inspections. Calculate the percent of time spent on an average day for each activity.

b. Considering the number of hours spent on each of the activities, for how many of them can the office bill a client, and how many hours are not project-related and therefore not billable?

3. Study the findings of the ASLA-sponsored 1989 Bridge Conference summarized in Table 7.3. Reflecting on your own experience, would you agree with items ranked in the top five under importance in practice? If not, describe why you believe a different ranking is more appropriate.

■■■■■ **CHAPTER 8**

Organizational Perspectives

1. Business as a Form of Marriage
2. Legal Forms of Business Structure
3. Office Organization Theory
4. Two Styles of Office Management
5. Business Structure for the Twenty-first Century
6. In-Basket

1. BUSINESS AS A FORM OF MARRIAGE

The expression "married to the business" describes several possible business relationships. For some landscape architects, their work is their life. They spend long hours at the office, bring their work home, and spend most of their waking moments on the job.

Other uses of the term "married to the business," refer to peoples' relations with their business associates. These marriages are long-standing relationships with a partner or with corporate business associates. Attaining a balance in life, both professionally and personally, seems to prolong a healthy relationship between people as well as promoting satisfying career results.

In this chapter, however, a business marriage will be discussed in the sense of a legal structure, that is, the business relationship formally established between the owners of a private consulting firm. It is deemed advisable to formalize relationships when two or more people have joined forces to become a business entity. Formalizing a business relationship is necessary for several important reasons, including assigning responsibilities to individuals in the business of the firm, sharing in financial liabilities, and, hopefully, reducing professional liabilities to the individual.

When considering entering into a legal business structure, the parties involved may initially be motivated for professional reasons. There are, however, additional considerations that need to be addressed.

Responsibility

Financial Accountability Legal business relations between two or more individuals usually involve money. Often business owners will supply or borrow money individually or as part of a joint business decision when starting up a new business. They may also borrow or supply capital at several points during the life of the business as additional money is needed to pay bills, make payroll, or expand the business. Of concern here is first documenting individual contributions or allocating responsibility in the case of the borrowing of money on behalf of the firm; and second, devising a legal structure that limits individual liability for actions that could place a financial burden on the firm or from such actions as a professional liability lawsuit.

Delegation of Authority   Decisions involving assigning areas of responsibility should be formalized among the principals of a business. Who is responsible for doing what, lines of communication, and a variety of checks and balances where responsibilities are divided among the individuals of the business, need to be formulated and agreed upon. All agreements need to be put in writing and made part of the package formalizing the creation of a business. This is true for partnerships as well as for corporations, and any other business structure involving two or more people.

Tax Liability

There are tax advantages for establishing a business entity that will separate business tax liabilities from the individual's tax circumstances. This is true regardless of the type of business relation involved (sole proprietorship, partnership, or corporation). In many cases there are advantages to separating the individual's personal tax base from his or her business. Often the basis for deciding which business structure to establish is in large part a response to the tax laws, although professional liability and other considerations have a strong influence on the ultimate decision.

Professional Practice Liability

In the United States there has been a growing concern for the litigious nature of society. Establishing a means of separating one's personal and family liability from one's professional liability often influences the business structure selected. A sole proprietorship provides the least protection of one's personal assets from liability claims that may be made against one's business assets. The corporate structure provides the best protection for the individual. However, full protection of personal assets is not always possible depending on the circumstances involved in a particular legal question.

Acquiring Complementary Skills

The knowledge and skills required to successfully meet the needs and requirements of a landscape architect's clients are generally greater than any one individual's capacity. People and organizations with different expertise might join together under a formal relationship in order to expand or broaden their capabilities to work in new areas, that is, to offer new services to their own clients or to clients in other geographic regions.

For example, a firm wanting to enter a new area of service, such as public park planning and design, which has a strong history working with residential and commercial clients, might bring in a new partner, senior person, or even acquire another firm to accomplish this goal.

Broadening Client Base

Individuals or already-existing business organizations will be motivated to join together (under one new entity or joint venture arrangement) as part of a strategy to expand their client base.

Recognizing Two Heads Are (Often) Better than One

Individuals may decide to join forces in business because of the belief that the whole will be greater than the sum of the individual parts. People willing to work with others may come to realize that sharing their goals with others through a joint business venture (partnership or corporation) might result in achieving these goals more easily.

2. LEGAL FORMS OF BUSINESS STRUCTURE

As is the practice of most design professions, landscape architectural firms are usually organized using the four basic business structures: (1) sole proprietorship, (2) partnership, (3) corporation, and (4) joint venture or association. These are the most common forms of business structure found in the United States today. Other forms may evolve as firms become more involved working in other countries.

A firm may change its structure several times during its lifetime, each time responding to changes in legislation or internal and external events. These could be any of the following:

- addition or withdrawal of partners or principal owners
- changes in the federal or state tax laws
- changes in liability laws and subsequent modifications of insurance companies' policies
- changes in market and economic climate

There are other reasons for a firm to change its business structure. A firm attempting to improve its position in a targeted market or with a particular clientele may change, for instance, from a partnership to a corporate structure as a strategy to attract clients in a market that places value on the corporate image.

Each of the major forms of business structure has its advantages and disadvantages. Which form is best for any particular firm or group of people considering starting their own business may not be an easy decision. An evaluation considering the pros and cons of each business form should be made; perhaps making an initial selection based on the costs and the time frame associated with implementing the selected form. If circumstances suggest another form be considered, the principal owners of the firm have the option to make a change. Issues involving taxes and professional liability more than likely will provide the framework for making the ultimate choice. The primary aspects of each business structure choice are discussed in the following.

Sole Proprietorship

The sole proprietorship is the simplest and least costly form of business to establish. A sole proprietor is a single individual running his or her own business. The simplest way for an individual to start a landscape architectural practice is to secure and furnish an office, purchase some supplies and equipment, print stationery, obtain a business license or permit, and begin working (assuming a clientele is already established). For tax purposes, a federal tax identification number (TIN) also should be obtained, particularly if the intent is to separate personal taxes from business tax obligations. Basically, in this form of business, the individual *is* the business and as such personally assumes all liabilities of the firm. The income generated by the business becomes the individual's personal income and, of course, all losses are the individual's losses.

Advantages of a Sole Proprietorship   This form of business organization entails little or no formality. There is no need for any written agreements or protocol to formalize relations when one person is the owner of an organization. The individual has virtually complete freedom in decisions involving the direction and operation of the company; it is unnecessary to obtain anyone else's consent.

All profits are the property of the owner and need not be shared except with employees and then at the discretion of the owner. Any earnings (profits) from the business may be retained in the business for its improvement and expansion in subsequent years. Business losses are deductible from the personal income of the owner.

As compared with a partnership, an owner's liability in a sole proprietorship is limited to the owner's errors or obligations, no one else's. Also, there is no danger of loss of the business or a portion of the financial resources of the business resulting from the death or withdrawal (as in retirement) of a partner.

As compared with a corporation, the owner of a sole proprietorship will not have to:

- pay double tax when profits are distributed
- pay capital stock tax
- prepare and submit corporate reports
- be concerned with restrictions on the nature of the business
- pay a penalty for retaining earnings in the business

Disadvantages of a Sole Proprietorship   The many abilities required for a successful, long-term business, such as marketing, management, administration, production, quality control, etc., are seldom possessed by one person. Therefore, the one-owner organization may have certain significant limitations restricting the firm's capabilities to expand in size or to obtain certain types of clients, or to borrow money.

Lenders, such as banks, may not be willing to provide needed capital for a one-owner business to grow or to make significant equipment purchases. Lenders require collateral as a condition of making most types of business loans. The personal assets of the sole proprietorship are often limited.

In the event of a business failure, the owner's personal assets, including home, other real estate, automobiles, and personal property are subject to claims by creditors. Additionally, it is not easy for a single owner to leave the business, particularly for extended periods of time, for vacation or personal or professional leave as in an organization that has multiple partners or principals.

Partnership

A business partnership may consist of two, twenty, one hundred, or even more partners. The number has as much to do with the scale or dollar volume of the business as with any other factor, such as expertise and services offered, multiple office locations, and response to client requirements. In a partnership, the owners share the risks, the profits, and the losses. Each partner has an unlimited liability, that is, any claim against one partner in the course of doing business is a claim against all partners. It may be necessary to draw from the assets of all the partners in the event a successful financial claim is made against the business.

For income tax purposes, the term *partnership* is more comprehensive than when taken in its ordinary sense. Partnerships created in response to certain tax laws may include syndicate, joint venture, and limited partnerships as well as an ordinary partnership. The ordinary partnership (the most common partnership form of landscape architecture firms) is when two or more persons pool their financial resources, knowledge, skill, and business contacts together in a co-ownership venture for profit.

There are many reasons for considering the partnership form of business. Frequently, professionals wanting to own their own consulting business are neither financially nor psychologically prepared to do so alone. They need help and encouragement. Having a partner might provide the necessary capital and encouragement to realize the dream of private ownership. In addition to capital and energy, you should consider two additional factors that come into play when entering into a business partnership: (1) that you have the right temperament to be a partner, and (2) that you are very selective in your choice of partner(s).

Prospective partners who are more interested in their own success and personal achievement than the firm's should be viewed as a less desirable partnership choice. Other negative indicators for the partnership venture include:

- too much desire for independence
- a dislike of sharing responsibility
- a preference for doing everything alone

The level of success of a partnership is directly proportional to the degree each partner is willing to:

- cooperate
- find a way to make things work
- maintain a positive attitude
- find common ground where all sides win in situations where differences exist

Advantages of a Partnership   This form of business organization has the potential of harnessing the synergistic benefits that come when two or more viewpoints and experiences come together in one business enterprise. If personal abilities are complementary, a partnership can lead to long-term business success. The assumption here is that no one individual could accomplish alone what could be accomplished with others.

A partnership has greater potential than a sole proprietorship for obtaining or amassing capital. The collective personal resources of the partners or their combined assets can been pooled as collateral for making loans.

As compared with the corporation form of business:

- Business losses are deductible from the personal income of each partner for income tax purposes.
- There are no state taxes, no capital stock tax, and no double tax on profits.
- Income may be divided equally or on a basis other than investments, such as time spent in the business.
- Partners' salary is not subject to payroll taxes.
- No penalty results from retaining earnings in the business.

Disadvantages of a Partnership   Each partner is liable for all debts incurred by the business. Likewise, the profits must be shared among the partners. Each partner is responsible for the actions of all other partners when they create an obligation for the business.

The partnership is automatically dissolved by the death, the disability, or voluntary withdrawal of a partner. There are steps the partners can take to prepare for the continuation of the business in the event of a partner's death, disability, or voluntary withdrawal. One common vehicle used is the execution of a "key man" agreement together with the purchase of "key man insurance" to fund cases involving death or disability. This method requires each partner to purchase an agreed-on face-value amount of insurance naming the other partner or partners as the beneficiary. In the event of a partner's death or disability, the insurance is paid to the beneficiary(s) with the funds used to pay whatever costs necessary to continue the business.

Corporation

Corporations are a legal form of organization governed by state laws. State laws govern the provisions under which a corporation is chartered, that is, authorized to operate as a business entity in the state. Since a corporation is the creation of state laws (called *corporate laws*), it is impersonal and exists without reference to the particular individuals who may share its ownership and direct and carry out its activities. Usually, those considered the owners of the business are the stockholders in the corporation. The ownership of the corporation shares does not have to be evenly distributed among the stockholders. In older companies, stock ownership may be held on two levels: senior partners holding larger percentages of the stock, and junior partners owning smaller percentages.

The motivation to establish a corporation in landscape architecture often has to do with limiting liability and realizing certain tax benefits (such as limiting the amount of taxes an individual would have to pay).

Advantages of a Corporation   Finding ways of limiting personal liability is a major consideration of individuals providing professional services in the private sector. The legal liability of the stockholders in a corporation for personal injury suits or other legal actions against the company, connected to its activities, is limited to the amount of funds each owner has invested in the corporation.

The corporation can continue existing indefinitely or as specified in its charter, whereas the other two forms of business cease with the death of the owner or one of the partners, except in cases where a partnership agreement is devised to circumvent this situation through the purchase of key man insurance.

Capital may be accumulated from many sources, such as through the sale of common or preferred stock, loans made by issuing bonds, exchange of assets, and the reservation of profits from the business. Ownership in a corporation is easily transferred by the sale or exchange of stock and entry of the new ownership on the books of the corporation.

Management of the firm may be delegated to one or more individuals even though ownership is evenly distributed.

Disadvantages of a Corporation   The business activities of the corporation are limited specifically to activities specified in the corporate charter. A firm incorporated to provide landscape architectural design services could not legally be engaged in the retail nursery trade without changing its charter to do so by receiving approval by the appropriate state administrative body responsible for regulating corporate activities.

The geographical area of a corporation's operations is limited to the state granting its charter. Permission must be secured from each state in which a corporate entity wishes to operate. This limitation does not exsist for sole proprietorship or partnership businesses; they may operate in other states. The limiting factor, in the case of landscape architectural services, would be securing the necessary business and professional licenses required by the individual states before practicing in those states.

A corporation is required to prepare numerous reports for taxation and other purposes. The reports are completed on a regular basis for each state in which the company does business. All meetings and or discussions involving company policy or business decisions must be documented in writing. Minutes must be taken, signed by the appropriate corporate officers, and entered in the official corporate record. Certain actions and decisions made by the corporation—as specified in the state charter—must be voted on with the action recorded in the corporate minutes.

Federal and state regulation of corporations has been increasing, making it mandatory that changes in the regulations be monitored and followed by the corporate officers. The changes often have a substantial impact on companies, to such an extent that the original reasons and benefits for incorporating may no longer be achievable. The changes may be such that it is in the interest of the stockholders to give serious consideration to changing the business to a partnership or other structure.

The corporate structure is subject to more taxes than is the sole proprietorship or partnership. The tax laws need to be continually reviewed and considered by the corporate officers to determine their extent and the most prudent course of action relative to the benefit of the company.

In small corporations—as in the case of many landscape architectural companies—the advantage of limited liability is often lost where business debts due to banks must be secured by the personal assets of the major stockholders.

Joint Venture and Associations

A joint venture or association is a legal entity that consists of a group of individuals, group of companies, or a combination of the two that unite for some special business purpose, such as to secure a contract and perform services that would not be possible for the individuals or companies to perform on their own. The formation of a joint venture or an association is common for smaller firms looking to gain access both to large government or private planning, and feasibility and design contracts. Joint ventures are also formed for projects having a mix of highly specialized or unique elements requiring a team effort with the appropriate expertise to undertake them adequately.

A joint venture can be set up with a specific time span. They may be established to join the resources and expertise of two or more individual companies for the purpose of tackling certain types of projects when they become available. Joint ventures require their own set of books including accounting, administrative, and management records. A joint venture is often as complicated to establish as a new corporation. It requires a working agreement (to be signed by each party) or charter (in the case of creating a corporate entity). The joint venture is taxed in the same manner as a corporation and must follow federal and state tax laws. The advantages and disadvantages are similar to those discussed under the corporation heading.

3. OFFICE ORGANIZATION THEORY

Office organization is the means of managing a firm's resources. It also provides the framework for guiding the business affairs of a firm. The resources include the physical spaces of the office, the equipment, the production and the support personnel, and the leadership. The business of the firm includes contract management, administration, personnel management, and financial management. Management's function is to establish an organizational structure and a set of procedures together with appropriate resources to assist people in achieving the goals set by the firm's leadership. As an example, in a professional design office, the manager manages the marketing activities of the firm to find the kind of clients desired, secure the desired mix of office personnel, allocate and manage the assignments, establish and monitor schedules and budgets, and guide all the activities necessary for the execution of services. Having an effective management structure should result in efficient productivity of services and contracted products. Efficient productivity should translate into an acceptable profit for the firm, and it should also enhance the firm's professional reputation in the markets in which it competes.

Many design professionals approach office management as simply working hard to get things done on time. Hard work and long hours are not the only keys to successfully managing a business, particularly in production activities associated with multiple, large, and complex projects. Successful design firms understand that management is a necessary activity to steer the course that the firm's leadership desires. Management is a deliberate process that involves planning, devising appropriate systems to husband the flow of information, and guiding the production of contracted products. Good management systems also include procedures for monitoring the progress of the activities that produce the products (plans, reports, and other documents) that represent the firm's services to the client.

When looking toward the future, successful managers define their goals in quantitative as well as in qualitative terms. Developing measurable project goals requires implementing deliberate steps to assess the degree of success in achieving them.

The work of design firms involves multiple disciplines and multiple functions. The role of management is to keep projects proceeding through the functions and disciplines in an efficient manner. By so doing, the hoped-for goal of producing quality products and services should result. By the same token, the production of the resulting products and services should result in profitability for the business. The choice of management structure for an office is a matter of optimizing the flow and coordination of information among the various participants within the office and design team members of subconsulting firms located in other offices. Ultimately, the flow of information should reach the client.

It is difficult to characterize the ways landscape architectural offices organize to perform for their clients. However, most offices use many different ways of organizing office personnel to accomplish required project work. They follow two basic organizational models. The first is based on an industrial efficiency model. Similar to an industrial factory production line, personnel are assigned to various production groups. A project progresses from start to finish from one group to the next. Each group is responsible for performing a certain task or cluster of tasks. When the group is finished, the project moves to the next production group.

The second model follows a sports team approach where projects are assigned to a team. There may be several teams or groups in an office. Each team is responsible for completing all phases of work for assigned projects. Team membership consists of a principal-in-charge, a project manager or job captain, and supporting professional staff. The staff assigned to a team will represent the breadth of skills, knowledge, and experience needed to complete each project.

4. TWO STYLES OF OFFICE MANAGEMENT

Management is the function of helping people achieve the goals set by the firm's leadership. Two styles define the extremes of management approaches in common use:

- facilitative structure, based on team building
- autocratic structure, based on top-down or vertical control

Organizations tend to utilize only one of the approaches but circumstances may require that a combination of the two be employed.

Facilitative Style

Firms following a facilitative management approach are the ones that foster team building. The team-building style promotes decision making at all levels of office structure, an approach that affirms the belief that those most directly involved in the design service affairs of the firm are capable of making important decisions. This approach reinforces another management premise, that office staff are just as serious about having responsibility delegated to them as they are about their salary and benefits. This desire to be given responsibility is certainly the case at the middle and advanced phases of the careers of most professional personnel.

The production of work following this structure is organized in project teams. Professional staff composed of owners, project managers, designers, production staff, and construction administration are assigned to specific projects. This approach encourages workers at all experience levels to make more decisions. Minimizing staff time spent waiting for decisions to be made by others ultimately speeds up production and increases profits. Principals as well as project managers and support staff are involved in the planning of each phase of work, as well as the execution and coordination with the client and outside consultants. Any of the people on the project team may be involved in direct client contact. This approach requires people willing to participate in a process where a high degree of coordination is involved.

Ultimately, a principal of the firm is responsible for the work produced and delivered to the client. Quality control is crucial in insuring that high standards of care are maintained. One advantage of the team approach is that in most cases team members are all sufficiently familiar with the project to minimize the chances of error or poor coordination of critical parts of a project.

The facilitative approach empowers staff to make decisions following objectives or criteria established by management.

Autocratic Style

This structure has a long history and is referred to as the *vertical* or *pyramidal* management structure. Under this structure a principal presides over all project management activities. Orders are passed down the chain of command and executed through hierarchical layers of staff. Work is segmented according to functions such as planning, design, drawing production, and construction administration. There is little overlap among the specialized functions. In an office that uses the autocratic structure, decisions are made by managers who retain tight control over what happens each step of the way. This structure follows a top-down chain of command, typical of an authoritarian leadership style.

This approach places most of the burden of project production on the managing partner or principal who in turn may delegate work to a project manager and down the line through job captain and so on to production staff. In the event that questions or problems come up and the principal is unavailable, they may not be dealt with until the principal is available.

For smaller firms, a variation or combination of the above two models might be used. Smaller, less complex projects will be assigned to one or a few people. People selected to work on these less complex projects might be entry level or have modest project experience. The more complex and large projects will go to the more experienced personnel. As projects become larger and more complex, the production or team model might be employed. Which model is selected may have as much to do with the management preference of the firm's principals as with the experience and availability of the staff at any particular time. Generally, firms assign personnel and select an organization model based on matching the best, most responsible and reliable people with the least experienced staff members. The speed with which people work may also be a consideration for making assignments. While a firm may consistently employ a particular model, in most situations, firm management is constantly adjusting and reorganizing staff to make the best use of personnel resources to match the particular needs of any given project.

5. BUSINESS STRUCTURE FOR THE TWENTY-FIRST CENTURY

How companies organize and conduct their business, and the type of structure they create, will most probably change in the future. As landscape architectural firms search to develop new markets and position themselves to meet new and changing markets for their services, they will most likely need to change their organizational structure. Striving for stability is no longer the critical organizational issue. Client needs and markets in general are rapidly changing as technological advances are made. The successful organizations will be the ones that are managed to accommodate change. Firms are moving away from the pyramidal structure with a company president at the top and staff along the bottom. The classic management ideal that big is beautiful is rapidly being rejected. Size alone will no longer be the desirable attribute as design firms organize to more effectively meet changing markets for their services. Whatever structure is sought, the key goal is to provide a structure that enables the professional staff and managers to find better ways of generating ideas to competitively meet market needs. Part of this matrix of change involves managing technology and information and cooperating toward achieving a common goal.

Encouraging employees to accept change requires establishing a new system of expectations and rewards. Companies will have to communicate their goals and objectives clearly and more fully to all personnel. To be effective, all levels of staff must be involved in the agenda-setting process. Lower-level staff have to adapt to assuming responsibility. Managers have to adjust to leading teams, not giving orders. Pay may no longer be tied to longevity with a company or to a job description or title. More and more people will be paid by the contribution they make toward achieving company goals and objectives. This approach gives people the opportunity of having a stake in the firm. The successful managers will be those who clearly make a strong connection between staff performance, the firm's financial success, and their own potential for reward.

With the establishment of the European Common Market and the North American Free Trade Agreement, landscape architecture firms in the United States will change in some very profound ways in order to better compete both in the United States and internationally. The world economic and political order is changing so fast that few in the design professions can comprehend the impact these changes will have on their business The successful firms will be those that devise a structure that will enable them to take advantage of changing conditions in the newly created global markets.

In the future, firms from several countries will probably join together, forming multinational joint ventures and associations composed of individuals and firms. Issues involving professional education, expertise, qualifications, experience, legalities, and taxation will need be understood and dealt with as practitioners from the United States seek new markets in other countries. Add to the list language, culture, and customs, as well as industry labor skills and materials standards, and it becomes apparent that design firms attempting to conduct business outside their own country's borders must accept a totally new form of practice. Quality control and standards of care issues will become enormously complex and design firms wishing to work in other countries will have to understand and address them. Marketing, too, will present incredible challenges. Thus, firms seeking success in the next century must devise a company business structure that can effectively deal with quality control, standards of care, and marketing. They must also devise strategies to enable them to remain profitable in business climates different from the ones to which they are already accustomed.

6. IN-BASKET

1. Imagine you are working for a landscape architectural firm that employs the industrial model for producing the firm's project work. You have been with the firm one year and have accumulated a total of five years' experience with other firms. Also, you have recently obtained your license.

   a. Consider that you were hired based on your expertise to design irrigation and outdoor lighting systems. Your responsibilities will be in these two areas. Describe how you would feel about continuing with the firm designing irrigation and outdoor lighting systems in view of your ultimate goal of owning your own firm or working toward becoming a partner in the existing firm.

   b. Next week you will be discussing your annual review with the firm. Devise a plan to suggest to the partners that will allow you to gain varied experience and expand your responsibilities.

2. Make an assessment of your personality traits and predict how well you would do as a partner or corporate owner.

   a. Do you predict success or do you feel you would be better off working alone as the sole proprietor in your own firm? Explain.

   b. What type of personality traits in other people allow you to work successfully on teams? If you had a partner or partners with these same traits do you think a partnership of some sort would work out for you? Explain.

3. You are a partner in a firm specializing in resort planning and design and are wishing to expand your market area by working in another country. You have been contacted by a firm located in Mexico City wishing to increase its expertise and better compete in the expanding tourism market in Mexico.

   a. Assuming that you and your partners see this as a favorable opportunity, what form of business structure would you recommend to bind the two firms together?

   b. Assuming that you are the cautious type, how would recommend working with the firm in Mexico on a trial basis? Would you consider drawing up a joint venture agreement with a limited time frame as a trial period before finalizing your business agreement? Outline the pros and cons of each alternative.

   c. Outline the steps you would take toward the final contractural agreement considering how you would ensure design quality control as well as the proper running of the business.

CHAPTER 9

Starting a Small Design Firm

1. The Dream of Running Your Own Firm
2. Elements of a Business Plan
3. Administrative and Managerial Plan
4. Business Plan Implementation
5. In-Basket

1. THE DREAM OF RUNNING YOUR OWN FIRM

Many landscape architects have given consideration to starting their own firm someday. As students, some have mentally tested the water as they visited the offices of alumni and/or other landscape architects during class field trips. Other classmates may have different professional goals, such as working in a government agency or becoming a teacher. Those with strong entrepreneurial leanings will most likely realize their need to own their own business. However, for most, the opportunity to start one's own private practice will be placed on the back burner until after graduating, working a few years, becoming licensed, and putting away a modest savings.

Landscape architects who own their own business have done so following many different paths. Each private firm owner has a story to tell. Some followed a long, arduous path, while others became a firm owner quickly. Regardless of the speed or the circumstances, the preparation required to start and maintain a successful private practice can be visualized in terms of a number of simple steps. Nevertheless, these steps may prove difficult to implement without devoting considerable time beforehand to planning and preparation.

The initial motivations for going into private practice and becoming an owner of a firm can be explained in terms of rewards and benefits. The rewards include control, independence, pride of ownership, and the fulfillment of a dream. Contrary to popular thinking, those choosing a public practice can also expect many of the same rewards and benefits of private practice. The potential of attaining independence, of being able to put your creative ideas to work, and developing direction within a government agency are distinct possibilities for public practitioners. A landscape architect working in an agency over a period of time can also achieve pride of ownership and find the fulfillment of a professional dream. However, there is a fundamental difference between starting your own private firm and being the head of a governmental unit. The basic difference is that, in most cases, a public practitioner steps into an already existing government agency. With very few exceptions, a landscape architect rarely has the opportunity of starting a new program or unit in a government agency at the ground floor.

This chapter focuses on the steps involved in starting a small, private landscape architectural firm. Anyone can start a business; but anyone wishing to start a business that has a chance to succeed and continue over a long time period should consider following a few basic, time-tested steps. Regardless of the startup plan one develops, the process followed, and the adequacy of the preparation, hard work is a must. Implementing and following a plan is not about getting rich quickly or easily.

Starting your own business requires hard work over a long time. It goes without saying that few have found success by being lazy. As a rule of thumb, two years is the minimum time needed for a newly created firm to financially break even. There are firms that have reached the break-even point earlier, but there are a greater number that have taken well beyond two years to reach a reasonable level of financial stability.

2. ELEMENTS OF A BUSINESS PLAN

You will need to make several decisions before setting up a firm. First, you must understand why you want to have your own firm and what you hope to accomplish with it. In the course of answering these questions, a plan should begin to form. The plan should outline in as much detail as possible the steps and decisions that need to be made in order for the dream to become a reality.

The first step in getting started establishing a firm is to develop a business startup plan. The material discussed in the following sections should serve as a framework to assist you in developing your own business startup plan. For items where alternatives are given, these are meant to suggest a range of options.

Concept of the Firm

What type of practice are you going to launch? Is the firm to be a design firm, a firm specializing in historic preservation, or is the goal to become a design-build office? Who are the type of clients you want to serve? These are initial questions that if clearly described will guide most subsequent elements of the business startup plan. The answers to these questions will yield a clear concept of the firm: type of practice, targeted client base, services offered, and geographic market area.

Table 9.1 outlines many of the possible areas of primary focus for a new firm. Check one or more of the areas of specialization that would best represent the primary focus of your practice.

Considering each box you checked, describe in as much detail as possible the proposed goals of the firm (for example: to be within three years the leading firm in the region, known for our use of state-of-the-art computer technology applied to urban design and large-scale land planning). Divide your discussion in terms of short-term goals (one to

TABLE 9.1   Primary Areas of Focus

☐ Landscape planning & design	☐ Riverfront planning & design	
☐ Design-Build	☐ Regional planning	
☐ Design-build/maintenance	☐ Park planning & design	
☐ Multidisciplinary firm	☐ Horticultural consultant	
☐ Restoration & mitigation	☐ Resort planning & design	
☐ Urban design	☐ Other _____	
☐ Golf course architect	☐ Other _____	

three years) and long-term goals (three to five years). Also include a discussion of the objectives of the firm (for example, reach within five years a professional staff of twelve to fifteen with annual contracts valued at one million dollars).

Target Customer Groups   Identify types of clients you wish to do work for using Table 9.2, considering your capabilities, expertise, and the needs of these clients. Most businesses just starting out will target a specific group of clients. Once the firm establishes itself and achieves a degree of notoriety, the owners may chose to expand their client base assuming they have acquired the necessary staff capabilities and operations capacity to handle the new clients.

Delineate Areas of Specialization—Professional Services   Describe in detail the qualities you believe will make your approach of doing business unique and hence competitive. Consider what you believe are the needs of your potential clients and what combination of services you wish to market to attract those customers. Landscape architectural services and the manner in which those services are delivered can be considered as a product—one that must be shown to satisfy the needs of prospective clients. Landscape architectural services can have any one or a combination of the following dimensions:

- **Special working relationship with the client**: Make sure that a principal is usually available to the client rather than giving the impression that the client will deal with staff after a contract is executed.
- **Unique approach in performing services or dealing with the client**: Provide a well-coordinated quality control procedure to ensure the accuracy and completeness of work performed.
- **Special qualities of your services and products**: Utilize the best state-of-the-art techniques appropriate to the service and delivery of products.
- **Special relationship of business owners to staff**: This might make a difference in the quality of service and products of the firm by enabling staff to participate fully in all aspects of a project rather than narrowly focusing on production activities. This helps staff better understand all aspects of design services activities and hence they are better able to help resolve problems and make decisions as a project progresses from design through construction.

Determine the services to be offered (area of specialization or market niche). Consider the types of services that best match the needs of the client types you intend to attract using Table 9.3.

TABLE 9.2   Target Customer Group Areas

☐ Private	☐ Residential	☐ Commercial	
☐ Corporate	☐ Industry	☐ Institutional	
☐ Government	☐ Local	☐ State	☐ Federal
☐ Land developer	☐ Attorneys (as expert witnesses)		
☐ Other consultants (as subconsultant for architects, engineers)			
☐ Other _____			

TABLE 9.3   Service Areas of Specialization

☐ Planning and feasibility studies	☐ Landscape design
☐ Research/consulting	☐ Expert witness
☐ Project design	☐ Maintenance management
☐ Historic preservation	☐ Environmental restoration
☐ Computer applications_____	☐ Other _____

Define Geographic Market   Delineate preferred geographic market area or areas in which the firm will practice. Research business permits, professional licenses, and taxes required to practice in each location. Most businesses starting out will target a specific geographic area. In the case of landscape architecture firms, the region will be defined by the city the firm is located in or perhaps by state boundaries. Once firms become established and achieve success in one region, they may chose to expand their client base into new geographic regions, even into other states or countries. They make this decision to expand assuming they have acquired the necessary staff capabilities and operations capacity to efficiently operate in the new regions.

Some cities, counties, and states require professional firms to maintain a business license to pay taxes in order to do business in the area. Examples of the license and tax requirements that might be required include:

- **City and County**: business license or permit, local taxes including business and sales taxes
- **State**: professional registration (license), state income taxes (personal and corporate), and sales taxes

Companies wishing to operate under the corporate structure will be required to file an application and other documents and pay certain fees to operate as a corporation in each state in which they intend to maintain a permanent office.

Information for permit and license requirements can be obtained from tax and assessment boards or economic and financial offices of city and county governments. State licensing agencies, such as occupational liscensing boards, and corporation commissions can provide information on professional and business licenses, taxes, and corporation requirements.

Competition

Knowing who you will be competing with in attracting the clients you have identified is important before solidifying your marketing strategy. The better you are able to understand the capabilities of the competition, the more likely you will be able to define your own firm's capabilities. Arriving at a clear understanding of your capabilities will make it easier to be more closely aligned with the needs of the clients you wish to attract. With this knowledge and understanding you should be capable of increasing your competitive advantage over other firms.

Identify Competitive Firms   List the types of firms you perceive as your competition. Identify the firms in each category of client type (such as land developer, commercial client, county parks department, etc.). Useful information to obtain about the competing firms include their names and the following information:

Figure 9.1 Small office building location presenting an intimate, personal-scale image of a quiet midtown street.

- firm concept: areas of expertise, market niche description
- composition of the professional staff: numbers, training and expertise
- clientele
- special technology utilization
- strengths and weaknesses

Information about firms you would be competing with can be obtained from several sources. As this information is not in a published form, acquiring it may require a certain degree of creative investigation. One source is through prospective clients. Interviews with clients might include questions asking which consultants they have used, would hire again, and would recommend. Finding out why clients would recommend these consultants and what attributes are attractive to them can help you assess your own capabilities and expertise relative to the competition's. Other sources of information about your competition might come from other consultants (who have worked with the firms you have identified as the competition), public records of government agencies on firms they have hired in the past, and other sources within your professional network or community of contacts.

Identify Market Niches Identify niches in desired markets that you believe you have the expertise to fill. The word *niche* is a marketing term that refers to an identifiable product or service that belongs to one type or class of product or service provided in an industry that contains a broad range of products or services. For instance, within the broad spectrum of services provided by landscape architects, one area, say land planning, may have a number of firms providing services in several subsets of land planning services. A niche within the land planning service area might be a service that utilizes computer technology together with remote sensing data to assist clients in the planning the development of their property. Although there may be many firms offering land planning services, yours might be the only one that provides these services with advanced technological capabilities.

By assessing the information collected about potential competitors, you should be able to identify a distinct set of services the firm might offer that will give it an advantage based on its specialized skills, expertise, and technological capabilities.

A market niche may represent a set of services, the application of technology, or a particular approach to business that a firm markets as being not only unique but also more efficient and cost-effective in meeting client needs. Considering that landscape architecture is a service profession, offering a unique service that produces efficient and cost-effective results is desirable from a marketing perspective. It might help establish a niche for a firm in a region already having many competing landscape architectural firms. Table 9.4 may be used to identify potential market niches for your consideration.

The Place of Business: Location and Setting

The decision of where to locate the office of a new business should be based on geographic attributes as well as image considerations (Figures 9.1 and 9.2). Each neighborhood or section of town has a visual quality and set of amenities unique to that area and offers a stock of potential office locations that can be described in the following terms:

- **building types**—including structures such as high-rise office buildings, low-rise office parks, downtown historical districts, or office space in structures converted for adaptive reuse
- **quality of construction**—including building design and prevalent building materials used
- **site amenities**—including onsite parking, landscaping, and outdoor use areas
- **visual quality** of surrounding buildings and neighborhood
- **Overall image** of location, building type, and design that reflects image sought as part of marketing strategy

TABLE 9.4   **Market Niches Data File**

1. Professional Service Niche _____ _____

   List resources that support the service:

      Staff/expertise _____

      Technology _____

      Specialized equipment _____

      Potential clients _____ _____

2. Professional Service Niche _____ _____

   List resources that support the service:

      Staff/expertise _____

      Technology _____

      Specialized equipment _____

      Potential clients _____ _____

      • **Continue with additional categories as necessary**

Figure 9.2   High-rise office building in a downtown location presenting a conservative, prosperous image that might appeal to corporate and governmental clients.

The spatial needs of the office are also important in determining where to establish. Table 9.5 contains a checklist of locational attributes that can assist in the fact-finding process involved in answering the question of where to locate. Table 9.6 can be used in defining office spatial requirements.

Financial Plan

It takes money—capital—to start a firm. This is true whether you intend to start conservatively, on a shoestring budget with a minimum initial investment, or whether you approach startup with a substantial capital outlay and hence, debt. Regardless of how you intend to start out, a financial plan must be prepared. The planning should begin with the preparation of a two-year income statement. The statement would be compiled by projecting expenses and income on a monthly basis for the two-year period.

Some of the items that would be covered under expenses would include salaries (yours and any employees), rent and utilities, lease or purchase expenses for furniture and equipment, supplies, telephone and other communication expenses, advertisement and marketing, travel, postage, and taxes.

Projecting income is much more difficult to do, particularly when starting a firm for the first time. Estimates of contract fees and charges for hourly consulting should be made based on conservative estimates of what your research indicates firms of similar size can bill per month. The difference between projected income and projected expenses should estimated. The projected difference is the amount of capital you may need to come up with

TABLE 9.5   Office Requirements Checklist

Location, considering:
1. Access to: ☐ clients ☐ support services ☐ airport
   ☐ public transportation ☐ other _____
2. Expansion potential ☐ Good ☐ Fair ☐ Will require move
3. Customer parking ☐ Good ☐ Fair ☐ Poor
4. Employee parking ☐ Good ☐ Fair ☐ Poor
5. Cost month or daily rate $ _____ per car, per _____

Size, considering:
1. Number of employees: Principals _____
   Professional staff _____ Support staff _____
2. Total square footage _____ SF
   Professional staff _____ SF Support staff _____ SF
3. Cost $ _____ per SF per month or year
4. Maintenance ☐ provided ☐ renter provides

Business Image to be Projected
Describe:

---

either from personal resources or loans. Before a bank will consider making a new firm a loan, a financial and business plan must be prepared and submitted together with a loan request.

TABLE 9.6   Office Plan Checklist

Office Plan
- Usable office space _____ SF
    Offices, number _____ Space _____ SF _____ SF _____ SF
    Production area _____ SF Number of stations _____
- Bathrooms, number: _____ • Conference room _____ SF
- Storage _____ SF ☐ Secured ☐ Unsecured
- Reproduction & supplies _____ SF
- Kitchen, lunchroom _____ SF
- Common areas, halls, etc. _____ SF

Office Setting, indicate preference:
☐ Open office and workstations
☐ Individually enclosed office and workstations
☐ Combination

Computer Requirements
1. Workstation configurations
    ☐ Centralized computer stations and peripherals
    ☐ Individual workstations
2. Networking requirements
    ☐ Describe _____

Marketing Plan

Develop a calendar for your marketing efforts. The calendar should include specific activities (preparation of office brochure, listing of potential client contacts), time frame allocated for each activity with a start and completion date, specific staff to assign to each task, and describe in as much detail as possible the expected outcome of each activity as it is accomplished.

Marketing consists of many different activities. Each may require a unique or tailored approach to execute. Basically, marketing means making known the firm's existence and services offered through any one or a combination of the following activities:

- Research and develop a list of potential clients, identifying key contacts.
- Mail promotional materials to potential clients.
- Make appointments to interview and inform potential clients.
- Research agencies and companies that maintain bidders' lists, learn about the submittal requirements (documentation/forms) the agencies use, and make arrangements to be included in bidders' lists for the type of work you are interested in doing.
- Subscribe to the *Commerce Business Daily* for a listing of all federal agencies' professional services contracts.
- Review the legal section of newspaper want ads for local government agency requests for professional services proposals.

Next, delegate responsibility for each marketing activity. Identify the lead person and supporting staff along with an estimate of the hours per week or month each will be given to carry out his or her assignment.

Most firms prepare a variety of promotional materials to be used in the marketing of the firm. These materials may include brochures, individually prepared and tailored informational packets, letters of introduction, and prepared graphic displays including slide, video, or multimedia presentations. A target budget should be established for each promotional element and for a total expenditure for the year. Staff assignments together with realistic time frames in which to develop and produce the promotional materials should be made.

3. ADMINISTRATIVE AND MANAGERIAL PLAN

The administration and management of a small consulting firm consists of four systems:

- records management
- financial management
- personnel management
- project management

A firm should have an organizational structure to manage personnel and the activities of the business, and should also establish a process for managing the flow of information for internal and external handling of documents and correspondence. The first job of managers is to establish a structure for each system and then to monitor the activities in each system. The strength and value of any system must be evaluated by ease of use and by how well the system enables a firm's managers to clarify activities and delegate responsibilities. Of particular concern, from the standpoint of a firm's longevity, is the manager's ability to effectively manage those activities that contribute to the firm's financial well-being.

The decision of what system to employ should be based on whether it is:

- user friendly, and therefore has a reasonable chance of being used
- easy to access (to add, modify, and remove information)
- expandable and capable of being modified to meet the changing needs of the business
- possible to monitor the activities involved in maintaining it
- capable of meeting appropriate fiduciary, governmental, and legal standards of care

The four primary systems needed to manage most landscape architectural office activities should each be carefully thought out to meet the needs of the owners in such a way that the systems are easy to manage and maintain. There are a number of ways to organize each system; some systems are fairly standard, such as keeping the financial records and related bookkeeping activities of a business. The ultimate success—or failure—of a firm will depend upon the effectiveness of the systems to adequately handle the plethora of paper passing through, recording keeping, financial activities, and project activities. Good systems will enable the owners to keep track of the status of all of the firm's staff activities and to make adjustments when necessary. The profitability and financial health of the firm is also dependent upon the effectiveness of the systems to enable the managers to track and monitor schedules, and personnel activities, and project progress.

Records Management

The topic of office record-keeping is covered in Chapter 11. The types of records maintained in a design office include project records, accounting, personnel and general business records, general correspondence, and product and technical data (Figure 9.3). Records are kept in series. Series categories might include:

- active project records
- inactive project files
- general business records
- documentation of policy and business decisions relative to a partnership or corporation
- marketing records and proposal materials
- product information, technical data, and reference materials
- computer files

Financial Management—Accounting System

Keeping track of financial and business accounting activities of a firm requires a team effort. Team members include the business owners, the firm's certified public accountant,

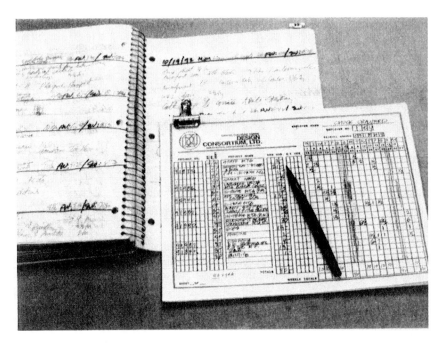

Figure 9.3   Having a system—regardless of its sophistication—and using it is vital to conducting business. A landscape architect keeps a daily journal and at the end of the week transfers important information to the appropriate file—such as project hours entered onto company time sheets.

and the staff assigned to maintain the accounting activities of the firm. All three need to understand the needs of the firm and which system is most desirable from the standpoint of business management, accounting, and income tax.

Personnel Management

Owners or managers of a firm establish business and professional objectives, develop strategies for accomplishing the firm's objectives, and then set priorities together with a schedule and timetable for implementing the objectives. The role of personnel management is to clarify activities that relate to the firm's objectives and delegate responsibilities for carrying them out. The effective manager, in addition to clarifying and delegating, establishes guidelines for performance of the activities and the criteria to be used in evaluating the quality of performance results (products and services).

Office Manual   An office manual states the goals and ethical basis of the firm, its mission with respect to the projects and clients it hopes to serve. Office manuals also contain valuable information such as company management and personnel policies, codes of conduct, and general information to help the new employee understand company goals and expectations. An important goal to consider when writing an office manual is to include information that would help employees to perform well.

Personnel Job Descriptions   Personnel management guidelines include both job descriptions and descriptions of responsibilities of professional and nonprofessional staff.

The guidelines should detail the range of expertise, experience, and qualifications deemed the minimum requirement for each staff position. Job descriptions should be written for each category of employee such as for the following:

Professional

- principals and associates
- project manager or team captain
- project landscape architect
- professionals in other disciplines such as engineering, environmental science, graphic arts, and agronomy
- seasonal assistance (student interns or short-term and part-time employees)

Support staff

- secretary
- bookkeeper
- receptionist
- errand runner

Equal Opportunity Policy Private firms are required to have in place equal opportunity polices to guide their hiring practices. These policies should include nondiscriminatory clauses, a policy on sexual harassment, as well as codes of behavior relative to interpersonal relations. Compliance with government-mandated laws may not always be deemed obligatory. However, if firms intend to contract for government work, most agencies require their consultants to adhere to state and federal equal opportunity and other so-called workplace laws. Those laws and policies that are required by government agencies are written into most government contracts.

Recruitment and Hiring Criteria Building and maintaining a strong professional and support staff is key to building a firm's reputation. As a firm grows, the staff requirements generally expand, which requires recruiting and hiring new people. Hiring requirements continue as a firm matures. With maturity comes the movement of people, such as by advancing in the firm itself, moving on to work elsewhere, retiring, and occasionally termination of employment.

Recruiting the right people for the firm is one of the more difficult responsibilities of the company's owners and managers. To find the right candidates for open positions requires having a clear idea about the combination of training, skills, and experience needed for the job. Of equal importance are the people skills of employee candidates. The following is a list of key elements for successful employee recruitment:

- **Resume and portfolio:** These are used first to screen potential applicants and later to assess the professional and technical abilities, skills, and qualifications of candidates seriously considered for potential employment.
- **Written communication:** Writing samples such as a letter or a short report are required as an effective means to determine a candidate's communication and organizational skills.
- **References:** Having a network of professional colleagues is an invaluable asset for obtaining good information about prospective candidates. Checking references is a

surprisingly underutilized recruiting tool. This is unfortunate, as it is a resource that can effectively screen a candidate for aspects that do not readily show up in resumes, portfolios, or even interviews. References not only confirm a candidate's professional abilities and skills, but they also shed some important light on a person's attitude, work habits, demeanor, and interpersonal skills.

- **Personal interview:** This gives the employer an opportunity to fine-tune and expand the evaluation of the candidate. The interview also gives both parties a chance to determine if the interpersonal chemistry is right for getting along in the office with existing staff. It is believed that people come to an initial decision about whether to hire a candidate within fifteen to twenty seconds of being introduced. The remaining time either confirms the initial impression of the candidate or reverses or alters it through the more in-depth and specific information exchange of the interview.

Salary, Benefits, and Incentive Pay Structure

- Establish salary ranges for each job description listing qualifications, work experience, licensing, and other criteria. Clarify criteria for salaried and hourly wage employees including overtime payment policies.
- List employee benefits and how benefits are determined for vacation, sick leave, maternity leave, and medical insurance.
- Describe pension and profit-sharing plans, and incentive or merit pay structure opportunities.
- Identify perks such as health club membership, personal use of firm's purchasing power, and personal use of company car or resort condominium.
- Describe professional development support, including reimbursement of continuing education tuition and membership dues to professional organizations. Also clarify the sabbatical leave policy.
- Define company expense reimbursement policy.

Performance Review

- Outline schedule for periodic employee performance review. Provide for one or more interim reviews for new employees or employees hired on provisional basis.
- Describe terms for promotion and for increased responsibility.
- Define termination policy including grounds for dismissal, resignation, and retirement.

Ownership Opportunities Outline the basis for offering ownership opportunities to employees in cases where owners intend to encourage these opportunities. Offering ownership in a firm is used as an incentive for encouraging staff longevity and fostering meritorious performance. Where owners want to keep certain employees who are valuable to a firm, ownership is sometimes the most effective way, where salary increases and various benefits may not be sufficient.

Out-of-office Policies Often entry and middle-level employees will supplement their income by seeking and performing work outside the office. There are offices that positively discourage this and others that say nothing to disallow it. Where work outside the office is not the preference of a firm, it is important to establish a policy on moonlighting and employees working for other firms or having their own clients. For example, a firm may discourage employees working after hours for competing firms or clients where issues of conflict of interest may arise.

It is to be expected that employees have other interests outside the office that may require a commitment of time on a regular basis. These interests might include involvement in community service projects, serving on boards or commissions, or supporting candidates or political groups. It may be necessary for a firm to define—or limit from the firm's point of view—guidelines for employees interested in performing community service or who are involved in political activities.

Project Management

Considerable variation exists among landscape architectural offices on how detailed project management procedures, production standards, and quality control measures, particularly construction drawings, specifications, and other project documents, are spelled out. Many offices compile an office procedures manual that is given to new employees to help them understand how things are expected to be done in the office. Contained in this manual are the following elements:

- chain of command and staff responsibilities
- document-production standards, including:
  - format, graphics, and layout standards
  - drafting standards
  - information and data requirements for each technical area
- quality control guidelines and procedures
- handling of communications with outside parties including written communication protocol and requirements, documentation of conversations at meetings, as well as telephone, fax, and other telecommunications (Figure 9.4)

4. BUSINESS PLAN IMPLEMENTATION

Many people who have decided to take the plunge and go forward with their new venture are full of energy and willing to jump right into startup activities. Willingness to work hard and unbridled enthusiasm are certainly assets but will not alone ensure success. Starting up a new firm involves preparation and the systematic implementation of many interrelated steps. Each step prepares the way for the next step. In planning for a new firm, the first step is clarifying what business you are going into, the market, the future of this market, appropriate services, the competition, and finally, what you see as your role or niche in this market. The second step is to prepare a realistic financial plan.

Having outlined the firm's goals and business concept, the next step is to identify and organize all the activities required to implement the startup. After this has been done, the next step is to prioritize the activities and prepare a timetable according to which each task is carried out. An important companion element to the timetable is identifying persons responsible for each task.

Figure 9.4   A landscape architect at a medium-sized A/E firm on the telephone with a client arranging a meeting to review the progress of a project.

The business plan should be reevaluated three to six months after startup, assuming the firm is operating with contracts and active projects. Any needed modifications to the plan, including its long-term objectives, should be considered. Appropriate adjustments to the timetable should also made. This timetable should be used to guide firm growth. A long-term plan must be flexible to take advantage of opportunities and changing markets. As a company matures, the activities scheduled in the timetable should provide the means for the owners to enhance the business and realize their own professional goals.

5. IN-BASKET

You are planning to open a landscape architectural office, consisting yourself and a second partner, a staff of two landscape architects, one secretary/bookkeeper, and a spare drafting station for use by a student intern or part-time employee. Assume the office will have two CAD work stations, a library, conference area, storage, and reproduction area with photocopier and blueprint machine.

1. Prepare a brief overview of the goals and objectives of your firm outlining the areas of service, project types, and clients you expect to serve.

2. Prepare a personnel management plan for your firm. Include in the plan a description of the areas of responsibility and duties for the partners, professional staff, and secretary, a brief job description, staff reporting hierarchy, project responsibilities (including

administrative, contracts, client contact, design, construction administration), and salary and benefits structure.

3. Research actual costs for office rent, utilities, furnishings, equipment, supplies, and everything else needed to establish your new office. Check the want-ad section of the newspaper for office rental rates, make telephone calls to local utilities and the telephone company for rates and installation costs, and check prices at office supply stores for furniture and supplies.

4. Develop an estimate of monthly costs for a twelve-month period incorporating the information researched above. Include in the estimate salaries for the five employees based on prevailing wage rates for professional and secretarial staff.

   a. What do you project your monthly expenses will be?

   b. Are the monthly expenses higher or lower than you would have estimated? If so, why the difference?

   c. What strategies could your implement to reduce these expenses and still be able to open the doors of you firm?

5. Prepare a floor plan of your office layout estimating square footage requirements for each work station and functional use area. Make an appointment to visit a small landscape architectural or architectural office and take measurements in order to obtain adequate data to project the square footage requirements of your office.

CHAPTER 10

Business Marketing

1. Marketing Is not Just for Companies Selling Soap
2. What Is Marketing Supposed to Do?
3. The Unique Characteristics of the Design Services Industry
4. What Is Marketing for Landscape Architectural Services?
5. Projects Don't Fall Out of the Sky
6. Marketing Is Something Everyone in the Firm Should Do
7. In-Basket

1. MARKETING IS NOT JUST FOR COMPANIES SELLING SOAP

I'm a designer; designers don't do marketing.

Private practice landscape architects who want to stay in business must be comfortable with the activity of marketing. It is through the activity of marketing that firms acquire clients that result in contracts for projects and fees for services rendered. Even landscape architects in public practice—and to some degree landscape architectural educators—rely on marketing to maintain their programs. Landscape architects in all forms of practice are competing for customers, looking for employment, and seeking financial resources. Marketing is an activity that can mean the very survival of any landscape architect regardless of the nature of his or her practice. To think otherwise is to think oneself out of the business.

For today's practitioner, marketing is not a four-letter word. Nor is it unique to companies selling soap, cereal, mouthwash, or other consumer goods. Concepts for marketing have changed dramatically in recent years. To be truly successful, everyone in an office—from secretary to office manager—must contribute to the marketing efforts of the business. Marketing can no longer be viewed as simply a sales tool. Rather, marketing must be understood as a means of satisfying customer needs through the exchange of professional services for compensation.

Marketing plays a central and critical role in all forms of landscape architectural practice. It is an important aspect of private practice. Government agencies also must market their services and programs to other agencies, the public they wish to serve, and to legislators, particularly when seeking acceptance of a budget or capital improvements program.

To a large extent, marketing is also necessary to maintain the viability of university programs. Landscape architecture programs must continually seek good students. They do this by marketing the profession as a career choice for high school students, incoming freshman, and undecided undergraduates. Landscape architecture programs use marketing techniques to vie for students seeking a career change and perhaps considering a second bachelor's or master's degree.

To ignore the need for marketing is to flirt with extinction. While marketing alone will not produce success, it is a key factor when one considers the small number and size of landscape architectural firms in the United States as compared with other professions offering similar, if not competing design services.

Clients do not necessarily know which firm, or even which profession, is appropriate for their project. It may not be obvious to clients that landscape architects are the appropriate professionals to execute their type of projects. Part of the marketing effort of landscape architects is educating potential clients that certain types of projects and services require their expertise. For example, it would seem obvious that a client would hire a landscape architect to design the garden at his or her residence, but a client may not think to call a landscape architect to develop a piece of land for a subdivision. Marketing landscape architectural services is as much a client education effort as it is an activity for obtaining clients for specific projects in a competitive environment.

2. WHAT IS MARKETING SUPPOSED TO DO?

The core concept to understanding marketing is to understand the product one is marketing. That statement may seem to be no more than a play on words; but taken seriously, it is truly what marketing professional services is all about. Marketing professional services must be understood in terms of value, needs, and products. The services and products a landscape architect provides must be of value to potential clients. Landscape architectural services must meet the following client- and market-driven criteria:

- Satisfy client's needs and desires.
- Be of use to clients or their user groups.
- Add value to the client's project.
- Be perceived as superior to the competition.

3. THE UNIQUE CHARACTERISTICS OF THE DESIGN SERVICES INDUSTRY

There are several unique aspects of a design services industry that require equally unique approaches for marketing professional design services. As part of the professional design services industry, landscape architecture firms must be mindful of their uniqueness when developing marketing strategies.

Tangible and Intangible Characteristics of Landscape Services

Even though landscape architects produce tangible items (or deliverables as they are referred to in contracts), such as reports, drawings, and specifications, the business of landscape architecture is really that of performing services which are intangible. A landscape architect's services result in ideas, recommendations, professional opinions or evaluations, and prescriptive suggestions. Nevertheless, although a landscape architectural firm may have a signed contract to provide services, the client generally expects certain physical products as well.

When formulating a marketing plan, remember that the products are not easily valued by a customer until—in the case of design work—the projects are built. In addition, clients are often unable to evaluate the quality of services to be performed. This places a burden on the marketing approach, requiring it to concentrate on explaining the often intangible benefits of hiring a particular firm. When marketing design services, it is important to stress the close relationship between the firm offering the services and the client contracting for the services.

The Perishable Nature of Landscape Services

Although landscape architects do not have a storage problem like a product manufacturer has, they do, however, have a limited capacity to perform services. To some extent their services are perishable. Landscape architects have a finite capacity for performing design services or meeting with a client to make certain suggestions and recommendations about a project. The usefulness of a landscape architect's services to a client is usually shortlived in that the services are site specific and valid for laws, client program, and market conditions at a particular time.

The services cannot be performed ahead of time, stored, and later sold according to the demand. Also unlike dry goods and appliances, landscape services cannot be purchased and resold or used by another client at another location. The services are site and program specific, with very few exceptions. They are also perishable in the sense that they are time specific. A project design, if not installed within a short time frame, may not be appropriate a year or two after the time the design was completed, perhaps because of changes in building codes and zoning regulations. Moreover, a limited availability of certain materials may not allow the design to be carried out at a later date.

The Performance of Services Is People Intensive

Landscape architectural services are performed by people, a fact that has become no less true with the advent of computer technology. The performance of landscape services is people intensive. As a result of this dependency, the services are subject to variations in quality of performance. But by instituting quality control measures consistently, a higher quality of service can be maintained. Landscape architectural firms are dependent on maintaining a reliable level of service quality in order to survive, in order to gain sufficient customer confidence to be considered for future work or to be given a positive recommendation through word of mouth to other potential clients.

4. WHAT IS MARKETING FOR LANDSCAPE ARCHITECTURAL SERVICES?

Northwestern University marketing professor, Philip Kotler, offers a summary of what marketing is:

> Companies cannot survive today by simply doing a good job. They must do an excellent job if they are to succeed in markets characterized by slow growth and fierce competition at home and abroad. Consumer and business buyers face an abundance of choices in seeking to satisfy their needs, and therefore look for excellence in quality or value or cost when they choose their suppliers. Recent studies have demonstrated that knowing and satisfying the customers with competitively superior offers is the key to profitable performance. And marketing is the company function charged with defining customer targets and the best way to satisfy their needs and wants competitively and profitably.[1]

[1]Kotler, *Marketing Management*, p. 30.

Let's look at an example of marketing, in light of this definition. Consider hamburger restaurants. What is the most popular hamburger restaurant in the world? If you said McDonald's you are correct but also consider that McDonald's doesn't just sell hamburgers. McDonald's success is not in serving the best hamburgers money can buy. If you were hungry for a really good hamburger, you would probably not go to a McDonald's. What McDonald's does sell is an acceptable hamburger, served quickly, at low cost, and in clean surroundings. Also, their stores are conveniently located and usually readily available to people who are thinking about stopping to eat.

What do customers consider when deciding which landscape architectural firms will satisfy their needs? To answer this question, suppose a city park department needs a master plan for a piece of undeveloped park property. They will, of course, consider the product itself, the master plan. But the board members realize there are probably many firms qualified to produce an acceptable quality plan. So the plan is really only one criterion of many that the park board will consider in making a final selection. They will assess the qualifications of the firms and their professional staff, and their past record of performance on similar projects with the board or with other cities in the area; they will consider how well the firms work with park staff and communities in arriving at master plan solutions. They will consider the interest the firms have in working on the project and will evaluate their degree of enthusiasm. Finally, they will determine how well firms understand and work under government policies and procedures as well as their willingness to satisfy the needs of the city. The timeliness of a firm's performance of the work, and its familiarity with costs that might impact project budgets, are also included in the final decision of whom to hire.

Often, a selection board will use a checklist for evaluating competing professional service firms. This checklist will include the evaluation criteria together with a point value system. Each member of the selection board will review the qualifications of the firms submitting proposals. They will assign a numerical value using a predetermined point scale to determine how well each firm meets the criteria. The firms will then be ranked according to the total point scores of each firm. The evaluation matrix in Table 10.1 is similar to a form that might be used for selecting a firm to prepare a park master plan.

5. PROJECTS DON'T FALL OUT OF THE SKY

Projects come into offices mostly through the marketing efforts of a firm's principals. In larger firms, a staff member with specific marketing skills is hired to function as a firm's marketing manager. This person is assigned to direct and in most instances conduct marketing activities of the firm.

Marketing is an activity consisting of a number of phases executed over time. Any one phase may vary in the length of time needed for its execution. Earlier phases are preparatory to and lay important ground for later phases. Devising a marketing strategy, developing marketing materials, and preparing for the launch of a marketing program could take as little as a few weeks or as long as six months or a year. Marketing programs involving new technologies could require a year or longer to develop and implement. Much of the work that goes into developing a marketing program is preparatory to the actual time when communication with the targeted clients begins. To illustrate a process for developing a successful marketing program a firm might follow these steps:

TABLE 10.1 Evaluation Matrix for Selecting Firms to Prepare Park Master Plan

Evaluation Criteria	Maximum Points	Firms Proposing			
		A	B	C	D
Past record of performance on similar projects	20				
Understanding of procedures and policies	15				
Interest and enthusiasm	15				
Firm qualifications	20				
Professional staff qualifications	15				
Cost estimating accuracy on previous projects	5				
Community facilitation skills	10				
Total Scores	**100**				

1. Define the clients and their need for services the firm wishes to provide. Develop a profile that translates these needs into specific services and products. Include the following:
   - potential clients, including private, public markets, and other consultant groups
   - where clients are not the user but are providing products for others (developers of subdivisions), identification of the needs of their user groups
   - financial resources of the private client company
   - funding sources of government agencies, including legislative appropriations, bonds, and general funds sources
   - one- and five-year capital improvement programs of local government agencies or long-range management plans of state and federal agencies
   - applicable government regulations, review procedures, and submittal requirements
   - description of the qualifications, expertise, and technological capabilities of firms currently doing work for targeted client groups (including consideration of geographic areas where these clients are located and locations where you wish to work.)

2. Systematically investigate in as precise detail as possible the nature of the targeted client's needs.

3. Describe the kinds of services and expertise the firm needs to serve the targeted clients.

4. Assess current expertise of the firm's professional staff to determine capability of servicing targeted client needs. Where deficiencies exist, obtain needed expertise through hiring of staff, training of existing staff, or a possible association with another firm having the expertise. Also consider acquiring specialized equipment that will enhance the firm's capabilities or that will meet client requirements better than competing firms.

5. As part of an overall marketing strategy, develop a cluster of communication actions for making known the capabilities and availability of the firm to targeted clients. The strategy should make clear to potential clients that the firm understands and has the

specific capabilities to satisfy the client's needs and requirements. Use language and terms familiar to the targeted clients.

6. MARKETING IS SOMETHING EVERYONE IN THE FIRM SHOULD DO

Marketing is something that each person in a firm should feel responsible to do on a continual basis. When the receptionist picks up the telephone receiver to answer or make a telephone call or greets a client coming into the office, the opportunity for marketing exists. The tone and energy in the voice should be positive and clear, communicating a "how can I help you" message. The person sent out on deliveries or to pick up plans should also be seen as complementing the marketing strategy of the firm. And, of course, the principals and professional staff should make sure they are communicating the marketing message of the firm. Once staff are associated with a firm by people in the community, all actions and conversations, whether in the course of business or during personal, off-hours, reflect on the firm.

Types of Marketing Activities for Private Firms

Firms get work through the marketing efforts of the people in the firm. Owners and staff with the responsibility for finding and getting contracts do so by several primary means: programmed activities, referrals, and solicited and unsolicited proposals. In the early days of establishing a firm, a great deal of time is spent in telling people of the firm's existence and communicating to potential clients the services and capabilities of the firm. Once a firm is known in the community or market area in which it has decided to work, less time is spent promoting the firm.

The marketing activities of a landscape architecture firm can take the full-time efforts of one or more professional staff hired for this purpose. One proposal can take as little as one week or as long as several weeks to prepare. The marketing activities of a firm whose owners are attempting to establish their business are discussed in the following sections.

Development and Distribution of Promotional Communications   For those just starting out, there are limited materials available to promote their firm since the firm does not have a track record of completed projects—and satisfied customers—to use in selling services. In the absence of completed projects, there are three approaches the firm's owners can take:

- **Areas of service:**

  They can indicate clearly and directly how the group of services they wish to provide will satisfy the needs of targeted customers.

- **Qualifications:**

  They can promote the professional qualifications of firm members, including their academic preparation, work experience, and unique skills.

- **Philosophy of the firm:**

  They can emphasize the unique aspects of the firm's approach to working with clients and their projects, stressing the attendant benefits to the client, and the goals of the firm in terms of quality control and cost effectiveness. Benefits should be presented in a language that would have meaning to the client.

Once the details of service, qualifications, and approach philosophy are spelled out, the firm owners must design promotional materials to be used in getting the word out. Certainly the location and design of the office should reinforce the image the firm wishes to project to target clients. As part of its marketing strategy, the firm might develop several promotional materials:

- **Brochure and firm identification materials:**

  These materials include letterhead, business cards, brochures, and other types of promotional materials. They are used to help make known your existence, unique qualifications, and expertise, and also to project an image that will make you attractive in the eyes of targeted clients.

Next comes the hard work of making client contacts through a variety of approaches that could include:

- telephone calls
- letters of introduction
- follow-up interviews responding to potential client interest
- information-seeking interviews regarding short- and long-range client needs

Referrals and Name Recognition   As a firm develops a good reputation, opportunities for contracted work will come through client referrals. A firm in business for five to ten years can also expect to realize the residual benefits of firm name recognition. A firm in business for some time can achieve a certain degree of fame through the visibility of its work or word-of-mouth accolades by satisfied clients. This recognition for certain services or expertise may result in new clients and contracts. Bad work has the opposite effect.

It is important to follow up in a timely manner on referrals or contacts made by potential clients familiar with your work. Once a client contact is made, it should be a matter of firm policy to execute at least two actions:

- thank-you letter with personal telephone call to the individual who made the referral
- telephone call with a follow-up letter to the potential client thanking them for the inquiry and letting them know of your interest to discuss their needs at their earliest convenience

Solicited Proposals   A solicited proposal is a client-initiated process for selecting consultants. Federal codes and state and local government procurement laws dictate the process and manner of soliciting proposals and selecting firms to perform planning and design services for government agencies. Although there are variations from state to state and region to region, there is enough uniformity to provide an overview of the process.

Each year, agencies (federal, state, and local government) have money in their budgets allocated for specific projects. The source of the money may be the sale of bonds, through an appropriation bill, or as a budget item funded through the governing body's general budget. Each year agencies that hire landscape architecture firms to perform planning and design services schedule work to be done by private firms. As the year progresses, the agencies advertise the proposed projects in local or regional newspapers and in local industry construction news services, post the advertisements in a purchasing or financing office bulletin board, or mail out announcements to firms who are on file with the agency. The advertisement is called a *Request for Proposals* (RFP), or *Request for Services*. All the agencies in the federal government advertise in the *Commerce Business Daily*. All requests for landscape architectural services fall under the heading of A/E Services (Architectural-Engineering Services).

In most RFPs there is a closing date for submitting proposals. The items to be included in the proposals and the criteria for making a selection by the contracting agency are also included in the RFP announcement. Other information relevant to the project and special features of the proposed contract are also published in the announcement. Often, a preproposal meeting is held by the contracting agency to answer questions and provide clarification about the proposed project, its requirements, and any special details regarding the consultant selection procedures. In most instances, the agency will interview a small number of the firms (from three to as many as seven firms or teams of firms) who submitted the best proposals. A final selection is made, followed by contract negotiations (including fee negotiations) and the award of a contract by the body of the agency authorized to enter into contract agreements for professional services.

The process for selecting landscape architectural firms in the private sector is generally less involved and less formalized. A private company or individual is not obligated in any way to follow any particular selection process. A company can offer a contract to provide services on a sole source basis; that is, they can offer the contract to one firm without receiving proposals or discussing the project with any other firm. With larger projects involving government oversight (such as energy generation, as in the case of a nuclear generating facility or oil pipeline system) the private company may closely follow a federal or state procurement of professional services process, similar to the RFP process outlined above.

Unsolicited Proposals   When a consultant approaches a potential client with a proposal to solve or deal with a particular problem or situation, it is considered an unsolicited proposal. The consultant defines the problem, outlines an approach to meet that problem, and describes the benefits to the client of the approach and services to be provided.

In the case where a private client is presented with an unsolicited proposal, the decision to accept, reject, or delay accepting the proposal is left up to the client. In the case of a government client, procurement rules under which the jurisdiction of the agency resides determine the manner and process by which they respond to an unsolicited proposal. If the agency staff sees merit in the proposal, most likely a formalized consultant selection process will be authorized.

Economic conditions and trends have become increasingly volative as national economies and political institutions are influenced by global events. The needs and requirements of today's clients can be expected to be equally volatile. A company's past success does not guarantee they will continue to be successful. A company that wishes to stay competitive and profitable must make every effort to understand current and prospective client needs. Part of understanding client requirements is understanding the shifts in economic trends at the regional, national, and global levels.

7. IN-BASKET

You have been made principal of a new landscape architectural section of an established environmental sciences firm. One of your first responsibilities is to develop a brochure for this new section and develop a new strategy for marketing landscape architectural services.

1. Your target is twofold: to gain new contracts from the existing client base and to attract new clients. What type of information would you include in the brochure? Would your approach be the same for both sets of market targets? Explain.

2. One strategy to generate potential contracts with this client base is to send an unsolicited letter. Outline the main points of the letter with the intent of using it to stimulate interest in your new group's services. Assume you will include a copy of the new brochure and that you hope this effort will result in a meeting with the clients to present the firm's new capabilities.

3. Explain the direction your approach might take if the brochure is being developed for a newly formed firm offering services primarily in landscape architecture in which you are a partner.

CHAPTER 11

Office Records

1. Office Record Keeping
2. Types of Records
3. Records Organization and Management
4. Systems for Archiving Office Records
5. In-Basket

1. OFFICE RECORD KEEPING

For the most part, the tangible products of a landscape architect are hard copy documents, such as notes, letters, contracts, specifications, drawings, and reports. These documents are also called the instruments of service, the records that make up the products of service of a landscape architect and staff. Keeping track of these records, that is, storing, indexing, and retrieving them, is of extreme importance (Figure 11.1).

In today's office, records and documents can be in two forms: hard copy (paper) or electronically stored in a magnetic format. Additionally, the design office maintains photographic media including slides, photographs (both negatives and reproductions), and video materials.

Storing and being able to retrieve the records and documents of service produced by an office or received from others (clients, contractors, vendors, consultants, and others) requires a system much like a library. A library requires a system for storing and retrieving books and other library holdings. Much of an office's success can be attributed to having an easy-to-use record-keeping and retrieval system. There are a variety of recording-keeping systems used by professional offices, designed to facilitate storage and retrieval.

What is important, regardless of the system used, is that people in an office know where to put the records for safe keeping and know how to go about finding a particular record when it is needed. For the newly established office, where there are few projects and clients, the need for an elaborate record-keeping system may not be a high priority (Figure 11.2). As projects continue over time, drawn out sometimes for several years, and as the number of clients and projects and records increases, the necessity for having a workable, easy-to-use record-keeping system becomes obvious.

Developing an efficient and effective record-keeping system is often the result of trial and error. An office might implement several systems until the right one is hit upon. If an office manager were to sit down and think about handling and accessing the company's records, the resulting list would include most, if not all, of the following record-keeping requirements:

Figure 11.1   Unmanaged paper clutter. What if the only person who knows what is in the stacks is sick or on vacation?

- **File and storage capability:**

  The system must be able to accommodate myriad documents and materials.

- **Retrievability:**

  Stored documents and materials should be accessible to all personnel requiring them.

- **Protection:**

  Stored materials must be kept safe from the elements, such as water, moisture, sun.

- **Security:**

  Control access to personnel files, financial records, and confidential documents.

- **Ease of use:**

  Provide a system that is organized in a logical manner and that can be understood and used by appropriate office staff.

Figure 11.2   A chair makes for a convenient temporary holding place or way of making sure the project folder is seen by the person for whom the information is intended. If the contents are valuable, there should be a more secure holding place. This is the type of situation an office records management system can take care of.

- **Archival needs:**

    Provide a system for storing away archival materials either in a less accessible area in the office or at a remote location.

There are many laws, contractual considerations, and governmental codes that structure landscape architecture practice. Legal and regulatory authorities mandate that both private and public practices maintain a good record-keeping system. To protect the office and its employees and managers, the activities associated with record keeping must be followed in a consistent, routine manner considering, among other things, statutes of limitations.[1]

---

[1]*Statute of limitations* is a legal term that establishes the length of time an individual or organization is responsible for certain actions and must therefore maintain adequate documentation in the event a claim is made against the individual or organization.

2. TYPES OF RECORDS

Records: The Knowledge Base of an Office

There are many types of records and documents generated and maintained in a design office. These materials represent the activities of an office, its recorded history of services rendered, correspondence, and communication during the life of a project and the life of the office. The history of records and documents of an office should be considered not only as a record of activities but also as a reference resource. The body of records maintained by an office is the knowledge base of that office. Members of the office refer to and utilize the many records and documents maintained in this knowledge base, applying the information contained in the records to new projects and activities.

Typical Office Records and Documents

The typical records maintained by an office consist of documents and correspondence generated by office personnel or received from other offices, individuals, or organizations. All materials must be held and maintained during the life of the project, or for specified periods prescribed by governmental regulations, as in the case of tax records. All documents of a project or specified governmental program constitute the historical and legal record of the project or program. All are necessary to make the project or program complete. The design drawings of a constructed project do not alone complete the record of the project. All correspondence, documentation of meetings and decisions, contracts, review documents, and other data complete the project file. Typical records maintained by landscape architects include:

General business management records and documents

- individual, partnership, and corporation agreements and records
- lease, purchase, and maintenance agreements related to office, equipment, and contracted services
- office management and administrative documents, such as the business and marketing plan, and the office procedure manual
- insurance contracts including general liability, automobile, workman's compensation, medical, and errors and omissions insurance
- business contracts and subcontracts
- general correspondence
- business suppliers and service contracts and records
- utilities and office maintenance records

Accounting and financial records

- accounts receivable
- accounts payable
- job tracking and cost performance histories, including contracted fees, job cost projections, and actual job costs
- contracts
- tax-related documents and records

- bank and other financial statements
- income and profit statements with supporting data

Personnel records

- job descriptions
- personnel records
- personnel performance evaluations

Marketing documents

- marketing plan
- promotion materials
  - brochures
  - completed project histories
  - staff resumes
  - federal, state, and local government forms (F 254/255)
  - slides, photographs
- marketing presentation materials

Project-related documents

- correspondence from clients, other consultants, contractor(s) and other individuals, companies, and organizations
- drawings, including hard copy and electronic media files
- specifications and bid documents
- quantity take-offs and estimates of probable construction costs
- geotechnical, land surveying, material testing, and other project- and site-related investigation reports
- shop drawings
- material and equipment submittals, including specifications and certificates of compliance
- letters of release, such as third-party hold-harmless releases
- bidding and construction administration job files
- as-built, project closeout, and final acceptance
- hand-written notes, journal entries, correspondence confirming conversations and decisions between all parties

Reference and technical documents

- material and equipment catalogues and samples
- reference manuals
- books and periodicals
- government codes, ordinances, guidelines, specifications, and zoning documents
- technical file of standard details
- completed office reports and printed, published, and unpublished documents

Types of communication   The primary types of office communication are written and verbal. Any substantive communication involving a decision, recommendation, directive, action, and commitment of labor or money must be put in writing. Anything put in writing should become a part of the office records (Figure 11.3).

Don't Just Say it—Put it in Writing   Any form of communication can become a part of the permanent record of a project if it is recorded and stored in an office filing system. Maintaining a personal journal or diary is a convenient way of recording telephone conversations as well as formal and informal discussions (Figure 11.4). Pertinent journal entries can be photocopied and placed as hard copy in a project or general office file. Any substantive discussion, verbal exchange, or agreement should be put into writing and sent to the parties involved including those potentially affected by the outcome of the conversation. Copies of these types of confirmation letters should be placed in an appropriate office file.

A personal journal might also contain a telephone log. It may be the preference of an office that a separate telephone log be maintained. Regardless of the method used, each person in an office should consider it standard operating procedure to record all verbal discussions. For important discussions, letters to the file with copies to the affected parties should also be an expected part of the routine. The legal implications of maintaining complete written records is of utmost importance. The private practitioner should maintain a complete written record of all verbal communication including telephone and in-person conversations.

For those who have not yet found themselves in court or involved in a legal deposition, the need for maintaining written records of all verbal agreements or decisions, if not all conversations, may not seem as much an imperative as it is for someone involved in a legal

Figure 11.3   To record and keep track of a variety of projects, personnel, and business activities, an office utilizes standard forms such as timesheets, transmittal forms, cost-estimating forms, and forms to track shop drawing and equipment submittal reviews.

Figure 11.4   A personal journal or daily calendar is needed to keep track of appointments and document important conversations.

action. For those who have not been involved in a conflict having legal implications, putting everything in writing may seem contradictory to another aspect of professional life, that of developing goodwill and trust between consultant and client. Inexperienced professionals may feel it is more important to follow through on a commitment, particularly if that commitment was made at a time when a sense of goodwill and collegiality seemed exceptionally clear. But what happens, later, after the actions are taken and the sense of goodwill has eroded due to misunderstandings and different interpretations of past events? Differences of opinion regarding past decisions and agreements often occur. People hear and interpret conversations differently. Sometimes the differences in interpretation occur when the original parties in a conversation delegate the follow-up actions to others. Those delegated to act may perform a different action than what was intended in the original conversation. Regardless of the reasons, these actions may be unexpected and hence unacceptable to the receiving party. No matter how much goodwill was felt at the time, if one party believes the wrong response was executed by the other party, previous feelings of goodwill may go by the wayside.

If the main points of discussion and agreement are put in writing before the agreed-upon actions are carried out, the party carrying out the actions has a basis upon which to justify itself should legal action be taken. Considering the adage that the customer is always right, any decision by a consultant to contest in this situation must be tempered by considering the long-term view. It could hurt the firm's reputation and ultimately its business if a client badmouths the firm. The decision to contest or not to contest a client's allegations is as much a business decision as it is simply convincing the client that the correct action was taken using the written record as proof. This is a matter that falls under ethics and professional codes of conduct.

3. RECORDS ORGANIZATION AND MANAGEMENT

Most projects and activities of an office generate a tremendous volume of documents and correspondence that necessitates a comprehensive filing system. The volume of material is compounded by materials received from a large number of different individuals or organizations in addition to the client groups served by the office.

Often, several sets of records or files are maintained in an office. The record sets may or may not be cross-referenced. Office records may also be maintained in active and inactive files. The active files are often "on the floor"—readily accessible to all within one office location. Inactive files might be placed somewhere out of the way from the daily routine or at a remote location such as a bank vault or secured storage facility.

Records Over the Life of a Project

The types of documents and correspondence will vary from phase to phase over the life of a project:

Marketing

- written proposals and presentations prepared for selection review boards

Contracts

- fee negotiations, signatures, and approvals

Planning and design

- submittal packages (such as plans for review) and various types of information and communication as well as exchanges, drawings, specifications, product review, and cost estimating; also documents associated with governmental permits, reviews, and approvals, and those associated with requirements of financial lending institutions

Bidding and negotiations

- advertisements of bid and bid documents, construction contracts, pre-bid meeting documentation, addenda, bid awards, and contract negotiations

Construction through warranty and final acceptance

- all written correspondence and records documenting:
  - material and equipment submittals
  - shop drawings
  - preexisting site conditions (such as a photographic and/or video record)
  - construction administration documentation
  - change orders and progress payment records
  - prefinal and final inspections, punch list, and project acceptance
  - warranty and maintenance period documentation
  - as-built drawings

4. SYSTEMS FOR ARCHIVING OFFICE RECORDS

Many offices maintain files that were not designed following a methodical process considering the record-keeping needs of the business. For most private offices, the filing system in place is based on someone's straightforward, logical way of storing what was becoming piles of correspondence and drawings. Many office record-keeping systems are more the product of common sense than the application of a systematic design process.

During the startup years of an office, an ad hoc system is serviceable, but it may not be adequate as the office matures. The flow of paper and correspondence can be prodigious. Regardless of the size of an office, the buildup of enormous amounts of varied types of records is inevitable (Figure 11.5).

Filing Systems

A filing system can be designed to integrate one or more variables. Most systems follow some type of taxonomic hierarchy with the first order of record keeping based on, perhaps, client name with subcategories of project name or project date. The common categories of most record-keeping taxonomies include the following primary headings:

- alphabetical by client name
- date

Figure 11.5   Much of an office's administrative records, written correspondence, and graphic documents are generated using computers and saved on floppy or hard disks. Maintaining an electronic filing system is a serious concern of landscape architects as they make the transition from traditional hard copy.

- assigned numeric system
- project type
- project location

One common record-keeping system maintains records in alphabetical order by client name. As additional projects are done for a particular client, a second tier for filing records might be alphabetical by project name or by chronological order. This record-keeping taxonomy would be organized in tiers or levels of information as shown in Figure 11.6.

Office Log for All Documents

All documents that come into or leave the office should be tracked by entering the transaction into a central log book. The responsibility of maintaining the log should be given to one individual or an assigned group. By implementing an office log for all documents, it will be possible to keep track of the existence of all office correspondence, documents, drawings, and other records of activity or action. It also provides easier access to needed information. Each piece of paper and every report, drawing, document, or hard copy (and electronically transferred) file should be catalogued for eventual retrieval.

Record-keeping taxonomy

Tier One: Client type and/or geographic location, examples:

1.   Government
    a.   Federal
    b.   State
    c.   Local
2.   Private
    a.   Corporate
    b.   Consultant (prime)
    c.   Family and private individual

Tier Two: Client names in alphabetic order

Tier Three: Project phases with each project having subdivisions following contracted phases of work such as:
    a.   Schematic design
    b.   Design development
    c.   Construction documents
    d.   Bidding
    e.   Construction administration

Tier Four: Chronological order

Figure 11.6   Record-keeping taxonomy.

The status of each item's whereabouts can be tracked by maintaining a log of all documents received and transmitted. An office log might include the following data sets:

- date item received
- date item transmitted and by what means: hand, mail, facsimile, or delivery service, and to whom, including where copies were sent
- description of item including name of originator
- action taken (if required)
- where item was filed and date filed

5. IN-BASKET

Imagine a collection of slides taken over the years documenting many projects worked on in the office and memorable visits to exciting cities around the world. Now, imagine the problem of selecting and organizing slides for presentations to clients and various groups. Most often, slides are kept in the original boxes they came in from the photo lab, perhaps in plastic folders, in carousel trays, or in metal slide-holding boxes. The photograph in Figure 11.7 shows a typical scene found in a design office, that of organizing slides for a presentation.

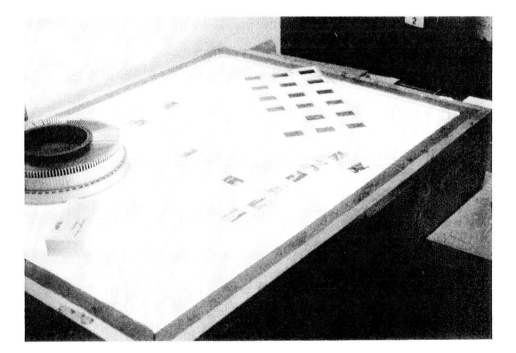

Figure 11.7   Light table with a slide presentation being prepared for a prospective client.

1. Considering your own slide collection, develop a catalogue system that will keep track of your slides and facilitate storing, retrieving, and returning them to storage as they are used. Develop a taxonomy that will allow you to identify each slide by project or site name, location, date, and other fields of information relative to specific items or attributes represented in the slides.

2. Based on the same set of slides, modify the catalogue system developed in exercise 1 so you can log in new slides taken at different times over several years for the same projects already included in your collection.

CHAPTER 12

Life of a Project

1. From an Idea to a Built and Functioning Project
2. Project Development as a Process
3. Standard Products of Performance
4. Concepts of Project Design Services
5. Phases of the Project Design Process
6. In-Basket

1. FROM AN IDEA TO A BUILT AND FUNCTIONING PROJECT

A design project has a life of its own. It might begin as an idea to meet a client's need or in response to a law or a governmental program. Next, the idea is developed into a detailed design proposal. The proposal might describe a function or group of functions, or definite purpose, and include a site or defined location, a budget, and a time frame for completion. After several intermediate stages of refinement, the design is translated into construction drawings and technical specifications. The final stage of a project's life is the process of executing the paper proposal—drawings and specifications—into the final, functioning product such as a park, urban plaza, or restored wetland marsh.

The process of design leading to construction is an important aspect of landscape architecture. Most private landscape architectural firms and design/construction sections of government entities are engaged daily in the process of design leading to construction. This process consists of a number of stages.

The First Stage

A project begins as an idea to satisfy a need or meet a requirement. It may originate in many ways, including:

- an entrepreneurial opportunity initiated by a corporate individual or board to design and build a resort-based community in a market area where demand for such a project is considered high and where a high rate of return on investment can be expected
- a governmental agency's or regulatory body's decision to meet a community need or to respond to a particular piece of legislation, for example, to design and build a park with an interpretive facility in a community demanding such facilities
- an individual's wish to improve and upgrade a residence by refurbishing or adding onto outdoor living areas with new gardens and a pool

A project scope and perhaps a budget are then defined during this first stage of a project. The scope includes the functional elements or purpose of the project and might identify built elements that relate to the functional elements. In the case of a proposed project for a private client, a feasibility study might then be initiated to determine if there is a market for the project and if the project is economically feasible. Although public projects are not thought of in terms of being market driven, public projects are generally designed to meet specific user group demands (such as public schools), serve a community need (such as a bicycle trail as an alternate transportation link), or perform a public service (such as roadway beautification).

Once the desirability and feasibility of a project are determined, a decision is made to hire a consultant or assign agency staff to carry out the design activities. A specific process is usually outlined together with schedules for completing incremental phases of design work, and a budget to pay for a consultant's services or to pay staff. A contract is written and signed when a consultant is hired to perform the design services for a client.

The Middle Stage

A project then reaches a middle period that may involve fact finding, analyzing the facts, and exploring possible solutions. The solutions are reviewed with the client and modifications made based on client input. Interaction with the client may involve more than one review phase. After each review, components of the design solution are refined and modified leading to the preparation of final construction documents. Final construction documents generally include drawings, specifications, and details. This document, called the *construction package*, is used to secure bids from contractors.

It is during the middle phase that the project's form is established. Form-giving is a process of transforming facts and ideas into some coherent framework called the *design solution*. The design solution is developed two-dimensionally on paper or with the use of computers as a scaled drawing (consisting of plans, sections, details, and perspective drawings), or as a three-dimensional scaled model. The plan and model are reviewed by the client, then revised by the landscape architect in a series of steps beginning with conceptual design and then design development, and finally ending as a set of construction drawings and specifications.

The middle stage involves considerable interaction between the client and the landscape architect. Other entities may also become involved, interacting with the consultant and sometimes in consultation with the client. The other entities are generally governmental reviewers whose administrative or regulatory functions include review and approval of specified aspects of a project. One of these aspects is adequacy of conformance to:

- land-use zoning ordinances
- specified codes, design standards, or regulatory guidelines involving public health and safety issues
- permitting requirements

The Final Stage

Implementation is the final state of a project's life. For most landscape architects, implementation consists of construction or some form of execution. Depending on the type of project, the client,[1] governmental requirements, funding sources, and many other circumstantial influences, the final stage of a project follows a process that is divided into discrete phases. Each phase consists of specified activities that produce prescribed products. The final phases might include the following elements:

- contract award and issuance of a written notice for the contractor to proceed with construction at a specific date
- review and approval of materials, equipment, and shop drawings submitted by the contractor to the landscape architect
- mobilization and construction startup by contractor of equipment and construction personnel
- construction with routine observation by landscape architect of work in progress, inspection and approval of certain preparatory work items such as the laying out of major elements (walks, paved areas, walls, etc.), location of plant materials, and concrete form work (prior to pouring concrete)
- evaluation by the landscape architect of completed work to determine acceptance or nonacceptance based on design intent, drawings and technical specifications (the landscape architect should consider approval of contractor requests for progress payments)
- preliminary inspection by the landscape architect of all work at 100 percent completion, and preparation of a punchlist[2] of inadequate or unacceptable work
- final inspection and acceptance; commencement of warranty and maintenance period
- acknowledgment of satisfactory completion of construction contract by sending contractor written notice of the acceptance of work and final payment (called *project closeout*)

2. PROJECT DEVELOPMENT AS A PROCESS

Design projects begin as ideas to satisfy or meet people's needs. The process of identifying needs can be a complex and often lengthy process when large groups of people such as community, corporate, and special-interest groups are affected. Idea formulation for landscape architecture projects also involves a complex process requiring the acquisition of a variety of information. Information is needed about the physical features of the project site, the governmental requirements, the economic and marketing context, and other environmental and temporal conditions. In order to be effective and produce relevant results, the design process must further provide for understanding the web of interrelationships of the dynamic systems, such as the social, cultural, and environmental systems in which the built project will serve and reside.

The path a project takes from its inception as an idea to the final coat of paint and ultimate use should be viewed as a process that may vary depending on an array of circumstances. Table 12.1 illustrates the seven key elements that a design process might contain.

---

[1]*Client* is used here to encompass both client and user. The user may not be the client and the client may not be the eventual user as in the case of the developer of a golf course for a residential community. The developer is the client, but the residents will be the users.

[2]The *punchlist* is a list of items determined by the landscape architect as not conforming to either the drawings or technical specifications, and that the contractor is obligated to correct. This list is drawn up in the form of a letter or memorandum and usually establishes a schedule of when remedial work is to be completed and inspected.

TABLE 12.1   Project Process: From a Program to Construction

Who	How	Results
1. Project Initiation		
Community groups	Direct communication to:	Bond
Special interest groups	• Agency or board	Capital improvement plan
Persons of influence	• Politicians	Law, enabling act, program
Politicians	Vote	Project approval
Agency staff	Hearing, participatory process	
Societal goals & demands	Pressure or influence	
	Research and surveys	
2. Project Definition		
Elected bodies	Public hearing	Project program
Boards and commissions	Programming and budgeting	Master plan or feasibility
Agency staff	Master planning and predesign	study
Hired consultant	Marketing research	Project budget and schedule
3. Project Budget		
Elected bodies	Project budgeting process	Appropriation
Boards and commissions	Estimate of probable costs of	Project construction budget
Agency staff	all items to be constructed	Tax or special assessment dis-
Hired consultant	within the project amount	trict
	budgeted	
4. Project Design Implementation		
Agency professional staff	Design Process	Construction bid package
A/E consultant	• Schematic design	Advertise bid
	• Design development	
	• Construction documents	
	• Bidding and negotiations	
	• Construction	
	Review by agency staff, the	
	public, and the governing	
	body	
	Design package approval	
	process	
5. Project Bid Process		
Agency staff	Advertise bids	Bid award
Procurement office	Pre-bid meeting	Contract executed
A/E consultant	Bid opening	Notice to proceed construction
Licensed or bonded	Contract negotiations	
contractors		
6. Project Construction		
Agency staff	Construction admininstration	Acceptance of construction
A/E consultant	Review submittals, pay	Punchlist
Contractor	requests and change orders	Occupancy permit
	Pre and final inspections	
	Warranty and maintenance	
	inspections	
7. Operations and Maintenance		
Owner's personnel	Scheduled maintenance	O & M activities protect capital
Contractors bycontract or	O & M budget	investment and serve users
force account	Evaluate O & M effectivenss	Repair, remodel, and adaptive
		reuse

Table 12.1 uses a government-administered project as a model, although a table constructed for a large project in the private sector would be similar.

3. STANDARD PRODUCTS OF PERFORMANCE

Clients, such as private individuals and corporations and governmental employers, have come to expect certain products and services when they hire a landscape architect as a consultant or as an employee. These are understood as the standard products of performance. The tangible products are referred to as deliverables. Deliverables are the instruments of practice which consist of:

- drawings together with details
- notes
- schedules
- specifications
- contract bid documents

A number of contractual and supporting documents are usually included to complete the design package. This package is used to secure bids from contractors and guide the efforts in constructing a project (Figure 12.1).

Whether acting as a consultant or as an employee, a landscape architect follows a sequence of phased work. Each phase produces a prescribed package of drawings together with supporting documents as well as a prescribed set of information. The information is

Figure 12.1   Cover sheet to a set of construction drawings. A set of drawings for a single project may be as few as two or as many as several hundred sheets.

developed to a level of detail and completeness deemed appropriate and, in many ways, unique to each phase. At the earliest phase of a design project the landscape architect is primarily developing and communicating ideas. The level of detail at the beginning phases is minimal but adequate to the extent that the client understands:

- the design intent, rationale, or conceptual framework
- the design solution, including appropriate alternatives
- the materials, including plants, paved surfaces, structures, and equipment
- the probable costs of all elements of the ultimately constructed project

As a project progresses to the preparation of the final construction design package, the documentation and level of detail becomes increasingly specific. The final construction design package, if it is to be used for securing competitive bids or as the basis for developing a contract with a contractor, must meet standards of performance appropriate for the project type and industry standards. Several sources prescribe these standards, including federal and state agency design services procurement codes, and the American Institute of Architects (AIA) and the American Society of Civil Engineers (ASCE) standard form documents. The level of detail and completeness of information contained in the final construction bid package must meet standards suitable for bidding purposes as well. The standards for bidding are prescribed in the sources listed above, such as the AIA documents.

4. CONCEPTS OF PROJECT DESIGN SERVICES

Design services provided under contract by a private landscape architectural firm or landscape architect working in a public agency generally follow a specified sequence (Figure 12.2). This sequence contains five basic phases of activity:

- schematic design
- design development
- construction drawings
- bidding
- contract administration of construction

Government agencies, such as local and state departments of public works, public facilities, parks and recreation, and federal agencies such as the U.S. Forest Service, the National Park Service, and the U.S. Army Corps of Engineers, have their own formalized design services format. Each agency has provisions under its professional design services contracts that provide for phased work, with periodic reviews of work in progress. The landscape architect will periodically submit portions of work completed, representing work in progress. These submissions of work in progress (often referred to as *submittals*) allow the client to review and provide input at key intervals in the design process. Each increment of work submitted to the client represents a percentage of work completed. Each submission has its anticipated aspects of work described in the design services contract.

The types of information, the level of detail contained in the submitted documents, the completeness of information supplied, and the degree of refinement become more comprehensive and closer to their final form as the project moves from the early design concept

Design Project Leading Through Construction

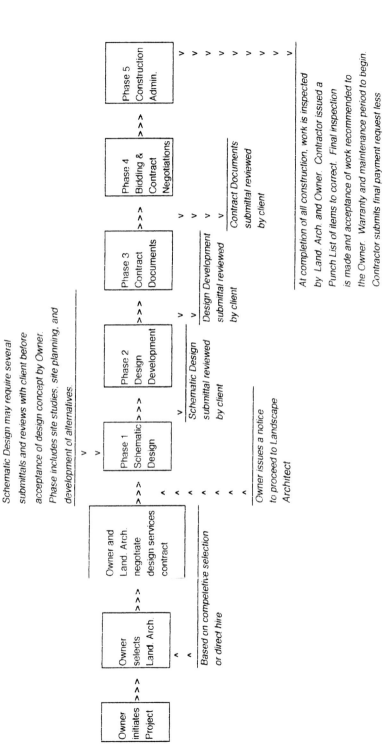

Figure 12.2 Overview of process.

phases through preparation of final construction documents. Each phase focuses on different aspects of a project's development and has a unique set of goals to be accomplished with respect to informing the owner and appropriate design review bodies about the project.

Depending on the nature of a project, additional phases may be considered, including an array of services and deliverable products. Each service and deliverable has its unique set of objectives, depending on the information requirements of individual phases and of project/client requirements. Services commonly provided under additional phases are discussed later in the chapter and include predesign, site analysis, postconstruction, and supplemental services.

AIA Document B163

The design industry's standard document outlining professional services used by most public agencies (federal, state, and local) is AIA document B163,[3] published by the American Institute of Architects. The American Society of Civil Engineers (ASCE) has a similar document and the American Society of Landscape Architects is currently developing its own standard services agreement. AIA Document B163 is often used as the basis for defining a scope of work in an A/E design services contract. The services in a design contract are referred to as *designated services*. The term refers to those services the consultant must perform on a particular type of project. The document presents a comprehensive outline of services together with descriptions of project phases. Used in conjunction with an owner-consultant contract, the AIA document provides a framework for identifying the particular set of services required for a specific project. Factors to consider when determining the scope of designated services required for any one project are presented in Table 12.2.

---

[3]"Standard Form of Agreement Between Owner and Architect for Designated Services," *AIA Document B163*, 1993 edition. American Institute of Architects, Washington, D.C.

TABLE 12.2   Considerations for Identifying Designated Services

1. The complexity and nature of the project **Example:**   Residential garden vs. highly complex mixed-use central business district streetscape and urban design project
2. The importance of the site relative to governing laws **Examples:**   Preservation wetlands, an endangered species habitat, a river flood plain
3. Legal, regulatory, or administrative requirements **Examples:**   Land-use zone change, an environmental impact statement, a nuclear power plant siting
4. Approval procedure and their requirements **Examples:**   Wetland fill permit from U.S. Army Corps of Engineers, or municipal sign ordinance
5. Project visibility or importance **Examples:**   Urban park in downtown, placement of art in public, a school site selection process, street landscape plan

5. PHASES OF THE PROJECT DESIGN PROCESS

Description of Basic Services

AIA Document B163 contains eight phases of designated services. Not all phases need to be included for every project. but all eight will be discussed in this chapter. There are three phases less frequently included in a contract involving landscape architects; these are pre-design, site analysis, and postconstruction. Items included in the scope of work of these three phases may be combined in the standard five-phase scope of work for landscape architects. For example, site analysis is usually included in the schematic design phase in a landscape architect's contract and is not designated as a standalone phase of work.

The eight phases in a scope-of-work agreement are listed below and are followed by an expanded explanation of each.

- pre-design
- site analysis
- schematic design
- design development
- construction documents
- bidding and negotiations
- construction contract administration
- postconstruction

Phase 1: Predesign Services   In the predesign phase the consultant provides the necessary assistance to the client in establishing or refining the client's program. The consultant may assist in establishing the financial and time requirements for a project, and may also assist in identifying limitations or restraints that come from outside the realm of the client and project that require action and response (such as zoning and plan review requirements or agency regulatory requirements).

Types of services included in this phase are:

Programming

- identifying the functional activities the design must satisfy

Space schematics of functional activities

- preparing spatial relation diagrams of functional activities, including circulation, access, and other important functional support requirements

Existing facilities and services survey

- preparing an inventory documenting existing conditions within the project boundaries and researching the type, capacity, and location of services such as water, electricity, gas, and sewer

Marketing studies

- assisting client in identifying potential market and service areas that could be served by the proposed project elements

Economic feasibility studies

- assessing the economic viability of the project, considering market demand, construction and operating expenses, projected income, and depreciation

Project development scheduling

- preparing a schedule (using critical path or other method) outlining required activities, time allocated to complete the project, milestone completion dates, and client/governmental review periods

Project budgeting (planning, design, and construction budget)

- preparing an estimate of probable costs of construction (based on best information available at this phase of work), which can be made on the basis of the known costs of comparable projects

Phase 2: Site Analysis   For most landscape architects, the services in this phase are often incorporated in phase 3, schematic design. The objectives of this phase are to establish site-related limitations based on an inventory and assessment of a site's physical attributes as well as the effect of off-site conditions. Some of the services unique to this phase are:

Site selection and site analysis

- assisting the client in selecting a suitable site for a project
- conducting an analysis of site conditions, including slope, drainage, existing structures, vegetative cover, views, and off-site factors

Site development planning

- analyzing activity utilization, circulation (pedestrian and vehicular), and functions

Needs assessment

- identifying requirements for land survey, geotechnical investigation, and conducting an environmental impact assessment

On- and off-site utility studies

- identifying and determining the available capacity of needed utilities

Zoning and permitting

- administering or assisting the client in processing documentation to secure needed zoning, ordinance, and permitting requirements

Phase 3: Schematic Design   The focus of the landscape architect in the schematic design phase of the design process is on understanding and defining the goals of the project. Landscape architectural services included in the predesign and site analysis phases outlined in AIA Document B163 are included under schematic design. The primary issue the consultant explores is the initial understanding of the influencing factors of the project and the resolution of these factors leading to the identification of one or more design concepts. When providing traditional landscape design services under an architectural contract, the landscape architect's services consist of identifying alternate materials, systems, and equipment as well as developing conceptual design solutions for land forms, drainage, hardscape, plantings, and other designed physical features to be incorporated into the project site.

Activities typically included under the schematic design phase are:

Project feasibility and constraints

- assessing the capability of the site to accommodate the proposed project program
- consideration to on- and off-site factors

Programming of functional elements

- using diagrams together with the quantitative area needs of functional elements
- preparing relational diagrams of functional activities to be accommodated within the project site

Design concepts

- utilizing the information and analysis conducted to this point, developing one or more design concepts that can be used in consultation with client to determine if client needs and requirements are met
- selecting an optimum design concept alternative

Materials and basic details

- selecting materials or material systems for project
- preparing preliminary construction details of critical components to help define final design qualities and quantities

Estimate of probable construction costs

- preparing estimate of probable costs based on preferred design concept, material selection, and preliminary details

Phase 4: Design Development   During this phase the landscape architect refines the concepts presented and approved by the client in the schematic design phase. At this stage, the project has advanced beyond the consideration of feasibility and acceptability (financially and in terms of meeting governmental guidelines, restraints, and requirements). The final scope-of-project work of preferred design alternates to be included in the construction package is determined together with:

Design development

- refining preferred schematic design concept, providing greater detail in all aspects related to construction details, dimensioning, grading and drainage, materials, structures, etc., paying particular attention to refining the grading, drainage, hardscape and landscape plans

Preliminary details

• beginning to prepare construction details

Outline specifications

• preparing outline specifications, including all elements of work that will require technical specifications

Preliminary design of equipment systems

• including product investigation and preliminary design of irrigation, lighting, specialized equipment, site furnishings, and signage

Estimate of probable construction cost

• preparing estimate of probable cost of construction based on information developed in this phase

Phase 5: Construction Documents   The scope of work included in this phase is based on approvals by the client and appropriate reviewing bodies from work submitted in the design development phase. Construction documents are prepared as a package, often called a *project manual*. The final package consists of drawings, technical specifications, bidding documents, special instructions, and other bidding materials. The package may also include a sample construction contract.

Activities typically included under design development are:

• preparing final construction drawings, specifications and bid package materials
• coordinating the drawings, specifications and other bid package materials prepared by subconsultants
• preparing an estimate of probable construction costs
• acquiring governmental approvals of project, utilizing documentation of final design package

Phase 6: Bidding and Negotiations   The degree of involvement by the landscape architect in this phase will be determined by the client. The client must sometimes be convinced of the necessity of the landscape architect's involvement during this phase. In the case of a private residential project, the landscape architect might have complete responsibility for administering and orchestrating the entire bidding and contract negotiation process. Where a government agency is involved, the landscape architect may simply assist and advise the contracting officer during the construction process.

Activities typically included under bidding and negotiations are the following:

• assisting the client in conducting the bid process and soliciting bids, which might be limited to answering specific questions or could involve administering the entire process
• organizing and handling the bidding materials:
  • reproducing project manuals
  • distributing project manuals directly to client procurement and bid-solicitation offices or to prospective contractors

- distributing or assisting in the distribution of addenda
- participating in pre-bid conference and bid opening by answering questions, clarifying design or technical issues, and preparing addenda for distribution to bidders
- assisting in the evaluations of bids and recommending contract awards, reviewing and evaluating the adequacy and completeness of bids, and recommending bidder for client to negotiate construction contract
- assisting the client in drafting the construction contract agreement (between the client and the contractor)

Phase 7: Construction Contract Administration This phase consists of three distinct subphases. Each subphase includes services requiring office and field activities by the landscape architect. These activities include: (1) evaluating contractor-supplied materials and equipment, (2) monitoring actual construction performance, and (3) documenting these evaluations, including pertinent communication between contractor, client, and any appropriate government entity. Written documentation of recommendations and decisions made by the landscape architect is required regarding contractor performance and submittals.

The landscape architect has the additional responsibility of representing the client and the client's interest in this phase. The landscape architect's role is to make sure that the intent of the project goals and design are fully realized by the contractor in the materials and equipment supplied by the contractor and the workmanship throughout the installation of the project.

Landscape architects carry out their responsibilities primarily by providing suggestions and recommendations to the contractor. The landscape architect should not direct the contractor. If the contractor follows the directives of the landscape architect and the results are not acceptable or the cost of execution is greater than anticipated and takes more time, the contractor may have a valid claim for additional compensation and for a time extension to complete the contract. Unacceptable work performed at the direction of the landscape architect may place the responsibility of correcting the poor workmanship on the landscape architect.

Conceptually, the landscape architect must allow the contractor to proceed, realizing that the responsibility to accept or reject completed work resides with the landscape architect. The contractor can seek advice and the landscape architect can offer advice. However, the advice and suggestions should be carefully offered so as not to be construed as a directive by the landscape architect to the contractor.

The subphases of construction contract administration discussed in the following:

- The first subphase is review of materials, fabricated elements, and equipment submitted by the contractor for the landscape architect's approval or denial. The contractor submits technical specifications, provided by the manufacturer or supplier, shop drawings, and material samples. On occasion, material and workmanship cannot be evaluated on paper, and the contractor may be required (in the technical specifications) to construct a sample of the work such as a masonry wall treated with special textured materials.
- Construction administration requires office administration and coordination, on-site field observations of work in progress or completed work, as well as the following (Figure 12.3):

Figure 12.3 At a construction site many different trades represented by subcontractors may be working side by side. The coordination of these activities is the responsibility of the prime contractor. However, the landscape architect must be sufficiently knowledgeable of the work in progress to be able to evaluate whether that work meets the intent of the design (as represented in the contract documents).

- preparing progress reports documenting field observations of contractor activities and progress
- reviewing and approving pay requests and change orders submitted by contractor
- monitoring contractor activities where potential or actual activities of the contractor may lead to third-party claims[4]
- participating in project scheduling where coordination is required between contractor, client, or other parties
- The third subphase encompasses final inspection, construction cost accounting, and project closeout:
  - conducting prefinal and final inspections including notification of any deficiencies (Figure 12.4)
  - accepting receipt of warranties, affidavits, and releases and waivers of any liens or bonds indemnifying the client against liens
  - preparing documentation and coordinating project closeout, including securing consent of surety companies to issue final certificate of payment

[4]Third-party claims are made against the contractor or project owner by another party for supposed damages to personal property brought on by the project contractor. An example would be the dumping of ususable fill on another site without prior permission of property owner. The claim could be in the form of a threat of probable legal action.

Figure 12.4 Sometimes hard decisions must be made by the landscape architect as the contract administrator. These large trees planted earlier in the season are showing extreme signs of stress. The landscape architect has to decide whether to accept the trees or require that they be replaced. The cost to the contractor to replace the trees will be high; on the other hand, the owner and the landscaper will have to replace them later if they are accepted but continue to decline.

Phase 8: Postconstruction Services   Once the contractor has completed construction, inspections are made by the landscape architect to determine the adequacy of materials and workmanship. Any deficiencies are noted and the contractor is directed to correct them, and if the project is acceptable to the landscape architect and owner, the maintenance and warranty period begins.

Services often provided by the landscape architect in the postconstruction phase include:

- *Providing periodic inspections of warranty items and work:* Items accepted under warranty, such as equipment or plant materials, normally require periodic inspection by the landscape architect to assess the performance of either the contractor—in the case of maintaining plant materials—or of equipment—such as children's outdoor play equipment. Warranty periods usually extend for one year, beginning from the time the work was accepted. Any deficiencies need to be reported to the contractor in writing by the landscape architect, with a time frame indicated for making corrections.

- *Coordinating execution of final payment and contractual closeout items:* Most professional services contracts require the landscape architect to review all payment submittals made by the contractor and to inspect the performance of the contractor in correcting all deficiencies of workmanship and materials. The landscape architect should then advise the client whether to make final payment to the contractor or withhold an amount as allowed under the general conditions of the contract and specifications.

- *Coordinating the preparation and receipt of as-built or record drawings:* Construction projects are rarely built exactly to the specifications prepared by the landscape architect. Adjustments and changes—both significant and minor—are invariably made. Most government clients and many private clients require either the landscape architect, the contractor, or a third-party to prepare a set of drawings that reflect what actually was constructed. When the landscape architects do not prepare the as-built drawings, they are still responsible for checking the accuracy of the drawings and recommending to the client any changes needed.

- *Monitoring contractor performance in connection with maintenance items:* The landscape architect generally has the responsibility to assess the performance of the contractor for items requiring maintenance during warranty periods. The landscape architect is responsible for arranging the correction of any deficiencies.

- *Conducting postconstruction evaluation:* The landscape architect is responsible for carrying out an evaluation of the functional and operational performance of the project with respect to maintenance and user satisfaction. Postconstruction evaluation provides an opportunity for the landscape architect to evaluate the effectiveness and adequacy of the design in meeting the hoped-for performance of design elements. An example would be to determine if an outdoor-use area is meeting the needs of the owner to provide a safe and attractive venue for employees or for the public.

Supplemental Services

Often there are projects or clients with unique or specialized needs that require services and provisions for acquiring products and materials not normally included in a design contract. The list of supplemental services can be very lengthy. A list of optional services might include selecting art or coordinating the activities of a percent-for-art jury,[5] providing promotional materials such as a marketing brochure, preparing mockups of custom equipment or site features, providing and coordinating the work of specialized consultants, and providing many other services requiring specialized knowledge, experience, and skill.

Typical supplemental services that may be considered for inclusion in a professional services contract or amended later into an existing contract include:

- renderings and models
- videotaping of project site or other subject
- special studies and reports
- life-cycle cost analysis
- expert witness testimony
- long-distance travel to inspect materials and equipment of potential suppliers and vendors

[5]Many city and state governments have legislation that requires a specified percentage of a public works construction budget be set aside for public art. Often the process of selecting the art piece or artist involves a committee that may include a representative of the user group, the sponsoring agency, the project designers, and an art council member.

6. IN-BASKET

You have met with a couple whose wishes to contract with you to design the landscape for their new home. You have just returned to your office.

1. Prepare a letter to your client's outlining the scope of work or steps you plan to follow in developing a final plan from concept to contract administration. Describe the expected products for each step of the process.

2. Describe what you think your client's would be most interested in knowing about the project at the schematic design phase. What would the deliverables be at this phase that could explain your design and answer your clients' questions about their project? How would the information differ from what the client would need to know at the end of the design development phase?

3. At the end of which phase would you expect the cost estimate for construction to be more accurate: schematic design or construction documents? What factors do you think allow for greatest accuracy?

CHAPTER 13

Legal Issues

1. The Legal Aspects of Practice
2. The U.S. Legal System
3. The Legal System's Impact on Design
4. The Legal System's Impact on Client-Consultant Relations
5. Increased Costs of Doing Business
6. Legal Considerations in Design and Construction
7. Tips to Minimize Trouble
8. In-Basket

1. THE LEGAL ASPECTS OF PRACTICE

Topics of legal concern comprise more than just contracts. Legal issues in a design environment pervade all areas of landscape architectural practice. Legal issues are of concern to the private landscape architectural consultant, including the owners of a firm and the staff. The activities of government personnel are also guided in large part by the legal environment. Legal concerns of landscape architects providing professional services for site design projects fall into several broad categories that include contracts, tort laws, business and tax laws, and administrative or public law. Legal terminology can be confusing sometimes. What is confusing is that in different regions people will use different terms for a similar law or will use various terms interchangeably. For instance, some cities refer to *zoning ordinances* as *zoning codes*. The word *statute* is generally used in place of the word *law*.

State and local laws will vary on such matters as professional registration, building codes, land use ordinances, permitting procedures, and liability. Readers should familiarize themselves with the local variations of legal concepts presented in this chapter.

Areas where landscape architects might anticipate running into legal difficulties fall into several broad categories that include contracts, tort law, administrative or public law, business and tax law, and communication.

Contracts

- **Breach of contract:** This happens when one party of a contract does not perform or adequately complete one of the services spelled out in the contract. For example: A landscape architect does not complete the contract documents as scheduled and does not notify the client in a timely manner. The result might be that the documents will not be delivered as agreed and the owner is not able to start construction as planned. The owner may file a claim for damages against the landscape architect for not meeting the schedule as agreed in the contract.

- **Liability:** In the case of a landscape architect contracted to design a project for a client, the landscape architect is responsible for preparing a design that should preclude third-party injury. If a third party is injured and can prove the injury was the result of poor design, the landscape architect is held liable and is responsible for paying damages to the injured person.

- **Responsibility:** A contract identifies the areas of responsibility of each party. For example, the owner is responsible for providing a property description and topographic survey of the project. The landscape architect is responsible for producing a design that meets applicable codes and that will receive bids within budget.

- **Performance:** The quality of the work and the manner in which it is performed are established in the contract. A contract must delineate performance expectations. These stated expectations may be used to judge the adequacy of each party's performance. For landscape architectural design services, industry standards of care guide the performance of a landscape architect in developing the drawings and technical specifications required for the construction bid document package.

Tort Law

- **Negligence:** Actions that can be proven to be careless performance of work with errors, designs that do not meet safety standards, and actions of poor judgment are cause for legal action. Acts of negligence are often decided by the courts.

- **Liability:** In the case of a landscape architect contracted to design a project for a client, the landscape architect is responsible for preparing a design that should preclude third-party injury. If a third party is injured and can prove the injury was the result of poor design, the landscape architect is held liable and is responsible for paying damages to the injured person.

- **Public safety and welfare:** Building codes, administrative policies, design guidelines, and other legislative and administrative actions define minimum standards for insuring the safety and welfare of the public. It is the responsibility of the landscape architect to be conversant with the codes and laws pertinent to work they have been contracted to design. For example, a landscape architect must know when handrails are required and their proper design in order to protect the public's health, safety, and welfare.

Administrative and Public Laws

- **Codes, ordinances, and regulations:** Federal, state, and local government through legislative or administrative actions produce laws and regulations that must be addressed in the design of a project. In the governmental review process (such as for land-use zoning matters) and during construction (such as for providing adequate siltation protection where required to protect adjacent water bodies) the landscape architect should know the permit and approval processes. Failure to satisfactorily address or meet the pertinent laws and regulations can lead to legal action against the landscape architect.

Business and Tax Laws

- **Business and tax law:** Businesses, including landscape architectural firms, are required to meet the requirements and have specific obligations under the prevailing business laws of a state or local government as well as state and federal tax laws. For example, a firm that practices in a city that requires a business license must properly secure that business license before offering and performing services. Likewise, a firm practicing in one or more states is obligated to pay the appropriate taxes as required by each state's tax laws. Failure to secure a necessary business license or pay an obligatory tax may result in legal action and penalties.

These legal concerns represent a broad landscape filled with numerous possibilities for legal action (Figure 13.1). Most contracts specify the landscape architect's responsibilities in regard to those concerns. However, as a practical matter, most legal problems involving landscape architects with their clients or with contractors usually arise as a result of poor communication. Most legal problems a landscape architect can expect to encounter are the result of inadequately addressing following the matters:

- **Money:** The actions and decisions of a landscape architect can have a financial impact on a client and other people involved with a project. Money issues include making sure a project is designed to fall within budget. For a private client who has borrowed money to finance a project, remaining on schedule is extremely important. On large projects, each day of delay can mean thousands of dollars in additional finance charges for the owners.
- **Time and schedule:** Most design services and construction contracts contain performance stipulations. Performance stipulations describe when phased items of work are

Figure 13.1   Most claims do not require a decision by the courts. Often claims are settled by the parties themselves, through a third-party arbitration board, or with settlements negotiated out of court by the attorneys representing each side.

to be completed together with a final completion date for all work. Schedules can be specified two ways: number of calendar days or specific milestone dates. Failure to meet contract dates can result in legal action by a client. Also, a contractor can file a claim for damages if he or she feels a decision or action by the client or landscape architect contributed to the delay in completion of a contract and that the delay caused additional expenses for which compensation might be claimed over and above the contract amount. A landscape architect should be mindful of the financial circumstances of a project and avoid unnecessary time extensions that can jeopardize the client-consultant relation.

- **Decisions or directives:** Landscape architects must make decisions or direct other people to perform work as part of their contractual obligations to a client. Certain decisions may result in impacts on other people's work performance, such as causing a delay to complete the work in the time frame specified by contract. The landscape architect, as the contract administrator for a construction contract, may be held responsible for delays in completing work if decisions by the landscape architect caused the contractor to extend a completion date. Damages due to additional time on the project may be claimed by the contractor. Damages could include requesting additional compensation or bringing legal action against the landscape architect.

- **Disagreements:** Each party to a contract will have an opinion that differs somewhat from what others think are the specifics of an event, the adequacy of an action or decision by others, and the assessment of the work performed by themselves or by others. These differences of opinion can result in legal action if not resolved. An example where a landscape architect might become involved in a dispute involving a difference of opinion is where the work of a contractor—such as the workmanship of paved concrete surface—is deemed unacceptable by the landscape architect, but is disputed by the contractor. If the specifications and drawings do not clearly describe the desired paving surface, leaving the decision to the landscape architect, a difference of opinion may not be resolved without reconciliation by a third party or legal decision.

- **Poor communication and misunderstandings:** Poor or inadequate communication can lead to misunderstandings between the parties of a contract. Legal action can result when misunderstandings occur and are not resolved in a timely manner. If a contractor fails to notify the landscape architect when certain critical items of work are to be performed and the landscape architect later visits the job site to find the work already in progress or completed, there may be cause not to accept the work even if on the surface it may appear adequate. For example, the form work and preparations for concrete retaining walls usually need to be inspected in order to assess that the specified reinforcement bar is properly placed prior to the pouring of the concrete.

  Letting a client know in advance of the need to extend a contract to allow more time to complete it is acceptable and granted, whereas allowing the scheduled date to pass before communicating that a late completion date will occur is not acceptable. Walking a contractor through a project, reviewing the design intent, explaining site constraints, and in general sharing areas of concern is time well spent. A preconstruction conference can reduce potential misunderstandings later on during construction due to poor communication.

- **Errors and unacceptable performance:** Disputes and legal action can result from work performed by landscape architects if that work, because of deficiencies or errors, results in injuries to third parties—such as causing bodily harm due to inappropriate design—or if that work is incomplete, inadequate, or has inaccuracies not acceptable to the client. Unacceptable performance by a contractor due to poor workmanship or the supply of unacceptable materials can also result in legal action.

2. THE U.S. LEGAL SYSTEM

The U.S. legal system is based on the English system of civil law, which is based on Roman law. The U.S. system follows a hierarchy with federal and state constitutions representing the first and highest tier of the system. The next tier consists of laws, codes, and regulations established by legislative bodies. These are followed by regulations and administrative instruments developed by government agencies and by governing boards.

The U.S. legal system can be divided into several areas: civil law, criminal law, and public (administrative) law. Criminal law, which only in the rarest circumstances involves actions of landscape architects, deals with the criminal actions of individuals considered a threat to society. More common legal actions involve civil, business and tax, and administrative law.

Civil Law

Civil law pertains to the dealings between individuals or groups. Civil law is concerned with the rights and obligations of individuals and corporations. For professional landscape architects, the primary areas of concern under civil law have to do with contract law and torts.

Civil law relies heavily on precedents, the prior decisions handed down from the court system in similar cases. It is the responsibility of the courts to examine and interpret the application of written codes and statutes in the legal process. The doctrine of legal precedence relies on the body of case law composed of previous written judicial decisions. The courts then rely on these past decisions to interpret the meaning and intent behind written laws of constitutional, legislative, and administrative origin. Current legal decisions are therefore often based on the precedents set by the determination of previous cases involving similar circumstances and events. Examples where civil law affects landscape architects include liability, negligence, breach of contract, and corporate laws.

Public or Administrative Law

Public or administrative law is concerned with the relationship between government and people (individuals or private organizations). The laws falling under this category deal with the operations and policies of government agencies. This branch of law is important for landscape architects working on projects involving government agencies or conditions where government regulations, codes, or administrative guidelines are applicable. There are many areas of service that require landscape architects to be knowledgeable of certain public laws such as design standards specified by law (Figure 13.2). These laws and standards fall under the rubric of protecting public health, safety, and welfare and include:

- accessibility design standards
- building permits, codes, and certificates of occupancy
- planning and design review

Figure 13.2   Landscape architects, whether in the public or private sector, must be familiar with government requirements, review processes, laws, and regulations in order to successfully carry out their work. Government offices, such as this city office, are both a good source of information as well as the location where much work takes place (reviewing and approving design projects under their jurisdiction).

- zoning and other land-use ordinances, such as green laws
- professional services procurement regulations
- wetland filling permits
- environmental impact statements

The Jurisdictional Hierarchy of Laws in the United States

Laws in the United States are created and carried out following a jurisdictional hierarchy beginning at the federal level with the Constitution and the laws passed by Congress. Next in the hierarchy are the constitutions and laws adopted by individual states, and finally at the local level are the charters, ordinances, and design standards adopted by city and county governments. Under each jurisdiction several types of laws are created and administered. These laws, the basis of our legal system, are summarized in Table 13.1.

3. THE LEGAL SYSTEM'S IMPACT ON DESIGN

The fear of lawsuits has increasingly affected the business, professional, and personal decisions and actions people make. To a significant degree, business and practice decisions made by landscape architects are influenced by the desire to reduce legal exposure and to

TABLE 13.1   Classification and Hierarchy of Law

Constitution—Federal and State

Establishes the manner and means by which power shall be exercised by the executive, legislative, and judicial branches of federal and state government.

Laws—Federal and State

Written and ratified by the Congress or state legislatures. Establishes rights and obligations of individuals, corporations, and other entities. Includes civil, criminal, and administrative laws. *Example:* Clean Water Act: A Federal law placing the responsibility of cleaning up the nation's waters on the Environmental Protection Agency. The EPA in turn establishd a regulatory body within the agency to carry out the intent of the enabling act and to enforce water quality standards.

Codes, regulations, and ordinances—Administrative Actions

Written by administrative staff of federal, state, and local government agencies or departments. Usually adopted to assist government authorities and their staff to carry out the intent of a specific law, ordinance, or statute. *Example:* Clean Water Act: EPA regulatory staff, using water quality guidelines, develops standards for measuring performance of waste discharge systems operated by local government agencies and private entitites. If waste discharge does not meet standards, EPA can direct that the noncomplying entity be modified and/or that it upgrade its facility so that standards will be met. Acts of noncompliance can result in plant shutdown, fines, or loss of cost-share funding.

---

minimize litigation. A private firm's business structure (sole proprietorship, partnership, or corporation) is also based on civil legal considerations. A firm's structure can minimize an individual's liability exposure and reduce one's personal financial obligations in the event of a legal claim. Firm structure can also alter the firm's and it's owner's personal tax responsibilities.

Legal considerations and the desire to limit legal exposure and financial obligations have had an impact on design. For example, rather than designing children's playground equipment, landscape architects will often specify the preengineered products of a manufacturer's play equipment. This is done to reduce the risk of liability for injuries. So, if a child falls and is injured, the injury could be attributed to a design flaw in the play equipment, not in the landscape architect's plan.[1] For this reason, design of public spaces is an area in which landscape architects have come to take a very cautious approach. Minimizing the potential for litigation tends to take precedence in some instances over aesthetic considerations.

4. THE LEGAL SYSTEM'S IMPACT ON CLIENT-CONSULTANT RELATIONS

Legal considerations also influence the relationship between the landscape architect and the client as well as the landscape architect and his or her employees. Fear of legal action has created a cautionary environment between people whereby one measures interpersonal relations in order to reduce the potential of legal action. This cautionary stance can be very uncomfortable, particularly in a profession that has attracted people who place great value in establishing close working relations with others. The writing of follow-up letters reiterating or confirming conversations or decisions makes sound business sense. Even though follow-up correspondence and contractual arrangements might suggest to one party that an

---

[1]Thus the manufacturer is held liable rather than the landscape architect or owner.

untrusting relationship exists, the protection that written confirmations afford are well worth the increased air of formality.

5. INCREASED COSTS OF DOING BUSINESS

The trend of increased litigation has also increased the costs of not only the products of landscape architectural services but also the cost of doing business. Insurance is an instrument used to reduce and distribute the liability and cost of legal action, which has risen dramatically in recent years. Insurance for all types of potential occurrences for which a professional might be held liable have been developed. Various types of insurance can be purchased for myriad legal actions, including the following:

- **Errors and omissions insurance,** which involves tort law, is used to cover claims by individuals, government agencies, or groups who claim poor, inadequate, or dysfunctional design was the cause of an injury.
- **General business liability insurance,** which involves contract and commercial law, is used for claims involving the adequacy and sufficiency of performance by a business, such as the failure of a business to meet specific terms of a contract.
- **Performance bonds,** which involve commercial law, are used for claims against firms that are engaged in design-build. This form of insurance provides a guarantee to an owner that contracted work that the design-build firm is not able to complete (for whatever reason) will be completed by another contractor.

6. LEGAL CONSIDERATIONS IN DESIGN AND CONSTRUCTION

Legal Concerns Unique to the Phases of Design

It is standard for projects designed by landscape architects to include five of the eight phases discussed in Chapter 12. Most standard design contracts identify these phases under basic services. The phases consist of:

- schematic design
- design development
- construction drawings
- bidding
- construction contract administration

The legal issues are generally similar for schematic design, design development, and construction drawings phases. One issue of concern is standards of care. This involves determining what is adequate performance of a landscape architect. Standards of care rely on evaluating the adequacy of the work performed by one landscape architect as measured against what is considered reasonable performance by other landscape architects providing similar services. The law of statutes of limitation is also of concern to landscape architects. It has to do with the time duration the landscape architect can be held legally responsible for a project after it has been built and accepted by the owner. The length of time a landscape architect can be held responsible varies from three to seven years or longer.

Another matter that landscape architects may encounter is the question of who owns the design documents, that is, the drawings and technical specifications. This is a question that should be resolved during contract negotiations between the owner and landscape architect. Documents for most landscape architecture projects should not be used for a second project by a client or by others without the prior agreement of the landscape architect. If reuse of the drawings and technical specifications by the owner occurs on another project without the involvement of the landscape architect, then he or she should not only be compensated but should seek release and indemnification for liability exposure that may arise out of such reuse.

These and other legal concerns, such as breach of contract and general liability and errors and omissions, focus primarily on performance and contractual issues. The contract, mutually agreed upon between the client and landscape architect, should spell out the expectations and desired results of both parties. The landscape architect is obliged to carry out prescribed services and provide specific deliverables (products such as reports, drawings, and other documentation) as part of his or her contract obligations. The contract should further indicate time periods for providing specified services and deliverables, such as planning or feasibility reports or a construction drawing package.

Standards of care, the accuracy and completeness of a landscape architect's work, are an important consideration that form the basis of judging the landscape architect's performance. It is important at each phase of a contract for the landscape architect to perform in a manner, and to produce results, that will set the standards by which the client can evaluate the quality of service to expect throughout the remainder of a project. The performance of both the client and the consultant sets the tone of their relationship for a current or future project. Exemplary performance in the early stages of a project will go a long way in establishing trust and confidence throughout all phases of a project. With a positive, trusting relationship each party is less likely to find fault in the other, thereby reducing potential legal claims.

Legal Issues Involving Public or Administrative Law

A landscape architect should know the requirements and be familiar with the reviewing processes of governmental laws, codes, and regulations, as well as the various permitting and design review processes of government. Governmental matters have potential legal consequences that require the careful attention of the landscape architect, particularly during the design and contract document preparation phases of a project.

Government agencies at the federal, state and local level promulgate laws, codes, and regulations as well as permitting and regulatory processes. The type of laws that landscape architects would need to be most familiar with are ones involving land use controls (zoning), building codes, design ordinances or guidelines (green laws), environmental protection, and public safety (accessibility). Landscape architects should be knowledgeable and address the requirements of the laws, codes, and regulations in their work. They should make sure their designs meet the requirements of the laws and that they follow the governmental review and approval processes required under each law. Public and administrative laws most often affecting the work of landscape architects include the following examples:

- **Zoning and land use controls:** Local governments that have plan and design review authority generally require proposed project plans (plat, master plan, site design, etc.) to be submitted for approval consideration. The planning and design body is empowered to review, perhaps conduct a public hearing or receive public comment, and accept or reject a subdivision plan or site master development plan. The process generally provides an appeals procedure in the event a project is denied. These laws are established and enforced by local government to guide the use, density, and design of land considered for development. Examples include subdivision, sign, and landscape ordinances.

- **Building codes and permits:** These are laws adopted by state and local governments that establish minimum design standards to protect human health, safety and welfare. Examples of design standards include fire, building design, and seismic codes. Prior to breaking ground, state and local jurisdictions require that building permits are obtained. Designs are submitted for review to determine whether or not they comply to pertinent codes and regulations. If they do, the owner receives an approval (or permit) to commence construction. During construction, inspections of work in progress may be required, for example, of building foundations, electrical, and plumbing installations. In order to permit occupancy of structures after they are completed, an inspection by the appropriate agency is required with that agency issuing a certificate of occupancy if all conditions of the building permit and codes are met.

- **OSHA:** The Occupational Safety and Health Administration, a federal agency, establishes various types of standards, including design standards to protect worker safety and to reduce hazardous conditions in the work environment.

- **Accessibility:** The ADA (Americans with Disabilities Act of 1991) and other federal design standards require designers to make public buildings and outdoor spaces (such as public gathering places) accessible to people with physical disabilities. The laws require mandatory application of the appropriate design standards in public-use areas and/or facilities that receive federal fiscal support such as health care and educational facilities, parks, or in private business establishments that are open to the general public, such as restaurants and retail shopping stores (Figure 13.3).

- **Environmental protection:** Certain actions involving the design and construction of a project located in or adjacent to an environmentally sensitive or protected area may require permits from one or more government agencies before construction can begin. These agencies have been given administrative authority to provide for the protection of environmental elements such as air, water, wetlands, and habitat of protected or endangered species. A permit application is often required as part of the design approval process. For example, a permit is needed before locating certain types of facilities involving construction and/or filling in wetlands. In this case, a permit application is submitted to the U.S. Army Corps of Engineers for their review and approval. Other types of projects, such as the construction of oil and gas pipelines, public utilities, buildings, and transportation facilities (such as highways), require that an environmental impact assessment be conducted prior to governmental approval of the design. Projects involving the handling or processing of hazardous materials or the sitting of public facilities on sites known or suspected to contain hazardous materials also require a permit before construction can take place.

- **Utilities and services permits:** Public and private utilities and agencies providing public services may need to be advised of a pending project before design work is finalized. Often permits are required to use or cross utility rights-of-way or easements. Review by utility companies may be required to determine the adequacy of existing service facilities to handle a new project and/or determine the feasibility of extending service to the project site.

Figure 13.3   The Americans with Disabilities Act requires that designs incorporate equal access to not only government projects but also most private facilities where the public will have reason for access. This includes buildings such as libraries, hospitals, and schools, and outdoor facilities such as parks.

Property Law

The landscape architect should be knowledgeable and be able to advise a client as to the requirements related to real property (real estate) ownership:

- **General warranty:** a surety instrument to secure title and to conduct a title search on the property on which the project is to be constructed
- **Special warranty:** a limited title search to the last owner of record of a piece of real property
- **Quitclaim:** a written agreement of the seller not to contest ownership of a piece of real property
- **Easements and covenants:** a method to designate certain rights of other parties to use a portion of the project property for access, utility construction and maintenance, or temporary construction easement, or to maintain a view or provide continued access to sunlight

Construction Bidding Period

The legal issues of concern during the bidding phase of a project have less to do with contractual matters and more with one's professional responsibilities to act on behalf of the owner in ensuring the intent of the design is met. The primary issues during construction include:

- **Confidentiality** of information relative to protecting the interests of the client: The concern here is making sure that proprietary information and certain financial information about the client or owner are kept confidential.

    Confidentiality must be maintained of contractor-provided information until a public notice of a construction award has been officially made and the contractual agreement between owner and contractor is finalized and signed. The concern here is to protect the bidders by making sure that the information they provided relative to their bid is kept confidential, in the event that an award is not made and a decision is made to rebid the project.

- **Fairness** in providing information to all parties: The landscape architect must provide equal access of information pertinent to a project to all bidders. Requests of information from individual bidders should be provided to all bidders. The landscape architect must take care not to give unfair advantage to one bidder over other potential bidders.

- **Government procurement** regulations and codes: The landscape architect must have a working understanding of government procurement regulations and codes in order to protect his or her own business and legal rights and those of potential bidders.

- **Timeliness** of decisions relevant to contractor's bonding: The concern here is for the landscape architect to recognize that an individual contractor's capacity to submit bids is governed by his or her bonding limitations. Once bids are submitted and opened, the landscape architect should facilitate a speedy decision awarding a contract. Failure to make a decision in a reasonable time can have an adverse effect on a contractor's ability to bid other projects that require bonding as contractors are limited to the total face value of their bonds, up to an amount established by their bonding companies.

    When contractors are required to submit a bid bond, timeliness in awarding a contract is important. Timely decision making is particularly important in awarding a construction contract for the contractors who provided certified checks in lieu of the bid bond. The checks are held by the owner until a contract award is made. Thus, during the time between the bid and the award, the contractor's capital is tied up.[2]

Construction Contract Administration

When a landscape architect's scope-of-work agreement includes contract administration, he or she assumes responsibility during the construction phase to see that the project is constructed on time, within the budget, and that the intent of the design is carried out in the execution. The landscape architect also makes sure that the quality of the workmanship and materials used by the contractor meet the intent of the specifications and design drawings.

If the landscape architect is not responsible for construction administration, then the responsibility to ensure timely completion, to meet budget goals, and to achieve design intent falls on the owner (or a representative) or another consultant—such as the project architect or engineer. Even on projects where he or she does provide contract administration, the landscape architect's responsibilities remain in a limited capacity. If problems arise during construction, the owner may feel the landscape architect is responsible. But

[2]The checks are returned to the other contractors who bid, after a contract agreement is negotiated and signed with the successful bidder.

without involvement in the ongoing decision making that transpires during construction, the landscape architect cannot defend or interpret the intent of his or her design. Decisions made in the field during construction may alter the design to an extent that the original design may no longer be valid or appropriate to the conditions originally addressed by the landscape architect. Not being a party in the decision making of an ongoing construction process may limit the landscape architect's legal responsibilities, but if the end result is not satisfactory to the owner, it may tarnish his or her reputation. Not participating in the construction administration process does, however, limit the designer's responsibilities in the event of litigation. The courts will determine the extent of a designer's responsibility on a project should a legal claim be initiated.

The responsibilities of the landscape architect who has been contracted to provide construction administration services during construction will focus primarily on the evaluation of the contractor's performance and the materials provided. The elements of a contractor's performance include at least the quality of workmanship, materials, and equipment furnished. Further, the landscape architect's construction administration responsibilities are to review and approve the materials and equipment supplied for the project as well as the workmanship of the contractor. Construction administration responsibilities are carried out through observation and review of work performed by the contractor. The landscape architect may also be required to provide interpretation of the design intent of the drawings for items of work being constructed. Often during construction, adjustments to the design must be made to improve it based on actual conditions found in the field and not accounted for in the design drawings. It is the responsibility of the landscape architect to assess these situations and provide reasonable resolution of the design to fit the actual conditions.

The landscape architect should be careful not to direct the contractor while carrying out construction administration duties. While the landscape architect may offer an opinion to the contractor, care should be taken not to mandate an action. An opinion offered of what to do or how best to do it should be based on the landscape architect's understanding and interpretation of the construction documents. This approach allows the contractor the latitude to apply his or her construction knowledge, skill, and experience. It is up to the landscape architect to assess a situation and express concerns related to the contractor's work. In the end, the landscape architect must evaluate the workmanship and the quality of installed materials, and then accept or reject the completed work or materials, based on that evaluation.

If the landscape architect directs items of work of the contractor, the responsibility for that work shifts from the contractor onto the landscape architect. The landscape architect, by directing the contractor's efforts, is tacitly accepting the responsibility of the contractor's actions. Should something go wrong—poor quality of the finished work, increased cost to the contractor, or time delays—the contractor can then submit a claim (for a time extension or additional compensation), arguing that the actions of the landscape architect caused poor workmanship, and increased cost, and resulted in time delays.

Other legal issues of concern to landscape architects during construction are the following:

- **Liability for workmen:** The landscape architect is also obligated to protect the employees of the contractor and subcontractors by insuring that they are paid on time. In cases where government labor laws establish wage rates, the construction administrator is responsible for making sure that the workers are paid according to these rates. Projects in which government wage rates are enforced require the contractor to submit a certified payroll, and the landscape architect has certain responsibilities to verify the accuracy of these submittals.

- **Liability for materials:** Suppliers of materials and equipment are paid by the contractor. Most states have laws that protect suppliers so that they get paid. If the contractor defaults on payments, the suppliers can place a lien against the owner and the project. A lien places the responsibility of payment on the owner and the owner must pay the suppliers even in the event that payment covering labor and supplies was made to a contractor but the contractor failed in turn to pay the supplier. The landscape architect's responsibility here is to make sure suppliers are paid by the contractor to the extent it is possible to track these payment transactions. This is done in order to protect the owner against a materials lien. Verification of payment to suppliers is accomplished by insisting that the contractor provide the landscape architect with receipts showing that payment of materials and supplies have been made before approving a payment request submitted by the contractor.

Important Relationships of Key Players

Figure 13.4 diagrams the important relationships of the key players in a design project. The landscape architect works on behalf of the owner and is, therefore, the owner's agent. As the owner's agent, the landscape architect must protect the interests of the owner, making sure the owner's goals for the project are met (to the extent that the owner has communicated the project goals) and that the project is constructed on time, within budget, and according to the drawings and technical specifications.

While it is the primary responsibility of the landscape architect to represent the owner's interests, the contractor must also be treated fairly. At a minimum, fairness is considered to be reasonable treatment given within the context of the construction contract. The landscape architect administering a construction contract should ensure, to the extent feasible, that the contractor is not made to perform beyond the intent of the contract documents, drawings, and specifications. Recognizing that a contractor, to remain in business, must be able to make a profit, the landscape architect should not prevent the contractor from doing so.

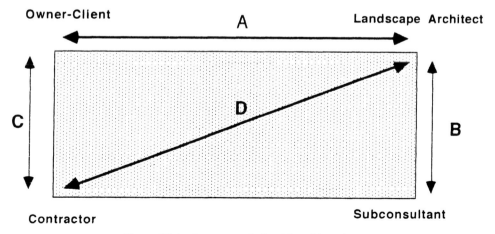

Figure 13.4   Important relationships of key players.

To carry out all responsibilities to both the owner and the contractor, the landscape architect must establish a nonconfrontational relationship. The landscape architect must be reasonable and fair when making decisions, ensure that the contractor conforms to governing laws and regulations and, when appropriate, provide supervision in the contractor's dealings with employees and subcontractors. This concern also applies to the prompt payment of companies supplying materials and equipment. It is in the interest of the project that these matters of payment for labor and materials are dealt with adequately so as not to adversely impact the project or affect the owner's interests.

Issues of Third-Party Legal Action during Construction

The landscape architect also has supervisory responsibility with respect to the contractor's actions in third-party matters. Steps must be taken to ensure that actions of the contractor do not result in damages to a third party, such as an adjacent property owner. Third-party damages could lead to litigation and claims not only against the contractor but also against the project owner. Third-party claims can be made by private individuals as well as private companies or a public agency—such as the U.S. Army Corps of Engineers. Some examples where contractor's actions could result in third-party claims include:

- dumping spoil material on wetlands without a government permit
- destroying private property such as a fence, building structure, or trees on an adjacent property

The landscape architect should, to the extent feasible, protect the interests of the owner and the project from claims or litigation as a result of a contractor's actions.

Surety Bonds

Most construction contracts require the contractor to provide several types of surety bonds. Bonds are a means of protecting the owner against incompetent, irresponsible, and financially troubled contractors. The General Conditions and the Instructions to Bidders included in the bid package and project manual should specify the bonding requirements for a project.

A surety bond is purchased by a contractor from companies that provide this service. The bond provides the project owner with assurance that the surety company will guarantee the faithful performance of the contractor to construct the project, pay the labor working on the project, and pay for the materials used in constructing the project. Three types of bonds commonly used in the construction industry are discussed in the following sections.

Bid Bonds

The contractor submits a bid bond together with the required bid and bid forms. The bid bond is a guarantee to the owner that the contractor will agree to the contract and perform all required work per the bid documents and for the dollar amount bid if the bid proposal is accepted. If the contractor withdraws the proposal after it is accepted by the owner, the surety company forfeits the amount of the bond, usually an amount equal to 5 to 10 percent of the contractor's bid amount. The bond amount is used by the owner to cover expenses to negotiate with another contractor or to re-bid the project.

There are any number of reasons for a contractor to withdraw a bid proposal. In the case of a competitive bid, the owner—if a government entity—is usually obligated to award the contract to the lowest bidder. If the contractor with the lowest bid is far below the next lowest bidder, has second thoughts, and then attempts to withdraw the bid proposal, the owner may elect to allow the contractor to withdraw if the next lowest bidder is within the project budget. If the owner does not accept an intent to withdraw, then the low-bid contractor is obligated to enter into a contract or default, thus forfeiting the bid bond. Surety companies do not look favorably on contractors who default, particularly ones who default often. When a contractor forfeits frequently, the cost of securing a bid bond goes up considerably or the surety companies may be unwilling to do business with the contractor altogether.

Performance Bonds

The performance bond provides the owner with a guarantee that the contractor will execute the work. It also protects the owner against defective work by the contractor. If the contractor does not perform satisfactorily or is unable to complete the work due to financial insolvency or other reasons, the surety company takes over and completes the contract or corrects the defective work.

The surety company has two basic options for completing the contract. The company can act as the general contractor and hire an alternate contractor or group of subcontractors to complete or correct the work. Alternately, the surety company may pay the owner the amount of the bond less a proportional amount of the bond for work already completed and accepted. In most cases, a performance bond is set at 100 percent of the contract bid amount.

Labor and Materials Payment Bonds

A labor and materials payment bond provides protection to the workers, subcontractors, and material suppliers. Its purpose is to assure they will get paid for work performed or for materials supplied to the contractor on a project. It is a guarantee that workers and suppliers will be paid by the bonding company in the event the contractor fails to do so. By not requiring a labor and materials payment bond, the responsibility to pay any liens falls to the project owner.

7. TIPS TO MINIMIZE TROUBLE

Write it Down

Maintain a written record of all formal and informal decisions, as well as communications with all parties. Maintain a personal journal and a daily telephone log, noting the telephone number and person or persons you've had conversations with. Summarize the main topics of discussion, outcomes, recommendations, agreements, and any decisions at meetings or from telephone conversations.

Also, maintain what is commonly referred to as a *paper trail*. Write down summary statements of all communications relative to a project, particularly communications where recommendations, directives, and any substantive information are given to you or provided by you. A paper trail should be kept from the early marketing and contract negotiation phases continuing throughout the remainder of the project until project closeout and final payment is made. The paper of a paper trail may consist of letters and memoranda summarizing conversations and decisions, written throughout the life of a project.

Adhere to Established Chains of Command

During all phases of contracted work, follow agreed-upon, established chains of command in all communications (written and verbal) with owner, client, contractor and subcontractors. For example, direct all communication regarding construction work to the contractor or the contractor's representative named in the construction contract. This means avoid giving directions, recommendations, or any instructions directly to laborers or to the subcontractors on a project construction site. All directions should be given to the representative of the prime contractor. This will reduce potential claims by the contractor for additional money or for time extensions.

Take Care of Liability Issues Even When Working for Free

Landscape architects are often asked to provide free professional services for community and nonprofit organizations. Doing design work for free does not limit one's professional liability. An eventual injury that can be attributed to faulty or inadequate design can result in a lawsuit. The landscape architect is responsible even when the design services were provided gratis. For instance, the parents of a child injured seriously on a piece of outdoor play apparatus would be just as likely to bring legal action whether the apparatus was designed free of charge for a community group or under contract for a parks department.

Take care of potential liability issues just as carefully when providing design services gratis as when providing services on a fee basis. The same degree of care is necessary for both small and large projects as well. The potential impact on a landscape architect in monetary and time losses from a legal action can be just as significant for a project with a construction cost of $1,500 as for one worth $1,500,000. What is at issue is the nature and severity of the injury or loss to the litigating party, not the dollar amount of project construction.

Regardless of the fee involved (including the gratis project) and the dollar amount of the project, the landscape architect should insist that a contract be drawn up and that the proper handling of professional liability be fully addressed prior to starting work and performing any services.

Act in a Timely Manner and Keep People Informed

Most of the work landscape architects perform involves others in some way. Clients hire a landscape architect with certain expectations as to what services and products to expect within an agreed-upon schedule and fee structure. Subconsultants to the landscape architect have similar expectations and rely on the landscape architect, as the prime consultant, to supply needed information so that the subconsultant can perform on schedule. The contractor also relies on the landscape architect, particularly in making the inspections of work critical to maintaining a tight construction schedule, reviewing submittals, and responding to special requests in the field as problems or questions arise.

In all cases, it is important for the landscape architect to perform and respond in the time frame expected, making sure that the client, subconsultant, and contractor know well in advance of any potential delays. It is far better to say you expect to be late on a submittal or scheduled meeting if you know in advance that a prearranged schedule is not going to be met. Delays can lead to claims and litigation against the landscape architect unless the landscape architect notifies the affected party in advance. If notification in advance of some delay can be made, verbally or in writing, an agreement for a time extension or to reschedule can usually be negotiated.

8. IN-BASKET

You are a partner in a landscape architecture consulting firm. The firm has two partners and a staff of landscape architects that fluctuates from seven to ten. As one of the principals, you are reviewing activities in the offices that have potential legal implications. Consider the following situations. Develop a short paragraph describing your reaction to each scenario and what you believe the legal ramifications are to you and your firm for each situation.

1. You are at the job site checking the planting and the location of several specimen trees. You decide that moving a group to a new location would provide a better screening effect. There are three laborers at the site and no foreman. How should you convey your wishes to shift the tree locations? Consider potential liabilities and problems. Also consider: chain of command, possible presence of underground utilities, and direction versus observation.

2. You have been asked by a client to change a particular detail of a wood deck you designed. It turns out the carpenter talked to the client while the client was out on the job and recommended changing a structural element, advising that the member size and spacing was overdesigned and would be very costly. Do you have any legal concerns? What course of action would you take in response to the client's request to change the detail? Consider: professional liability, structural integrity, change order, chain of command, and design intent.

3. You have just gotten off the telephone with a contractor. She has suggested changing the play equipment for a city park you designed and her firm is constructing. She claims the equipment she wants to use is equal to the one shown on the drawings. What is your reaction, the professional basis of your reaction, and the legal ramifications? Consider: change order, or-equal issues, documentation and specifications, costs, safety, and contract addendum.

4. You have found out that your partner, during lunch with one the firm's long-standing clients, verbally agreed to prepare a design for the entry of the client's office building. On a handshake your partner agreed to do the required work for a fee of $3,500 and promised to have a concept drawing next week. Do you think it is necessary that you take any steps to formalize your partner's action in order to protect your firm from any possible misunderstanding? What are the possible areas of misunderstanding that may later cause a legal problem for you and your client? Consider: contracts, written documentation, and professional conduct.

5. You have been asked by the principal at your child's school to prepare a free design for a small children's play area at the school to be constructed by PTA fathers and mothers. What is your reaction to this request and can you imagine any possible legal questions

that might come in to play? What steps should you take to protect yourself from possible legal action in case a child is seriously injured at some future date? Consider: professional liability, safety, quality control responsibilities, and professional reputation.

6. You have received notice from your client to begin working on the schematic design phase of a golf course subdivision located in some bottom lands on an old farm. Think about what research you believe is necessary before you begin this phase. Consider: legal description of property, regulatory and permit requirements, codes, flood and wetland delineation, and local ordinances.

CHAPTER 14

Professional Services Contracts

1. A Contract Is More than a Handshake
2. The Different Clients in a Contract Agreement
3. Elements of a Professional Services Contract
4. Use of Standard Contract Forms
5. In-Basket

1. A CONTRACT IS MORE THAN A HANDSHAKE

A handshake or nod of the head seals many agreements. A person's word is sometimes all that is necessary to close a deal for many people offering or receiving goods or services from others. Some business dealings are still conducted on the basis of a person's word; however, one should not count on the courts to uphold this casual basis of binding an agreement between two parties. The world has become far too complicated to indulge such a simple means of binding an agreement. Nor is it good business practice.

Many consultants—landscape architects included—continue to provide and receive services based on an oral promise made in person or by telephone. In their enthusiasm to please—to be a team player—landscape architects will often begin a project for a client without any written agreement documenting what was agreed upon on prior to doing the work and delivering the products.

Legal issues, however, go beyond agreements and differences between two people. Usually the relationship between people at the outset of a project is good. A feeling of goodwill generally exists between client and consultant, paralleling the euphoria of a new project and a new beginning. The excitement and enthusiasm of the client is because the project is finally beginning; for the consultant it comes from the opportunity of a job with new design possibilities. But any number of things can go wrong once a project is underway, such as differences of opinion between the landscape architect and client, costly delays by review agencies, and unacceptable performance by a contractor.

Preparations to deal with legal matters must be made in advance, before a problem occurs. Once a dispute develops, it is very difficult for people to agree on much. Involved parties will attempt to ensure their own interests when serious disagreements occur. Each party believes he or she is right and that a misdeed or injustice was caused by the other. The reason for preparing a contract at the beginning of a project is that the parties concerned are in a positive frame of mind. Feelings toward each other are usually positive, and their mindset is focused on the merits and objectives of the project. It is at this stage that the process for resolving disputes should be established.

2. THE DIFFERENT CLIENTS IN A CONTRACT AGREEMENT

There are several types of clients that a landscape architectural firm may do business with. The project owner is one type of client, and may range from a private individual to a corporation. The project client might also be a government agency. Other types of clients include architectural and engineering firms seeking the specialized services of a landscape architect on their project team. In this case, the landscape architect is a subconsultant who provides services to the prime consultant who in turn has a contract and is providing services directly to the client.

Sometimes the landscape architect will be the prime consultant of a project team. When this is the case, the landscape architect will invite the participation of other consultants, such as architectural or engineering firms. This will in turn require that separate contracts with each subconsultant be drawn up together with their individual terms and agreements.

3. ELEMENTS OF A PROFESSIONAL SERVICES CONTRACT

The complexity of events over time in a client–landscape architect relationship, require that written agreements be made prior to proceeding with a project. A landscape architect should be very cautious about working for a client without a written contract agreement. When one considers the degree of uncertainty that accompanies a new project or new client, it becomes clear that working with a contract makes good business sense.

Each project begins with a program, budget, and a set of objectives established by the client. These elements are used by the landscape architect as the basis for identifying a scope of work to be incorporated in a professional services contract. The scope of work may be later revised as a project advances through the various phases. These revisions may be the result of changes made by the client that are caused by intervening government regulations and administrative requirements, changing market conditions, and other influences. The unique physical qualities, the environmental setting, and the history of a project site can also alter a project program and, hence, the scope of work for the landscape architect. With all the potential for change, it is good advice to have a written contract to protect the landscape architect who might otherwise become overextended in time and money beyond what would be profitable. The chances for misunderstanding, and changes and modifications of a host of conditions require that a document of force, written with foresight, should be executed in order to steer the client and the landscape architect along the complex and changing conditions of a project's life.

The purpose of a contract is to minimize any misunderstandings by clarifying what is expected of the client and of the landscape architect, the elements of which should be arrived at through mutual consent. Contracts between a client and a landscape architect must be lawful; that is, the elements, terms, and conditions must be within the law. Both parties signing a contract must be legally competent to enter into a contract. Criteria for legal competency might include age, professional registration, and possession of a valid business license. Also, a contract must provide for a valid exchange of value such as the payment of fees by the client in exchange for services and professional instruments of service such as drawings, reports, and construction inspection from the landscape architect. To the extent practicable, a contract needs to be fair to both parties.

A landscape architect should insist on a written contract for all clients and for each project, regardless of whether the client remains the same. There are two types of contracts that a landscape architect should be familiar with:

- **Design services contracts:** These are used for consulting services between a landscape architect and a client or between a landscape architect and other consultants. Where the landscape architect is the prime consultant and employs the services of subconsultants, contracts should be made between each subconsultant. These subcontracts should reference the prime contract and avoid conflicts with the prime contract. Particular attention to professional liability insurance requirements should be made. Most insurance companies require all subconsultants to maintain professional liability insurance in amounts at least equal to the requirements in the prime contract.

- **Construction contracts:** These differ significantly from design services contracts. Building industry practices and government procurement regulations together influence terms and conditions of construction contracts. Most government entities have standardized contracts and contract conditions.

  Construction contracts in the private sector have been formalized by the construction industry involving the Associated General Contractors (a national organization with state chapters), the American Institute of Architects, and the American Society of Civil Engineers. Each entity has developed standard construction contract forms that are in common use in both the public and the private sector.

Elements of Design Services Contracts

Contracts can be lengthy and detailed or they can be a few short pages and of a general nature. The contents of a document are called the *conditions and terms*, which can vary greatly from one contract to another. However, there is a great deal of similarity in most design services contracts, at least on the surface. Most design services contracts begin by identifying both parties—owner or client, and the landscape architect. When the owner is a government agency or private corporation, the individual authorized to represent the owner is named together with his or her title.

Other elements that are normally considered essential in a professional service contract are discussed in the following sections.

Project Description   The opening sections of a contract should describe the nature of the project and its intended use, identify the project by name and location (address and legal property description), and include any other pertinent information that will clarify any unusual or important conditions relative to the project, such as land use or zoning and deed or other restrictions.

Responsibilities   This section should clearly indicate responsibilities of both the client and the consultant. It should also detail what information both the client and consultant are responsible for providing. The client is often responsible for providing such information as a site survey, a soils survey, a property description, and a project program. The landscape architect secures any other information required to perform contracted services.

Also in this section, lines of communication are formalized. A project manager or primary contact person authorized to represent both the client and the consultant are assigned. The responsible person named by each party must have the authority to answer questions and make decisions on behalf of the party represented.

Among other obligations, the client is to pay the consultant for services rendered and for making decisions in a timely manner during the design and construction process. The client is also required to give approvals of work completed at the end of each phase of service. Normally, the client is responsible for providing the following information to the landscape architect:

- project program and objectives
- project construction budget
- topographic and property boundary surveys, legal description, and soils engineering report of the property[1]

Scope of Work   The section of the contract that contains the scope of work outlines services to be provided by the landscape architect. Care should be given to indicate specific services adequate to produce all the work under the contract. The items included in a scope of work are to establish the fees in the contract negotiations process. Services fall under two categories:

- **Basic services:** These include project programming, schematic through final design and construction document preparation, and construction administration.
- **Additional services:** These include post-construction evaluation, display model building, marketing brochure design, and landscape maintenance programming.

The contract should delineate specific deliverables developed by the landscape architect under each phase of work. The number of copies of each deliverable item should be indicated with a method of determining costs to the client for additional copies.

This section of the contract should also contain a project schedule with either specific milestone dates or numbers of calendar days indicated for each phase of work.

Fees   The contract establishes basis and method of payment by the client to the landscape architect for services and products included under the scope of work. There are three standard methods for establishing fees when an owner reimburses the consultant for the actual cost of completing work under the contract:

- **Percentage basis:** A fee is calculated on the basis of the percentage of project construction costs, for example 6,8, or 12 percent of the cost of construction. The more complex design such as a zoo exhibit, may require a higher fee percentage. The simpler, more common design, such as a planting plan for a subdivision residence, will have a lower fee based percentage.
- **Fixed-fee basis:** A fee is negotiated as a fixed price, often based on an estimate of projected labor hours and expenses.
- **Multiplier basis:** A fee is based on an agreed-upon multiple of direct personnel expenses that is in turn based on an estimate of labor time, materials and billable expenses, The multiplier generally covers expenses over and above salary or payroll expenses to cover business overhead costs, administrative and marketing costs, and profit. A common multiplier is 2.5 to 3.0 times direct salary and labor costs.

[1]If the client does not have these already, the landscape architect may be asked by the client to include the securing of this information as part of the scope of work. The landscape architect would then subcontract to other consultants to prepare the needed land survey and soils engineering report.

This section of the contract should contain format instructions for submitting billing statements, that is, when and where to submit billing statements, and with what substantiating documentation. In the case of a fixed-fee contract, the contract usually breaks down the price by phases of work, or provides for payment on the basis of percentage of work completed. This enables the consultant to submit partial payment requests as each phase or percentage of work is completed rather than waiting until 100 percent of the work is completed. This is an important consideration in the case of projects requiring six months to a year or more to complete.

Liability Limitations and Insurance Requirements   This section assigns liability in specific terms. A contract can be written to limit or spread out liability among the parties of a contract. The liability section can also describe the dollar amount of each type of liability insurance required. Types of liability insurance typically required include general business, errors and omission, and automobile and personal injury.

Effective Date   The effective date of the agreement should be identified. This information is included either in the main body of the contract or with a written notice to proceed, which the client must issue to establish a starting date and to authorize the landscape architect to commence work.

Changes   A method or process for amending the contract for the purpose of adding or deleting services should be contained in the contract.

Termination   Valid circumstances and processes for terminating the contract by either party should be included in the contract. Terms of termination usually contain notification methods and processes, an allowable time frame for notification, and other conditions. Also, the contract should provide for the handling of the transfer of business ownership of either party, by sale or otherwise. Finally, it should indicate whether a transfer of ownership of the landscape architectural firm is or is not acceptable and what must transpire should an acceptable or unacceptable transfer occur.

Judicial Jurisdiction   This section indicates under which court system the contract falls. It is customary for the state and local court system in which either the project or client is named to be selected.

Arbitration   Methods to resolve disputes prior to taking legal action may also be spelled out in the contract. In addition to method and procedure, the contract generally identifies an arbitration board mutually agreed upon by both parties to the contract.

Clarifying Use of Documents   The landscape architect, as the author of the design drawing and technical specification documents, owns the copyright to the documents. The rights of ownership include the power to control subsequent use of the documents by the client or by others without the prior agreement of the landscape architect. If reuse by the client of the documents is allowed on another project or site, the landscape architect should not only be compensated but should seek written release from the owner for any liability exposure that may arise out of the reuse of the documents that occurs without the direct involvement of the landscape architect.

Signature   A signature block for both parties is contained at the conclusion of a contract. The signature space should be indicated with the name, title, and organization represented by each signature. Often, a contract requires that each signatory sign in the presence of a notary public. A date should also be written in for each person signing.

4. USE OF STANDARD CONTRACT FORMS

The professional organizations of allied design fields, such as the American Institute of Architects, have developed and published standard forms of agreement, specifically for professional services contracts. These and other standard documents are adaptable for use by landscape architects.

AIA Document B727, *Standard Form of Agreement between Owner and Architect for Special Services* 1988 edition, is an example of a standard contract document used by landscape architects (see Appendix II). It is best used for projects that have a well-defined scope of services. Copies of the documents are available for sale by the local AIA chapter. When a standard document is used, the landscape architect should check the edition to make sure it is the latest edition. As with any contractual document, it is good business to consult with a lawyer and an insurance firm before using a standard contract or signing a contract prepared by a client.

The terms of all contracts are negotiable and as such can be changed. The landscape architect should fully understand and agree with each term in a contract before signing the document.

5. IN-BASKET

As a partner in a modest size landscape architecture firm you have been asked by the owner of a commercial real estate developer to provide full design services for a small office park. The project is to be located in a low-lying area of town. Before preparing a contract agreement, you made a visit to the site and suspect that it is located in wetlands.

1. In addition to the obligations of the client normally included in an agreement, what other information would you wish to include given the circumstances found at the site? Briefly describe why this information is important and discuss what additional services you might need to include under the scope of work to cover additional work in dealing with wetland issues.

2. Consider that you will be hired to prepare a master plan, secure approvals of that plan from the city, and then prepare all necessary landscape design and construction implementation documents. Prepare an itemized scope of work. Divide that scope into basic services and additional services.

3. Prepare a payment schedule based on the itemized scope of work described above. Group the payment schedule to correspond to phases of work and estimate the percentage of the total fee each phase might represent.

4. Well into the design phases of your work, just prior to preparing construction implementation documents, the client informs you that she plans to purchase an adjoining piece of property that will add another group of buildings to the existing project. Assume that the addition requires some modification of the existing design. Outline what new work will be required for you to make adjustments to the existing plans and to incorporate the additional property into a complete design.

CHAPTER 15

Technical Specifications

1. Communicating Design Intent with Words
2. The Interrelationship between Drawings and Technical Specifications
3. Types of Technical Specifications
4. Specification Pointers
5. In-Basket

1. COMMUNICATING DESIGN INTENT WITH WORDS

Modes of Communicating Design Ideas

The primary topic of this chapter is technical specifications, one form of written communication that represents an important area of the services of landscape architects. However, it is important to understand that much of the work of a landscape architect involves the communication of ideas—presented in written and other forms—that will achieve a physical form. Communication is accomplished in several ways, including written, verbal, and graphic forms. The standard communication methods in the design professions rely on written and graphic representation. Both the written and graphic methods of representing ideas and concepts and the transferral of information constitute, in large part, the services rendered by landscape architects. Ultimately, the services rendered must be in the form of hard copy, capable of undergoing the scrutiny of a court of law or arbitration board. Hard-copy communication provides a tangible record or evidence should another party present a claim against a landscape architect.

The products of the services rendered by landscape architects that require written and graphic communication forms generally include feasibility and master planning studies, design proposals, construction documents, and expert opinion assessments. These services result in specific products that might include the following types of documents:

- **Bound reports** with written text, figures, graphs, plans, three-dimensional representations, and photographs and possibly backup materials stored on computer-generated files and video cassette tapes
- **Construction documents** with plan and detail drawings, notes, schedules, technical specifications, and bid and contract documents
- **Standard business communication devices** such as letters, memoranda, contracts, forms, and financial accounting statements

The Designer's Audience

The audience to whom a landscape architect communicates is varied. Landscape architects in an office situation most often communicate to:

- **Prospective clients**, through a variety of marketing activities including written proposals and verbal exchanges
- **Clients or administrative bodies**, through verbal and written exchanges, as well as graphic communication such as drawings
- **Government regulatory and administrative agencies, boards and commissions**, through written and verbal presentations and the submittal of drawings to secure permits and design review or other approvals
- **Contractors,** using written and graphic materials delineating work to be constructed, supplemented by verbal exchanges during the execution of the work
- **Vendors**, and others who represent or manufacture equipment and materials, through written and verbal communication

Graphic and written forms of communication are required for the construction of projects designed by a landscape architect. This is true for design services rendered by professional practitioners in private as well as in public practice. Both written and graphic communication devices are used to convey the design intent for projects to be constructed through competitive or selective bidding processes. The landscape architect prepares, as part of a design services contract, a package that includes construction drawings, technical specifications, contracts, and general conditions. This package is used to secure competitive bids from contractors and then is used to guide the work of the contractor selected to construct the project. The requirements for technical specifications are the subject of this chapter.

2. THE INTERRELATIONSHIP BETWEEN DRAWINGS AND TECHNICAL SPECIFICATIONS

The Need for Drawings and Specifications

Construction drawings (*drawings*) and technical specifications (*specifications*) are required for most projects that are to be built by a contractor. Drawings and specifications are particularly important for projects that are to be built by a contractor selected through a competitive or selective bidding process. Each element of a construction bid document performs a unique role in communicating the design intent and objectives of a design project. Together, the drawings and specifications (the *documents* or *construction documents*) guide the contractor through *where*, *what*, and *how* a project is to be built. The documents are used by the contractor to put together a bid price. Therefore, the two together communicate the design intent and the client's project requirements.

The Different Purposes of Drawings and Technical Specifications

The *drawings* rely on graphic representation to communicate the work to be performed. Drawings explain the following:

- location of elements
- shape, precise form, and size
- dimensioning and layout
- details of elements and subelements

The *technical specifications* spell out in writing the nuts and bolts of the work to be performed by the contractor. The specifications describe what is not easily shown in the drawings. They are concerned with the *what* (materials and equipment) and *how* (desired process) of construction, in varying degrees of detail, and usually include the following:

- type and quality of materials and workmanship
- methods of installation and construction
- testing and inspection requirements

In the event of any discrepancies between the drawings and specifications, the courts will generally give priority to the specifications over the drawings, unless the specifications or general provisions provide for the contrary.

3. TYPES OF TECHNICAL SPECIFICATIONS

There are two basic types of specification: *descriptive* and *performance*. Both are commonly used, and each has its appropriate application. Descriptive specifications describe in detail a method of execution, much like a recipe. A performance specification, on the other hand, describes in a fair amount of detail the desired results. This approach leaves the choice of most of the materials and methods of construction up to the contractor, as long as the desired performance standards are met. (See Figure 15.1 for contractors submittal.)

In the construction industry, the two basic types of specifications have evolved into four different technical specification formats. Each has characteristics developed to communicate what is specified and illustrate how to determine quality and acceptability of materials and workmanship. The four types of specification are: *descriptive, performance, proprietary*, and *reference*. Often, more than one type may be merged into a single set of specifications. Both the proprietary and reference specifications are commonly found in a set of specifications following either the descriptive or performance format.

The Four Specification Formats

Descriptive Specifications   This type of specification describes in a logical and thorough manner the materials needed and methods of their installation. This approach also outlines standards of workmanship used for installing each specified item. The descriptive specification provides the landscape architect with the greatest degree of control, as these specifications prescribe a more or less step by step procedure.

Performance Specifications   The performance specification is used in situations where the design intent is to replicate existing conditions. This situation is common where

Figure 15.1   As called for in the technical specifications, the contractor submits a sample of materials for approval of the landscape architects. The samples are evaluated for their conformance to the specifications. For special materials or unique appliction technique, the contractor will construct a sample of the system specified for review and approval.

the majority of project work involves remodeling, restoration, or phased construction of preexisting building conditions.

This type of specification focuses on describing the end result and the method of verifying the standards for accepting these results. The contractor, on the other hand, has the latitude of selecting the materials, the methods of installation, and techniques of construction. (See Figure 15.2 for a landscape architect's evaluation of work in progress.)

Proprietary Specifications   These specifications are prepared by the manufacturer of the materials, supplies, and equipment to be used on a project. Proprietary specifications are either incorporated in total into the project specifications or rewritten and adapted to parallel the format of the project specifications. They may also be incorporated by reference. Incorporation by reference requires that copies of the manufacturer's specifications are readily available to ensure that competitive bidding is achieved.

Reference Specifications   Reference specifications are standard specifications prepared by many governmental agencies and nongovernmental organizations, nationally certified testing laboratories, and professional institutions. Reference specifications contain descriptions of standardized materials, execution techniques, and testing procedures. It is common, for instance, for a city or state public works department to have a published set of standard specifications for materials and items of work that are routinely constructed. They are developed over a long period by the agency and have proven to be a reliable basis for specifying particular materials or executing specific standard items of work.

In addition to local and state standard technical specifications, there are many other

Figure 15.2 As portions of the work are installed, the landscape architect will visit the job site to examine work in progress, evaluating the workmanship and materials for conformance to the drawings and specifications. The landscape architect may make recommendations to improve the work based on the design intent.

types of reference standards. Many of these standards are used to ensure that certain health, safety, and welfare standards are met in the design of a built project. Examples of this type of reference specification include the Uniform Building Code and the American Society for Testing and Materials (ASTM). Reference specifications are also used as a basis for testing materials and workmanship. For example, the American National Standards Institute (ANSI) is a common reference for governmental construction projects.

The use of reference specifications considerably shortens the length of a project specification. The incorporation of reference standards also greatly reduces the instances of error by reducing typographical errors and errors caused by omission or inadequate information.

Complete standard specifications are readily available and used throughout the construction industry in ever-increasing frequency. These standards are produced and sold by sponsoring agencies or private companies. Most of the products can be purchased as books, or on floppy computer disks and other electronic media. Some are also available through an electronic data distribution network via computer hookup through Ethernet or a telephone modem. Standard specification products include:

- The Construction Specification Institute (CSI)
- Sweet's Catalogue Service
- Master Spec
- The American Institute of Architects
- Associated General Contractors

Although the building industry is not at the point of a national standard specification, the CSI system comes closest. The CSI system contains sixteen major divisions, each of which contains a number of subheadings. A listing of the most commonly used divisions and subdivisions contained in the CSI system is presented in Table 15.1.

Each division or subdivision in the CSI Format is organized into three parts:

- **Part 1—General**: This describes the main work, related work, applicable standard references, quality assurance measures, submittal handling process, and product/equipment care and protection.
- **Part 2—Products:** This describes the products, including ancillary materials.
- **Part 3—Installation**: This describes workmanship and installation procedures.

Specifications are organized in many ways depending on client requirements, the size of the project, its complexity, and the nature of the work. Methods of organization have evolved to a handful of standard frameworks. The use of standards (referred to as *industry standards*) makes it easier for reviewers and contractors to understand the work required in a particular project. Using standard forms of organizing specifications can influence the cost of a construction bid; the more familiar bidders are with the organizational format or a set of specifications, the lower their bids can be. This is lower because the contractors can provide a greater degree of accuracy if they prepare their bids based on a familiar format.

4. SPECIFICATION POINTERS

Cautionary Note: Say it Only Once

Although it easier said than done, there should not be any contradictions between the drawings and specifications. Often, when describing an item both in the specifications and in the drawing, there is the chance that conflicting information for the same item may inadvertently appear. The resulting inconsistencies can raise legitimate questions from the con-

TABLE 15.1   CSI Format Divisions

Division 0	Bidding requirements, contract forms, and general conditions of the contract
Division 1	General requirements
Division 2	Site Work
Division 3	Concrete
Division 4	Masonry
Division 5	Metals
Division 6	Wood and Plastics
Division 7	Thermal and moisture protection
Division 8	Doors and windows
Division 9	Finishes
Division 10	Specialties
Division 11	Equipment
Division 12	Furnishings
Division 13	Special construction
Division 14	Conveying systems
Division 15	Mechanical
Division 16	Electrical

tractor. In a competitive bidding situation, the contractor can be expected not only to point out the discrepancy but to seek additional compensation by arguing that his or her bid was based on the lesser-quality, less-expensive item.

As a rule of thumb, whatever is to be communicated (in writing or with graphics) should be said only once. Information clarifying the nature of a particular item detailed in the drawings (such as the specific type of material, dimension, quantity, physical qualities) should not be repeated in the specifications, or vice versa. The problem arises whenever more than one written or drawn reference for a particular item is made and subsequent changes are made during the review and revision process of preparing the construction bid package. An error can result when a change or modification is made to a reference in one place but not in others. For example, when specifying the numbers of coats of paint for a fence, if two coats are called for on the drawings and one coat is identified in the specifications, how many coats would the contractor be expected to apply? Usually, however, the general provisions of the specifications describe how to resolve such conflicts.

Government and Other Client Specification Requirements

For most private clients, the format and type of specifications used are most often determined by the landscape architect, who generally follows what is considered standard practice in a particular region or construction trade. Occasionally, however, someone other than the landscape architect or primary design consultant will make the decision.

Government agencies at all levels quite often require consultants to use their in-house specifications as well as their general condition, drawing format, and bid and contract forms. Most agency specifications follow standard practices. Some agencies may have unique circumstances or a past history of activity that has influenced the form and content requirements of bid documents (specifications included).

The landscape architectural firm doing design work under contract for an agency with unique specification requirements will most likely be made aware of the agency's requirements by the contracting officer or agency project manager. If not, it would be prudent for the landscape architect to ask for the requirements of the agency to eliminate surprises later on. Usually, the bid document requirements are discussed prior to contract negotiations. The willingness of an agency to alter its bid document requirements is very rare, and the need to adhere to an agency's requirements should be anticipated.

Specifications Should Always Accompany a Set of Drawings

Regardless of the size and construction dollar amount of the project, it is in the best interest of all parties involved (client, contractor, and landscape architect) to accompany drawings with specifications. In the event of any discrepancies, this minimizes the potential for litigation.

Make Sure There Is an Equal Before Specifying "Or Equal"

Most government agencies specify in their consulting services contracts that the landscape architect include the term "or equal" when specifying proprietary materials or equipment. This requirement has become standard practice particularly where government clients are involved. It is done to increase competition among bidders and suppliers, thus reducing construction costs.

Even though landscape architects generally agree to write in an "or equal" clause, they are not so willing to accept substitutions submitted by contractors of another manufacturer's product as an equal product. However, the landscape architect must carefully review all aspects of a substitution request submitted as an equal to products specified, making sure the materials used, quality of fabrication, finishes, and other physical attributes of the products indeed are equal. Sloppy evaluations followed by the denial of a substitution request can result in legal action. The landscape architect should carefully research the products specified and be willing to accept a product that is truly equal or clearly state the bases for denial.

Quality Assurance Coordination

A system for quality assurance and plan coordination should be in place and routinely followed by any office or individual practicing landscape architecture. Many firms have developed a checklist system for guiding their quality efforts to ensure that standards of care have been achieved in producing the drawings and specifictaions for each project. Equally important, a final check of all construction document elements should be made to ensure that all necessary coordination of items cross-referened in the specifications has been made and checked for accuracy and consistency with plans, drawings, and other contract documents before letting a construction package out to bid.

The following is a list of common items and areas to include in any construction document coordination checkout procedure.

1. All references to the thickness and quantities of materials should be made only in the plans and drawings and not in the specifications. For example: The specification section of rough carpentry should spell out the type, grade, and other aspects related to the physical qualities of the wood products, leaving the size or dimensioning of lumber required to the drawings and details. For example, specify 2x4 dimensional lumber in the drawings, and leave the description of the species and grade of wood for the specifications.

2. All references to size of materials where gradation or a specified mixture of component materials is involved, such as gravel fill, or references to percentage composition of materials such as in topsoil, should be made in the specifications and not in the plans and drawings. In the drawings, the type of gravel fill (such as Type II fill) can be designated. The composition and component materials that meet Type II fill requirements will be spelled out in the specifications.

3. Verify that cross-referenced specification sections exist and have been included in the bid package. For example, if a reference is made in the concrete section specifying the fill material to be used to construct the sub-base in the site work section, make sure that the specifications for fill materials have been included and are adequate.

4. Make sure bid items including additive alternates or deductive alternates[1] are noted in the specifications and are clearly marked and coordinated with the drawings.

5. Check plant materials listed in the plans and in the plant material schedule. Make sure that plant materials noted in the plans are included in the plant schedule. Pay

---

[1]An *additive alternate* is an item of work that can be split out from the basic bid, be made a separate bid item, and be bidded by the contractor. If there are sufficient funds to cover the base bid and the additive alternates, they may be added by the owner to the contract award amount in the construction contract. A *deductive alternate* is an item of work that is included in the base bid but can be subtracted by the owner from the contract award in the construction contract. There may be more than one additive or deductive bid item in a set of contract documents.

particular attention in the specifications to detailing the quality of the plants and their care and condition, leaving reference to size and quantity in the plant schedule. Rely on the planting plan to indicate desired location of plants listed in the plant material schedule.

6. Verify that where the term "as indicated" is used in the specifications the items are in fact indicated on the plans and drawings.

7. Check items of equipment included in the specifications, making sure that they are adequately coordinated with the drawings. Pay particular attention to technical details such as voltage requirements, flow requirements and sizes, and the adequacy of points of utility connection or service (such as for electricity or water service).

8. Avoid duplicating information in the drawings with information already included in the specifications. If duplications are made, establish a procedure for ensuring that changes made in the drawings (or specifications) are immediately tracked and revised to coordinate with the other document.

Specifications and other written communication are tools that can be an effective means in explaining or presenting the design intent of a project to others. Used with drawings, the specifications help to clarify the planned-for results of the project as intended by the landscape architect. Contractors rely on the specifications to an extent often not fully appreciated by the landscape architect. As a result, careful attention to coordinating the information contained in the drawings and the specification should be made. A process for ensuring that this coordination is achieved should be given very high priority by the landscape architect. The success of a design is absolutely dependent on both the quality and attention to detail of the information contained in drawings and specifications, as well as the careful coordination of the information.

5. IN-BASKET

Locate an example of exposed aggregate paving that you find attractive. Note the color and size of the aggregate, the density distribution of the aggregate, the depth of exposure (how much of the aggregate is revealed), and any other physical characteristics you believe are important.

1. Write several paragraphs following the three-part CSI format describing the physical characteristics of the exposed aggregate paving. Write the paragraphs in the form of a set of directions that you would give to a contractor to use in constructing the desired paving surface. Consider how you would go about describing the color and size of the aggregate, the amount of reveal, and the density distribution of aggregate material.

2. Assume that a contractor has constructed an exposed aggregate pavement for a project you designed and that you have been asked to inspect the results. How you would go about determining whether or not the exposed aggregate surface met your design intent and what would you look for to support your case in the event the installation did not meet your expectations?

3. Assume the pavement you have specified for an exposed aggregate treatment is not acceptable because of the wrong color, size, and density distribution. Prepare a letter addressed to the contractor outlining why the paving is not acceptable and what corrections need to be made, making sure you relate your comments to the specifications.

CHAPTER 16

Contract Administration

1. Introduction
2. Construction Contract
3. Construction Administration Responsibilities
4. Construction Administration Activities
5. In-Basket

1. INTRODUCTION

There are five phases of work performed by a landscape architect that would be included under a basic services design contract:

- schematic design
- design development
- contract documents
- bidding and contract negotiations
- construction administration

The services provided by a landscape architect during each phase are described in Chapter 12. The work accomplished in the first and second phases (schematic design and design development) focuses on defining a project and establishing its design direction. It is during the third phase of a project that the landscape architect prepares and finalizes the construction documents. The construction document package is used to guide the actual construction. This package contains all the written documents (technical specifications and general contract conditions), graphic documents (drawings, details, and material schedules), bidding documents (invitation, bid forms, instructions), bonding requirements, and the proposed contract. The construction documents serve multiple purposes, including these five factors:

- They communicate to the owner what the project encompasses, including the design program and scheme with an estimate of probable costs.
- They serve as the basis for establishing the responsibilities and contractual obligations of the owner and contractor to each other, as well as the landscape architect.
- They communicate to the contractor the design intent of the project and all work required to be constructed. The construction documents are the basis for obtaining bids by detailing the quantities, qualities, and relationship of all work to be constructed.

- They are used to obtaining financing. In the case of private projects, the source of financing would be from private lenders and financial institutions. In the case of government-sponsored projects, the source of funds would come from the sale of bonds, appropriated from general funds, or taxes, or from government grants.
- They are needed for obtaining governmental regulatory approvals before proceeding to construction.

2. CONSTRUCTION CONTRACT

After a project is designed and construction documents are prepared, the bidding and negotiation phase commences. During this phase, the bidding and contract documents are made available to prospective contractors to review and to submit bids or quotations. After the bids are received, they are evaluated by the owner and landscape architect. One contractor is selected, and contract negotiations between the owner and the chosen contractor follow. Often a sample construction contract is included with the bid package. The bid price prepared by each contractor will be determined using estimated costs of labor, materials, and equipment, but also contract conditions. Contract conditions such as bonding requirements, labor pay scales, and reporting requirements can increase a contractor's costs and thus increase the bid price. Although a sample contract may be included in the bid package, final terms of a construction contract are negotiated between the owner and the selected contractor.

The project landscape architect may or may not be involved in contract negotiations. When the project owner is a government entity, contract negotiations exclude the landscape architect. For projects involving private clients, the landscape architect may have the main responsibility of negotiating and preparing a construction contract. The American Institute of Architects has several standard contract forms that are commonly used throughout the design industry. AIA Document A201 is one standard used for developing a construction contract.

Subsequent to the signing of the construction contract, the implementation phase of a project begins. It is during the implementation phase that a project is transformed from a paper plan into a built reality. At this stage, the landscape architect's role and responsibilities may vary depending on the needs of the client. For some projects, the client may take full responsibility of construction administration or may engage other professionals to perform the required services of administering the construction project. Construction administration services could be performed by any one or a combination of the following professionals:

- a landscape architect, either as the prime or subconsultant
- an architectural or engineering firm having the prime contract
- a project management firm (a professional service organization having specialized expertise in project management and administration)

A construction contract is often between a client and a general contractor. For most projects, the general contractor will have several subcontractors, each representing a specific trade. In addition to subcontractors, the general contractor will contract with a number of suppliers, each providing materials and specialized equipment. Most government projects will require the company names of both the subcontractors and the materials and equipment suppliers. In states that have strong labor and material lien laws, it is imperative that the companies providing subcontracting services, materials, and equipment are identified and written into the primary construction contract. In the event that the contractor fails to pay the subcontractors, the owner has the information to contact these companies.

3. CONSTRUCTION ADMINISTRATION RESPONSIBILITIES

The responsibilities of a landscape architect during the construction administration phase are primarily administrative in nature. The landscape architect who is assigned to administer a construction contract must observe the progress of work, evaluate the adequacy of the materials and workmanship, and be available to resolve conflicts involving the interpretation of the drawings and technical specifications. These responsibilities require considerable field experience and familiarity with construction practices, workmanship, and materials. This phase of a project involves interaction among a variety of people; therefore, communication and decision-making skills are needed for dealing with fast-moving situations where changes require mutually agreeable resolution. Those assuming the responsibility of administering a construction contract must display a keen interest and attention to detail.

The construction administration phase of a project can require a considerable amount of paperwork, many meetings, and frequent travel to the project site. Travel will sometimes also be required to the place of business of some of the material and equipment suppliers. This is done to verify that certain materials and equipment intended for use on the project meet the technical specification requirements.

During the construction period, the landscape architect is hired to work on the behalf of the client/owner. In this capacity, the landscape architecture firm will assign a member of the firm to perform the duties of construction administrator (CA). The landscape architect assigned the duties of CA will be acting in place of the client, and will be responsible for protecting the interests of the client. This responsibility requires the CA to ensure that the quality of the equipment and materials and workmanship of construction meet the intent of the design drawings and technical specifications. No less important is the objective that the project be constructed within the time frame and budget anticipated by the client and specified in the construction contract. The successful CA is able to protect the interests not only of the client but of the contractor as well. A balanced decision-making process insures that all parties are treated fairly and are not taken advantage of. The contractor administrator must apply good judgment to many complicated situations. Any situation has the potential to escalate from a difference of opinion into a lawsuit. To accomplish this balance requires someone with not only technical knowledge and experience but also a great deal of skill working with people.

To be successful, the contract administrator must be quick in completing required paperwork and making decisions. The CA must have good organizational and time-management skills, and be able to keep track of the considerable volume of documents that accumulate quickly during the course of the construction period.

The activities involved in construction administration are some times lumped together and referred to as *inspection*. This word is purposefully absent from the list of responsibilities of a construction administrator in a professional services contract. The activity of inspection refers to a specific governmental function, a function that requires agency personnel to review work in progress or completed. Government agency personnel perform inspections to determine whether elements of construction meet codes, design standards, or provisions specified in a building permit. Government inspection activities involve determining whether the materials, equipment, and workmanship of a particular trade or aspect of a constructed work are acceptable and meet the minimum standards established under the appropriate governing entity. Landscape architects contracted to perform construction administration duties do not perform inspections; they can only observe work in progress and recommend to the client whether to accept or reject the work.

Landscape architects acting in the capacity of construction administrator will travel to a construction site to observe and document items of construction work in progress. Their responsibility is to observe the progress and the quality of the work performed and the materials installed with the objective of determining whether the work meets the intent of the project design, technical specifications, and construction contract. Workmanship determined not acceptable or not adequate is identified both verbally and in writing by the landscape architect CA. The decision to accept or reject is conveyed to the general contractor's designated representative (so named and identified in the construction contract). Only the *decision* is conveyed, not what to do in the case of rejection or where corrective actions are necessary.

The CA must be careful not to direct the contractor or subcontractors in what to do. The wording to convey that work is rejected or unacceptable must be carefully chosen so as to identify what is wrong and what needs to be corrected without giving directions. By directing the contractor in what to do, the CA of the landscape architecture firm is then assuming the responsibility of the contractor's actions. In the event that something goes wrong, the contractor may be justified in naming the landscape architect responsible. The contractor may also be justified in claiming additional compensation or in requesting a time extension beyond what was specified in the construction contract.

4. CONSTRUCTION ADMINISTRATION ACTIVITIES

The construction administration responsibilities of a landscape architect involve a variety of activities performed at different times during the construction contract performance period. Small, less-complex construction projects may have a performance period of one to three months. Large, complex projects that involve a number of different trades and the installation of specialized equipment, and which fall under government review and inspection requirements, can take anywhere from three to six months to a year or longer to construct. Construction commences with the landscape architect issuing a written notice to proceed, and ends with final acceptance and final payment after any warranty periods have elapsed.

The responsibilities of the project CA during the construction phase fall into several distinct areas:

- project administration
- field administration
- review of contractor applications
- project closeout

Project Administration

Preconstruction Conference   Soon after the construction contract has been signed, the project CA will, on behalf of the owner, transmit to the contractor a written notice to proceed. Contained in this notice is the official date that sets the clock in motion regarding the agreed-upon construction performance time period. The notice will indicate a date, time, and place for a preconstruction conference. The purpose of this conference is to discuss procedural details, such as the appropriate chain of command. Also reviewed at this time are the clarification of responsibilities among the owner, CA, and contractor (Figure 16.1 is an example of one of the contractor's responsibilities); operating procedures; and scheduling matters. Figure 16.2 outlines a checklist of the agenda that is normally covered in a preconstruction conference.[1]

Review of Submittals   There are provisions in the General Conditions of the specifications that enumerate specified items of work that require the contractor to submit some form of documentation to be reviewed by the project CA. The project CA evaluates the submittals to determine if they meet the design intent or the technical specifications. The project CA must approve the submittals or find cause for their nonacceptance. Examples of items often requiring contractor submitted documentation include:

- bonds
- lists of subcontractors and materials and equipment providers
- product data and samples
- shop drawings
- material test results
- warranties and equipment manuals
- field measurement data
- maintenance manuals

The process of handling the submittals, particularly shop drawings and products (equipment and materials), between the contractor and landscape architect should be agreed upon and scheduled (Figure 16.3). When a project landscape architect reviews contractor-furnished drawings and product materials, he or she is reviewing for conformance with the design intent of the project and with the information provided in the contract documents (technical specifications and construction drawings). The landscape architect should be specific when rejecting a submittal, outlining in detail the nature of the inadequacies and recommending corrective measures for the contractor to consider.

Scheduling and Coordination   The time period established for the contractor to complete all work is specified either in the construction contract, bid notice document, or the specifications. It is the responsibility of the contractor to provide the project CA with a construction schedule. This schedule should include the sequence and timing of submittals, construction work items, and the timing when owner-furnished equipment and materials are required.

---

[1]AIA, *Architect's Handbook of Professional Practice*, volume 2, section 2.8.

Figure 16.1 The contractor is responsible for maintaining the security of a job site. On larger projects involving a considerable amount of work and many subcontractors, traffic will be controlled onto the site. Any damage to work in progress or loss of materials, due to vandalis, or other causes, are the responsibility of the contractor.

Precontruction Agenda	
1. Explanation of Chain-of-command	13. Parking
2. Duties of the owner and contractor	14. Storage
3. Insurance	15. Permits
4. Submittals	16. Right-of-way
5. Progress payments	17. Testing
6. List of subcontractors	18. Overtime
7. Employment practices	19. Cleanup
8. Utilities	20. Owner furnished items
9. Scheduling	21. Record documents
10. Contract changes and clarification	22. Public relations & project signs
11. Security	23. Emergency telephone numbers
12. Third-party letters of nonobjection	24. Milestone dates

Figure 16.2 Precontruction conference adenda checklist.

Figure 16.3 The contractor is required by the General Conditions section of the contract to submit samples of specified materials and equipment for review and approval by the landscape architect prior to installing them. For some materials, the contractor is required to submit laboratory tests along with the samples. The nature and purpose of the tests are explained in the technical specifications.

During the preconstruction conference, the project CA should indicate to the contractor critical work that the landscape architect desires to observe. The contractor should give adequate notification to the landscape architect prior to delivering the specific materials or to commencing certain items of work identified by the landscape architect.[2]

Documenting Existing Conditions It is beneficial for the project CA to make a photographic (video or still picture) record of the project site prior to breaking ground. Photography is an excellent method for recording existing conditions as well as for documenting the physical status of work elements and construction activities. The project CA should routinely photograph work in progress, recording conditions found at each site visit. Recording conditions in written and photographic form is particularly important when checking key phases of certain items such as form work prior to pouring concrete, sub-base preparation before paving, and conditions uncovered prior to installing the point of connection of a water system.

Several brands of cameras can be purchased with a built-in date imprint device. The date and, with some models, the time is exposed onto the film as each frame is taken.

---

[2]For example, the landscape architect may want to inspect the plant materials at the nursery to assess their condition and qualify before they are delivered to the project site. Once at the site, the landscape architect may want to inspect their condition, particularly for plants that have been transported over long distances. The landscape architect may then want to be notified before the contractor installs the plant materials to spot or designate the location of the plants, and to inspect the planting holes and backfill material prior to installing the plants.

The project CA should maintain both a written and photographic record on a regular and systematic basis. This may be important later, in the event that a difference of opinion develops between the contractor and the project CA. Differences can and often do arise regarding the condition of items of work (either the preparation, workmanship, or materials) or the status of existing site features such as trees, other vegetation, and structures that the plans indicated were to remain and be protected. For projects where new work is supposed to tie into existing structures, such as paving, walls, and built structures, photographing the condition of these preexisting elements is necessary. Photographs convincingly validate any claims the project CA may make regarding damage that may need to be repaired due to contractor negligence.

Field Administration

During construction, the contract administration responsibilities of the landscape architect consist of periodic visits to the construction site in order to become familiar with the progress and quality of the work and to assess whether the work is proceeding in accordance with the contract documents. The frequency of these site visits is determined by the complexity, dollar volume, and special conditions of the project. For some projects, daily full-time visits to the site may be required throughout or for specified stages of work. For other projects, site visits may be timed to coincide with the milestone items of work.

For larger projects involving many trades, subcontractors, and lengthy construction periods, the contractor may be required to provide an office on site. Figure 16.4 is typical of a structure used as a field office.

Field Observation   Site visits should be scheduled at intervals, with a frequency appropriate to each stage of construction. The number and frequency of site visits is based on the judgment of the landscape architect as agreed upon by the client. The level of effort is negotiated and is written into the construction administration phase of the professional services contract. As there are fees associated with this area of service, the fee should be adequate to compensate the landscape architect for these services. Compensation for site visits is usually on a lump-sum or cost-plus basis.

After each site visit, the project CA should prepare and submit a field report. This report contains observations of work reviewed along with supporting photographic documentation. In addition, the field report should summarize any discussion or concluding decisions as well as describing construction difficulties encountered and remedial measures agreed upon. Much of the information that is contained in a field report is drawn from a *daily log*. A daily log should be routinely, consistently, and carefully maintained by the construction administrator.

Figure 16.5 illustrates the contents of a project CA's daily log.[3] The entries into a daily log should be incorporated into the permanent record of each project. The permanent records of a project may be reviewed by a number of people should a dispute for any reason occur against any party involved. Many government clients require that the contents of a daily log be transmitted by the project CA, if not daily, then on a weekly or monthly basis.

[3] AIA, *Architect's Handbook of Professional Practice,* volume 2, section 2.8.

Figure 16.4   The contractor may be required to install a field office complete with telephone, conference and meeting area, desk with complete set of contract documents, and other items called for in the specifications.

Critical Elements Requiring Field Observation   There are various items of work that usually require the presence of the landscape architect at the job site prior to their construction. These items should be identified in the construction documents and reinforced during the preconstruction meeting. The project CA should coordinate with the contractor the dates when these work items are to commence. It is the contractor's responsibility to notify the project CA before the actual work is to begin. Examples of items requiring the input of the landscape architect prior to commencing installation include:

- verifying the limits of work
- staking the location of existing trees and other features that are to remain and need protection from possible damage
- staking the location of certain construction features, such as entry roads, trails, and walks
- verifying the location of trees and planting beds, adjusting specimen or other plants whose location is critical to the intent of the planting design

Progress of Work   As the contractor completes work, the project CA must assess this work to determine whether it is acceptable and conforms to the contract documents (Figure 16.6–16.9). The project CA has several options regarding the acceptability of the work:

- accepting the work
- rejecting nonconforming work
- stopping the work

Daily Log

Project Name _____   **Client** _____

Date: _____   Time: _____   Contractor: _____

1. Weather, and site ground conditions.

2. Work performed: including the start and completion of any unit of work.

3. Construction difficulties encountered and corrective measures considered and mutually agreed upon.

4. Description of significant delays together with their cause.

5. Materials and equipment delivered to project site.

6. Number and classification of contractor and subcontractor workers present on site.

7. Description (written and photographic record) of any work or material in place that does not correspond with the drawings or specifications. Describe any action taken, listing any problems or abnormal occurrences that arose during each day.

8. Description of any disputes between contractor and landscape architect or contractor and government inspector or other third party.

9. Oral suggestions* given to contractor by the construction administrator.

10. Description of any accident, including names of witnesses, particularly when there are personal injuries or other matters that could result in litigation.

11. Detailed description of materials used and work performed in connection with extra work or any other item for which there is reason to anticipate that a claim for additional compensation may be made by the contractor.

12. Summary of telephone calls producing or affecting project decisions.

---

* The landscape architect must be careful never to direct or instruct a contractor to do any work. By doing so the landscape architect may be assuming responsibility for the contractor's actions, which might possibly result in disputed claims by the contractor. If the actions produce unacceptable results or the contractor claims additional payment, due to added costs for work performed, the landscape architect may be held responsible for these claims.

Figure 16.5   Daily log contents for a construction administrator.

As long as the project CA finds the work of the contractor acceptable, there are generally few problems. Once the contractor completes items of work, he or she may then request partial payment, and if the work is acceptable, the payment is made.

When the project CA encounters work that is not acceptable, differences of opinion may ensue; the contractor may attempt to argue the point. Problems involving unacceptable work that may arise during construction include:

- poor workmanship or nonconforming work
- materials and installed equipment that do not conform to specifications
- differences in interpretation of the construction documents
- unforeseen circumstances

Figure 16.6 The landscape architect should schedule an adequate number of visits in order to keep up with the work in progress and be able to make timely recommendations. The site observations provide the landscape architect the opportunity of checking workmanship, of making field adjustments to conform to existing or unforeseen conditions, and of maintaining positive communication with the contractor.

Figure 16.7 Carpenter constructing concrete forms. Work is checked against drawings.

Figure 16.8 Landscape architect should check all form work prior to pouring of concrete. Forms should be checked for their ability to maintain their shape once the wet concrete is poured. The check should also verify reinforcing bar is in place.

Unforeseen circumstances may include site conditions found to be different from those shown on the drawings, or site conditions altered by natural phenomena, such as flood damage and severe erosion or slope failure caused by excessive rains.

Most construction projects take months or years to complete. During the process it is often possible to correct nonconforming work, eventually producing work that is acceptable. In other instances, early errors may become worse as the work proceeds, thus producing a result that is not acceptable. The experienced project CA knows when to intervene, usually at the time when defective work is observed during a routine site visit, and knows when to reject work and when to recommend issuing a stop-work order to the contractor in order to provide time to resolve the nonconforming situations.

- **Rejected work:** The contractor, by contract, is required to provide access to the site and to work inprogress. Most construction contracts contain provisions that give the project CA the authority to have the contractor uncover work where the contract specifies observation by the project CA of work in progress. The project CA also has the right to request additional testing or inspection of work believed to be nonconforming. The contractor has the obligation to correct the work in a timely manner at no additional cost to the owner and with no allowances for extending the construction time period.

  In circumstances where the project CA is willing to recommend acceptance of nonconforming work, it is appropriate that the contract sum be adjusted accordingly. Acceptance of marginally acceptable or nonconforming work is a judgment call in a case in which the nature of the nonconforming work does not pose a health or safety

Figure 16.9 Spot checking to make sure lines and grades conform to drawings.

problem, and where circumstances bring the project CA to conclude that the aesthetics or functionality of the situation can be lived with in light of other considerations.[4]

• **Stop work:** The project CA may elect to notify the contractor to cease working on all or a portion of work for a project. This is done as a last resort to give the project CA time to resolve nonconforming work, to stop actions by the contractor that are deemed unacceptable, or to allow time to work out the details for disputes that need to

---

[4]This would be the case when the nonconforming work is deemed by the project CA as the best the contractor is capable of doing, or when by tearing out the work and attempting to redo it more damage may result to adjoining work than is justified.

be resolved. A stop-work order must be made in writing. It must be issued with the knowledge and most often with the approval of the owner.

The written stop-work order should describe the specific reasons for the order and outline the steps that must be taken by the contractor in order to correct the situation. The specified corrective work must be completed and be acceptable to the CA before the contractor will be allowed to resume work. Where specific action is also necessary by the owner, the landscape architect, or a third party, this information should also be included in the stop-work notice as well. Usually the landscape architect will request that the contractor prepare a plan to resolve the issue by submitting a written response describing what steps and schedule the contractor intends to follow. Once the disputed work is completed and viewed on site by the landscape architect, the project CA will issue a resume-work order in writing.

- **Liquidated damages:** In most construction contracts an owner may require compensation for each day a contractor fails to meet the contract completion schedule. This is done to penalize contractors and is a negative incentive to complete work on schedule. A dollar amount is established as a penalty; the amount will vary depending on the size of the contract and/or the necessity for completing the project on time. The project CA should notify the contractor in writing whether a time extension will be considered for most change-order requests at any time work in progress is being evaluated for possible changes. The contractor must be notified, in the case of a stop-work order, whether the contract completion date will be extended. If not, then the CA must inform the contractor that there is a possibility that liquidated damages may be applied.

Testing   The requirements for testing materials, equipment, or installed systems are described in the contract documents. Scheduling and, when necessary, coordinating the required testing is an item discussed in the preconstruction conference. It is the contractor's responsibility to arrange and pay for test items identified in the technical specifications. The contractor is obligated to notify the project CA of the company doing the tests and the exact time and place of the tests. This gives the project CA the option of observing the testing activities or reviewing the procedures with the testing company. The contractor must provide test results in a format described in the construction documents.

In some instances, the landscape architect may elect to arrange and pay for some tests. It is customary for the project CA to notify the contractor of these activities, although in the case of a dispute, the testing may be arranged without this notification.

It is customary to perform tests for a variety of items in a construction contract (Figure 16.10). Some examples of testing include:

- concrete and asphalt material and strength
- soil pH and content analysis
- base fill material content and sieve analysis
- irrigation system pressure and leak test

Contractor Applications

The contractor has the opportunity during the construction period to submit requests to the CA for consideration and action. These requests are submitted in writing following the procedures and format described in the specifications.

Figure 16.10 Slump testing of concrete—one of many material tests during construction that might include testing of soil compaction, testing the depth of asphalt pavement, soils tests (pH and composition), and tests of water pressure of installed irrigation system.

Changes Changes in contracted work may be required to accommodate unforeseen site conditions (such as a building being located differently from the way it was indicated in a survey or a building site plan), or in response to construction procedures and methods that make it reasonable to make the changes (such as the decision to utilize on-site fill material previously judged inaccessible due to unstable site ground conditions but determined suitable using specialized moving equipment provided by the contractor).

Minor changes in work may be authorized by the project CA where the contractor agrees to the changes. Minor changes are those that are consistent with the construction documents. These can usually be made within the contract sum and may not require an extension of the contract time.

Where major changes in the work are required, the project CA may initiate a *change order* request (Figure 16.11). A change order is issued by the project CA when changes to elements of the project design affect the contract sum or imply an extension of the contract. Design changes can arise from several sources, including:

- an owner's request
- a contractor's suggested changes to facilitate construction, to better meet site conditions, or to take advantage of opportunities afforded by utilizing alternate construction methods or procedures
- a contractor's request to clarify the construction documents made by the landscape architect.
- the result of a solution to a problem encountered during construction.

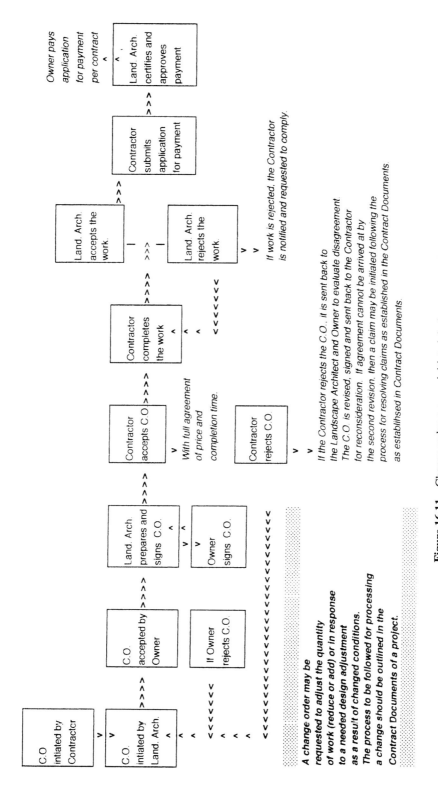

C.O.
initiated by
Contractor

C.O.
initiated by
Land. Arch.

C.O.
accepted by > > > >
Owner

If Owner
rejects C.O.

Land. Arch.
prepares and > > >
signs C.O.

Owner
signs C.O.

Contractor
accepts C.O. > > > >

With full agreement
of price and
completion time.

Contractor
rejects C.O.

Contractor
completes
the work

Land. Arch.
accepts the
work

Land. Arch.
rejects the
work

If work is rejected, the Contractor
is notified and requested to comply.

Contractor
submits
application
for payment

Owner pays
application
for payment
per contract

Land. Arch.
certifies and
approves
payment

*A change order may be
requested to adjust the quantity
of work (reduce or add) or in response
to a needed design adjustment
as a result of changed conditions.
The process to be followed for processing
a change should be outlined in the
Contract Documents of a project.*

*If the Contractor rejects the C.O. it is sent back to
the Landscape Architect and Owner to evaluate disagreement.
The C.O. is revised, signed and sent back to the Contractor
for reconsideration. If agreement cannot be arrived at by
the second revision, then a claim may be initiated following the
process for resolving claims as established in the Contract Documents.
as establihsed in Contract Documents*

Figure 16.11   Change order process initiated during construction.

Both minor and major changes, together with their written documentation, are binding addenda to the primary construction contract between the owner and contractor.

The change order process generally follows a sequence whereby the contractor submits a change order proposal following the written directives of the project CA. The change order proposal includes a description of the work, materials, and equipment, a revised work schedule, a request for time extension if necessary, and the price (which will adjust the contract price). This proposal is reviewed by the owner in consultation with the project CA. A decision to accept, deny, or request a resubmission of the change order proposal is made. In the case of acceptance of the proposal a written acceptance is issued. Where a denial is made or a resubmission is requested, written notice of the decision is made by the project CA. A change, once accepted, becomes part of the contract documents. All work to be performed under the change order must adhere to all appropriate conditions of the construction contract and contract documents.

Applications for Payment

- **Partial payment:** Most construction contracts have provisions allowing the contractor to apply for and receive partial payments. The amount of a partial payment is for work completed with payment based on:
  - actual work items accepted
  - a percentage of work accepted calculated by measuring quantities of materials or units of work in place

  Partial payments may also be made for materials and equipment purchased and delivered to the project site. Materials and equipment are normally not paid for until they are installed. However, in cases where the construction period will extend for a long period of time, the owner may agree to pay for these purchased and delivered items in advance of their installation.

- **Retainages:** Retainages of 5 to 10 percent may be withheld from each of the partial payments made to the contractor. The percentage is specified in the construction contract. The same percentage is subtracted from each application for payment submitted by the contractor. The retainages may be held until final payment or at some point when the contractor has satisfactorily completed most of the project.

  The retainage provides the owner with leverage to ensure that all work is satisfactorily completed. Retainages may be used to pay any lien claims made by subcontractors or suppliers against the project owner. Any retainages remaining at the time of the decision to make final payment are included in the final payment. In construction contracts where the dollar amounts are sizable, a contractor may request partial release of a specified percentage of the retainage at the time of substantial completion. A partial release of retainages can be made earlier, at a milestone point negotiated into the contract document.

Project Closeout

As the contractor approaches the point of completing the project, a process to closeout the contract may be started. The process is initiated by the contractor with the written request for the project CA and owner to inspect the completed work and determine its acceptability.

Substantial Completion   The contractor is obligated by contract to inform the project CA when the project is completed and is ready for inspection (Figure 16.12). At this juncture, all construction and installation is completed as delineated in the drawings and the specifications. This stage of the project is called *substantial completion.* The landscape architect reviews the request and, if satisfied that the work called for in the contract is substantially completed, will then schedule a date to inspect the work with the concurrence of the owner.

On the date of the inspection, the project CA will make a thorough inspection of the work and prepare a list of items found not to be in conformance to the drawings and specifications. This detailed list is called a *punchlist.* It contains a summary assessment of each nonconforming item of work, together with appropriate references to the contract documents. A time frame is given by the project CA in which the contractor is to correct all nonconforming work.

Final Completion   Once the contractor has corrected and brought into conformance all punchlist items and has satisfied all other contract requirements, a request can be made for the project CA to conduct a final inspection of work. If, after final inspection, the project CA agrees that all work is acceptable and in conformance with the contract requirements, the contractor may then apply for final payment.

As-built Drawings   In most construction contracts, the contractor is required to submit a revised set of drawings. These drawings are called *as-built drawings,* and show all work

Figure 16.12   Final days of construction with the installation of grass sod. Contractor is required to maintain job site free of debris and to provide ongoing maintenance, including watering of landscape materials installed, until project is accepted and turned over to the owner.

that was constructed, noting any changes in location, size, shape, or other qualities in elements that were constructed or installed differently from what was shown on the original drawings. Of concern here is to have a set of drawings that show the actual location of all the elements in the realized project.

The project CA should make certain that the location of all underground utilities and other systems installed by the contractor are accurately shown in the as-built drawings. Any changes to the location, shape, or critical dimensions of paving, walls, and structures should be shown. Any equipment installed that differs from the equipment specified must also be noted on the as-built drawings. In most construction contracts, the responsibility of maintaining and accurately updating a field set of construction drawings is assigned to the contractor. The project CA must also maintain a field set of drawings, and schedule periodic reviews with the contractor to confirm changes.

Final Payment   After the final inspection has been made and the project is accepted by the project CA and owner, the contractor may request final payment. The payment amount is contained in the contract and may include an increase or reduction of the contract price if there were any change orders approved during the construction period. Before the project CA approves the final payment, the contractor must supply certification that all labor wages, equipment, and materials have been paid by the contractor to his or her subcontractors and to the material and equipment suppliers. In states having stringent material and labor lien laws, it is advisable that an attorney review the certificates of payment prior to approving final payment. There are many legal issues involved with labor and material lien laws that must be thoroughly checked by an attorney familiar with this area of law before the project CA instructs the owner to make the final payment.

If a surety bond was a contract requirement, the project CA should receive the written consent of an authorized official of the surety company prior to making a final payment to the contractor. The written consent, in the form of an affidavit, verifies that the contractor has fulfilled and met all obligations to the satisfaction of the surety company.

With the final payment made to the contractor, the contract time ends and the maintenance and warranty period begins.

Maintenance and Warranty Period   Certain materials or equipment supplied under the terms of the contract may be guaranteed for a specified period. Should some of these items fail to meet the performance standards specified, during the warranty period they can be replaced in a timely manner at no cost to the owner. For items, such as plant materials, on which the contractor is to perform routine maintenance, the cost of the maintenance activities are separated out and identified in the construction contract. The contractor is paid for plant material maintenance executed on a schedule described in the landscape technical specifications prepared by the landscape architect.

Specific systems and equipment are warranted by their manufacturer. The length of the warranty period is described by the manufacturer in its product specifications. The landscape architect may require that other items of work be guaranteed and maintained for a specified period (six months or a year). The landscape architect will write these maintenance requirements into the technical specifications.

The contractor will be compensated for certain maintenance items in one of two ways. Often an allowance or retainage is deducted from the final payment to cover maintenance, guarantees, and warranty items. A second method of handling payment for certain maintenance items is to require that the contractor submit a separate price at the time of bid. The bid price for maintenance should be sufficient to cover the contractor's performance of all maintenance, guarantees, and warranty items specified in the technical specifications.

Postcompletion Generally, the basic services agreement of a design service contract ends with the issuance of final payment. Most standard design service contracts provide that the landscape architect be compensated for additional items of work when authorized by the owner. Postcompletion services may be requested by the owner, including an assessment of the owner's landscape maintenance program performance, user satisfaction of designed program elements, or an assessment of the performance of certain systems, such as an irrigation or lighting system. Additional design services may also be requested, and if they require minor effort, can sometimes be added to the original contract by amendment. Major design services may be best handled with the negotiation of a new professional services contract.

5. IN-BASKET

1. In situations where the landscape architectural firm is the prime consultant to a client, the proper chain of command is for the project CA to report to the client. On projects where the landscape architect is a subconsultant to an A/E firm, what is the reporting chain of command? How would the landscape architect in the subconsultant position go about getting an approval for a proposed field design change?

2. The project CA has the responsibility of looking out for the interests of the client. The project CA also needs to seek a balance at times that also protects the contractor's interest. If the CA were to force a series of decisions which caused the Contractor to declare bankruptcy prior to completing the work, how would the work be completed?

3. During construction, the CA has the option of accepting or rejecting items of work completed by the Contractor. When the workmanship and materials are acceptable, but not in exact conformance to the drawings, the CA has the option of accepting the work. Using the example of a concrete walk mistakenly installed by the Contractor with a broom finish rather than a salt finish, as specified in the drawings, describe a process the CA should follow to accept the change still meeting the client's interests. Would there be a change in the contract dollar amount and, if so, how would that be determined?

4. Discuss a strategy for requesting that the Contractor change the location of several trees from one location shown on the plan (near the side of a building) to a new location, to screen an unsightly, large electrical transformer existing on site. Consider the possible existence of underground electrical service to the transformer and the question of who would be liable if damages were to occur to the underground electrical lines.

CHAPTER 17

Concluding Thoughts

Langiappe is a Louisiana Cajun word meaning a little something extra. It is often used at the end of a meal, when the hosts offer their guests a little something more in the way of food, a story, or entertainment.

The word has gained wider usage in a variety of situations in contemporary Louisiana. It has found its way into the lecture and concert hall as well as other settings involving education, entertainment, and social events. Although not a native to Louisiana, I would like to offer the reader Langiappe, a little something extra that hopefully will help students as they prepare to graduate and start their careers in their first real job.

I have prepared a list of things students may find helpful to keep in mind as they embark on the real-life phase of their professional careers. This list contains a variety of thoughts that I felt would be of benefit if they were grouped together in one place. Many of them are the result of hard-learned lessons during my career as a landscape architect. Each idea has a long story behind it; each should prove helpful when dealing with people, something landscape architects do a great deal of. Most of the ideas were developed more fully throughout the chapters of this book.

It is in the spirit of sharing that I offer this list to the reader. As this is a personal list, the insight they are meant to represent may not have universal application. At the least, they may stimulate some interesting discussion.

The order in which the thoughts are presented is not of significance; there is neither order nor hierarchy implied.

- Above all, be honest. Once lost, the respect and trust of people you work with is close to impossible to regain.
- Maintain and protect your integrity. Your professional integrity is your most valuable asset.
- Protect the interests of the client.
- Remember that what you do is to provide a service.
- Never assume that the client or board to which you are presenting knows anything about the project.
- In preparing for an interview, don't assume that the employer, client, or board know who you are, even though you may have worked with them before.
- Strive to make it to the short list, then win the job in the interview.
- Be innovative in everything you do, particularly when seeking employment and proposing a project.
- Be willing to accept any of your proposed design alternatives; a client just might suggest the least desirable one. Be ready to suggest the best alternative if asked.

- Limit your liability, but not your responsibility.
- The most important person in an office is the one who answers the phone and has first contact with clients.
- Maintain your health. Be active, do something aerobic at least three times a week.
- Your education has prepared you to be a leader. Be a leader.
- Insist on a design survey before beginning any project that will be built.
- Calculate your anticipated time, schedule, and fee requirements to complete a job. Then multiply by four. You will be closer to being correct.
- Make sure that the material suppliers and laborers are paid by the general contractor before paying the contractor.
- Don't sign a contract with a hold-harmless clause.
- Never direct a laborer in the field unless you are willing to assume total responsibility for any cost overruns or unforeseen calamities.
- Write it down once in one place, either in the specifications, on the drawings, or in the details.
- Put everything you say over the telephone or in conversation in writing.
- Never work for free; certainly never in situations where professional liability will be assumed for the work you do. If you assign no price to your services, people will

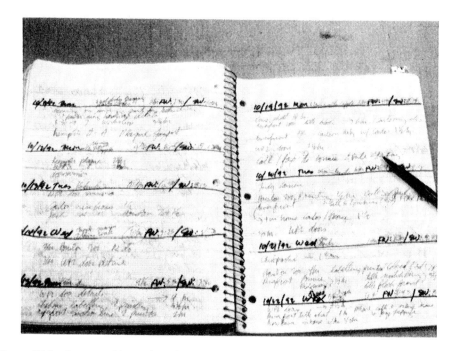

Figure 17.1 A personal journal can be something as simple as a spiral notebook or as formal as a hardbound blank book. How it is organized and the manner in which you make your entries are choices you make. What is important is that you maintain your journal on a daily basis, preferably keeping it with you so that it is convenient to make entries while on the telephone or at a meeting, or during any discussions throughout the day.

place little or no value on your suggestions and efforts; it will also reflect on your profession.

- Always establish a professional basis for working with a client.

- Never assume that a building will be located as shown on the plans. If you do so without checking, you can be certain to receive a late-night call from the contractor telling you that the parking lot won't fit because the distance between the building entry and the property line is 12 feet less than shown on the drawings.

- Always look into a hole, trench, or the form work before the concrete is poured or the asphalt is laid. Corollary: The R-bar won't be in or the specified materials and compaction will not have been put in place unless you see that it is before the pour.

Finally, maintain a personal journal (Figure 17.1). Record all telephone and other conversations. Bring your journal to all meetings and out to the field. Note at least the time, date, and persons involved. Jot down the main topics and summarize all decisions. Safeguard your journals, keep them as a part of your personal archives. Don't hide the fact that you maintain a journal; instead, make it obvious.

There should always be time in your busy life to invest in the next generation. Landscape architecture is a wonderful field, truly a profession for the twenty-first century. Involve yourself, to whatever degree you can, in education. As a practitioner, this can be accomplished by offering to share your knowledge and experience in the public schools during career day or as a guest in the classroom. Another activity for developing an awareness and appreciation of landscape architecture is to lead students on field trips to see outstanding park and public places designed by landscape architects. From these trips, the students will learn how these projects contribute to the enhancement of their community. A field trip might also inspire some of the students to pursue a career in landscape architecture.

Appendix I

AIA Document B163, *Standard Form of Agreement Between Owner and Architect for Designated Services,* 1993.

SAMPLE

AIA Document B163

Standard Form of Agreement Between Owner and Architect with Descriptions of Designated Services and Terms and Conditions

THIS DOCUMENT HAS IMPORTANT LEGAL CONSEQUENCES; CONSULTATION WITH AN ATTORNEY IS ENCOURAGED WITH RESPECT TO ITS COMPLETION OR MODIFICATION.

1993 EDITION

TABLE OF ARTICLES

PART 1—FORM OF AGREEMENT

ARTICLE 1.1   SCHEDULE OF DESIGNATED SERVICES
ARTICLE 1.2   COMPENSATION
ARTICLE 1.3   PAYMENTS
ARTICLE 1.4   TIME AND COST
ARTICLE 1.5   ENUMERATION OF DOCUMENTS
ARTICLE 1.6   OTHER CONDITIONS OR SERVICES

PART 2—DESCRIPTIONS OF DESIGNATED SERVICES

ARTICLE 2.1   DESIGNATED SERVICES
ARTICLE 2.2   PHASES OF DESIGNATED SERVICES
ARTICLE 2.3   DESCRIPTIONS OF DESIGNATED SERVICES
ARTICLE 2.4   DESCRIPTIONS OF SUPPLEMENTAL SERVICES

PART 3—TERMS AND CONDITIONS

ARTICLE 3.1   ARCHITECT'S RESPONSIBILITIES
ARTICLE 3.2   OWNER'S RESPONSIBILITIES
ARTICLE 3.3   CONTRACT ADMINISTRATION
ARTICLE 3.4   USE OF PROJECT DRAWINGS, SPECIFICATIONS AND OTHER DOCUMENTS
ARTICLE 3.5   COST OF THE WORK
ARTICLE 3.6   PAYMENTS TO THE ARCHITECT
ARTICLE 3.7   DISPUTE RESOLUTION
ARTICLE 3.8   MISCELLANEOUS PROVISIONS
ARTICLE 3.9   TERMINATION, SUSPENSION OR ABANDONMENT

B163—1993   1

FORM OF AGREEMENT
Between Owner and Architect
for Designated Services

AGREEMENT

made as of the   day of   in the year of
(In words, indicate day, month and year.)

BETWEEN the Owner:
(Name and address)

and the Architect:
(Name and address)

For the following Project:
(Include a detailed description of Project, location, address and scope.)

The Owner and the Architect agree as set forth below.

B163—1993   2

212

ARTICLE 1.1: SCHEDULE OF DESIGNATED SERVICES

PROJECT:

PROJECT #:

DATE:

Phases (columns 1–8):
1. Pre-Design Phase
2. Site Analysis Phase
3. Schematic Design Phase
4. Design Development Phase
5. Contract Documents Phase
6. Bidding or Negotiations Phase
7. Contract Administration Phase
8. Post-Contract Phase

"R: RESPONSIBILITY   "M: METHOD OF COMPENSATION

Category	Service	1 R/M	2 R/M	3 R/M	4 R/M	5 R/M	6 R/M	7 R/M	8 R/M	Remarks and Exceptions
Project Admin. & Mgmt. Services	.01 Project Administration									
	.02 Disciplines Coordination/Document Checking									
	.03 Agency Consulting/Review/Approval									
	.04 Owner-Supplied Data Coordination									
	.05 Schedule Development/Monitoring									
	.06 Preliminary Estimate of Cost of the Work									
	.07 Presentation									
Pre-Design Services	.08 Programming									
	.09 Space Schematics/Flow Diagrams									
	.10 Existing Facilities Surveys									
	.11 Marketing Studies									
	.12 Economic Feasibility Studies									
	.13 Project Financing									
Site Development Services	.14 Site Analysis and Selection									
	.15 Site Development Planning									
	.16 Detailed Site Utilization Studies									
	.17 On-Site Utility Studies									
	.18 Off-Site Utility Studies									
	.19 Environmental Studies and Reports									
	.20 Zoning Processing Assistance									
	.21 Geotechnical Engineering									
	.22 Site Surveying									
Design Services	.23 Architectural Design/Documentation									
	.24 Structural Design/Documentation									
	.25 Mechanical Design/Documentation									
	.26 Electrical Design/Documentation									
	.27 Civil Design/Documentation									
	.28 Landscape Design/Documentation									
	.29 Interior Design/Documentation									
	.30 Special Design/Documentation									
	.31 Materials Research/Specifications									
Bidding or Negotiation Services	.32 Bidding Materials									
	.33 Addenda									
	.34 Bidding/Negotiation									
	.35 Analysis of Alternates/Substitutions									
	.36 Special Bidding									
	.37 Bid Evaluation									
	.38 Contract Award									
Contract Administration Services	.39 Submittal Services									
	.40 Observation Services									
	.41 Project Representation									
	.42 Testing and Inspection Administration									
	.43 Supplemental Documentation									
	.44 Quotation Requests/Change Orders									
	.45 Contract Cost Accounting									
	.46 FF&E Installation Administration									
	.47 Interpretations and Decisions									
	.48 Project Closeout									
Post-Contract Services	.49 Maintenance and Operational Programming									
	.50 Start-Up Assistance									
	.51 Record Drawing									
	.52 Warranty Review									
	.53 Post-Contract Evaluation									

B163—1993   3

ARTICLE 1.1: SCHEDULE OF DESIGNATED SERVICES (continued)

PROJECT:	Supplemental Services
PROJECT #:	
DATE:	9

*R: RESPONSIBILITY **M: METHOD OF COMPENSATION	R	M	Remarks and Exceptions
.54 Special Studies			
.55 Tenant-Related Services			
.56 Special Furnishings Design			
.57 FF&E Services			
.58 Special Disciplines Consultation			
.59 Special Building Type Consultation			
.60 Fine Arts and Crafts			
.61 Graphic Design			
.62 Renderings			
.63 Model Construction			
.64 Still Photography			
.65 Motion Picture and Videotape			
.66 Life Cycle Cost Analysis			
.67 Value Analysis			
.68 Energy Studies			
.69 Quantity Surveys			
.70 Detailed Cost Estimating			
.71 Environmental Monitoring			
.72 Expert Witness			
.73 Materials and Systems Testing			
.74 Demolition Services			
.75 Mock-Up Services			
.76 Coordination of Designated Services			
.77 FF&E Purchasing/Installation			
.78 Computer Applications			
.79 Project Promotion/Public Relations			
.80 Leasing Brochures			
.81 Pre-Contract Administration/Management			
.82 Extended Bidding			
.83 Extended Contract Administration/Management			

Supplemental Services (vertical label)

Other Services (vertical label)

*R: RESPONSIBILITY	**M: METHOD OF COMPENSATION
A Architect	1. Multiple of Direct Personnel Expense
O Owner	2. Professional Fee Plus Expenses
N Not Provided	3. Percentage of Construction Cost
	4. Stipulated Sum
	5. Hourly Billing Rates
	6. Multiple of Amounts Billed to Architect
	7. Other: _____

In conjunction with the descriptions of terms and conditions of this Agreement, the Designated Services, where identified above by appropriate initial, shall be provided by the Owner or the Architect or not at all. In conjunction with the compensation and payment terms of this Agreement, the Owner shall compensate the Architect for such designated services performed by the Architect on the basis of the Method of Compensation identified above by an appropriately keyed number.

KEY

☐ All services performed in normal chronological order.

▨ Services performed out of normal sequence, or not typically provided during these phases, as in FAST-TRACK construction. Such services may warrant special requirements as to responsibility and/or compensation.

OWNER _____
(Signature)

ARCHITECT _____
(Signature)

ARTICLE 1.2

COMPENSATION

The Owner shall compensate the Architect as follows.

1.2.1 For Designated Services, as identified in the Schedule of Designated Services, described in the Description of Designated Services, and any other services included in Article 1.6, compensation shall be computed as follows:

(Insert basis of compensation, including stipulated sums, multiples or percentages, and identify phases to which particular methods of compensation apply, if necessary.)

1.2.2 For Contingent Additional Services of the Architect, as described in the Terms and Conditions, but excluding Contingent Additional Services of Consultants, compensation shall be computed as follows:

(Insert basis of compensation, including rates and multiples of Direct Personnel Expense for Principals and employees, and identify Principals and classify employees, if required. Identify specific services to which particular methods of compensation apply, if necessary.)

1.2.3 For Contingent Additional Services of the Architect's Consultants, including additional structural, mechanical and electrical engineering, and those identified in Article 1.6 and in the Schedule of Designated Services or as part of the Architect's Contingent Additional Services under the Terms and Conditions, compensation shall be computed as a multiple of
(   ) times the amounts billed to the Architect for such services.

(Identify specific types of consultants in Article 6, if required.)

1.2.4 For Reimbursable Expenses, as described in Article 3.7 of the Terms and Conditions, and any other items included in Article 1.6 as a Reimbursable Expense, the compensations shall be computed as a multiple of
(   ) times the expense incurred by the Architect, the Architect's employees and consultants in the interest of the Project.

1.2.5 If the Designated Services identified in the Schedule of Designated Services have not been completed within
(   ) months of the date hereof, through no fault of the Architect, extension of the Architect's services beyond that time shall be compensated as provided in Paragraph 1.2.2.

1.2.6 The rates and multiples set forth for Contingent Additional Services shall be annually adjusted in accordance with normal salary review practices of the Architect.

B163—1993   5

ARTICLE 1.3

PAYMENTS

1.3.1 An initial payment of   dollars ($)
shall be made upon execution of this Agreement and is the minimum payment under this Agreement. It shall be credited to the Owner's account at final payment. Subsequent payments for Designated Services shall be made monthly, and where applicable, shall be in proportion to services performed within each phase of service, on the basis set forth in the Agreement.

1.3.2 Where compensation is based on a stipulated sum or percentage of Construction Cost, progress payments for Designated Services in each phase shall be made monthly and shall be in proportion to services performed within each Phase of Services, so that Compensation for each Phase shall equal the following amounts or percentages of the total compensation payable for such Designated Services.

(Insert or delete phases as appropriate.)

Phase	Amount or Percentage
Pre-Design Phase:	
Site Analysis Phase:	
Schematic Design Phase:	
Design Development Phase:	
Contract Documents Phase:	
Bidding or Negotiation Phase:	
Contract Administration Phase:	
Post-Contract Phase:	

1.3.3 Payments are due and payable   (   ) days from the date of the Architect's invoice.
Amounts unpaid   (   ) days after the invoice date shall bear interest at the rate entered below, or in the absence thereof at the legal rate prevailing from time to time at the principal place of business of the Architect.
(Insert rate of interest agreed upon.)

(Usury laws and requirements under the Federal Truth in Lending Act, similar state and local consumer credit laws and other regulations at the Owner's and Architect's principal places of business, the location of the Project and elsewhere may affect the validity of this provision. Specific legal advice should be obtained with respect to deletion or modifications, and also regarding requirements such as written disclosures or waivers.)

ARTICLE 1.4

TIME AND COST

1.4.1 Unless otherwise indicated, the Owner and the Architect shall perform their respective obligations as expeditiously as is consistent with normal skill and care and the orderly progress of the Project. Upon the request of the Owner, the Architect shall prepare a schedule for the performance of the Designated Services which may be adjusted as the Project proceeds, and shall include allowances for periods of time required for the Owner's review and for approval of submissions by authorities having jurisdiction over the Project. Time limits established by this schedule upon approval by the Owner shall not, except for reasonable cause, be exceeded by the Architect or Owner. If the Architect is delayed in the performance of services under this Agreement by the Owner, the Owner's Consultants, or any other cause not within the control of the Architect, any applicable schedule shall be adjusted accordingly.

(Insert time requirements, if any.)

B163—1993   6

1.4.2 The Owner shall establish and update an overall budget for the Project, which shall include the Cost of the Work; contingencies for design, bidding and changes in the Work during construction; compensation of the Architect, Architect's consultants and the Owner's other consultants; cost of the land, rights-of-way and financing; and other costs that are the responsibility of the Owner as indicated by the Terms and Conditions or Designated Services. Prior to the establishment of such a budget, the Owner and the Architect may agree on Designated Services that include the utilization of the Architect's or other consultants' services to assist the Owner with market, financing and feasibility studies deemed necessary for development of such a budget for the Project.

1.4.3 No fixed limit of the Cost of the Work shall be established as a condition of this Agreement by the furnishing, proposal or establishment of a Project budget unless such fixed limit has been agreed to below or by separate Amendment made in writing and signed by the parties hereto. Any fixed limit of the Cost of the Work shall be subject to the limitations and definitions contained in the Terms and Conditions under Part 3 of this Agreement.

(If no fixed limit, leave blank.)

ARTICLE 1.5

ENUMERATION OF DOCUMENTS

1.5.1 This Agreement represents the entire and integrated agreement between the Owner and Architect and supersedes all prior negotiations, representations or agreements, either written or oral. This Agreement may be amended only by written instrument signed by both Owner and Architect.

1.5.2 The parts of this Agreement between the Owner and Architect, except for amendments issued after execution of this Agreement, are enumerated as follows:

1.5.2.1 Form of Agreement Between Owner and Architect, AIA Document B163—Part 1, 1993 Edition;

1.5.2.2 Descriptions of Designated Services for AIA Document B163, AIA Document B163—Part 2, 1993 Edition;

1.5.2.3 Terms and Conditions of AIA Document B163, AIA Document B163—Part 3, 1993 Edition.

1.5.2.4 Other Documents, if any, forming a part of the contract are as follows:

(Insert any additional documents, but only if they are intended to be part of the contract between the Owner and the Architect.)

ARTICLE 1.6

OTHER CONDITIONS OR SERVICES

(Insert modifications to the Descriptions of Services contained in Part 2 and to the Terms and Conditions contained in Part 3 of this Agreement.)

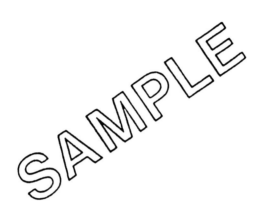

This Agreement entered into as of the day and year first written above.

OWNER   ARCHITECT

_____   _____
(Signature)   *(Signature)*

_____   _____
(Printed name and title)   *(Printed name and title)*

AIA DOCUMENT B163 • OWNER-ARCHITECT AGREEMENT FOR DESIGNATED SERVICES
AIA® • ©1993 • THE AMERICAN INSTITUTE OF ARCHITECTS, 1735 NEW YORK AVENUE,
N.W., WASHINGTON, D.C. 20006-5292 • **WARNING: Unlicensed photocopying
violates U.S. copyright laws and will subject the violator to legal prosecution.**   B163—1993   8

DESCRIPTIONS OF DESIGNATED SERVICES
for the Agreement
Between Owner and Architect

The current edition of AIA Document A201, General Conditions of the Contract for Construction, is adopted by reference under the Construction Phase of this document. Do not use with other general conditions unless this document is modified.

ARTICLE 2.1
DESIGNATED SERVICES

2.1.1 In accordance with the Schedule of Designated Services completed under Part 1 of this Agreement, the Owner and Architect shall provide the phases and services designated therein and described herein. Unless the responsibility for a Project phase or service is specifically allocated in the Schedule of Designated Services to the Owner or Architect, such phase or service shall not be a requirement of this Agreement.

ARTICLE 2.2
PHASES OF DESIGNATED SERVICES

2.2.1 Pre-Design Phase. The Pre-Design Phase is the stage in which the Owner's program, the financial and time requirements, and the scope of the Project are established.

2.2.2 Site Analysis Phase. The Site Analysis Phase is the stage in which site-related limitations and requirements for the Project are established.

2.2.3 Schematic Design Phase. The Schematic Design Phase is the stage in which the general scope, conceptual design, and the scale and relationship of components of the Project are established.

2.2.4 Design Development Phase. The Design Development Phase is the stage in which the size and character of the Project are further refined and described, including architectural, structural, mechanical and electrical systems, materials, and such other elements as may be appropriate.

2.2.5 Contract Documents Phase. The Contract Documents Phase is the stage in which the requirements for the Work are set forth in detail.

2.2.6 Bidding or Negotiations Phase. The Bidding or Negotiation Phase is the stage in which bids or negotiated proposals are solicited and obtained and in which contracts are awarded.

2.2.7 Contract Administration Phase. The Contract Administration Phase is the stage in which the Work is performed by one or more Contractors.

2.2.8 Post-Contract Phase. The Post-Contract Phase is the stage in which assistance in the Owner's use and occupancy of the Project is provided.

2.2.9 Sequence of Phases. The services for the above phases are generally performed in a chronological sequence following the order of phases shown in Paragraphs 2.2.1 through 2.2.8.

2.2.9.1 Normal Sequence. The Owner and Architect shall commence the performance of their respective responsibilities with the services assigned to the foremost sequential phase under the completed Schedule of Designated Services of Part 1 to this Agreement. Except as provided under Subparagraphs 2.2.9.2 and 2.2.9.3, subsequent phases shall not be commenced until the Owner has approved the results of the Architect's services for the preceding phase. Such approvals shall not be unreasonably withheld. When phases or services are to be combined or compressed, their chronology shall continue to follow that shown above, unless otherwise provided in this Agreement.

2.2.9.2 Fast Track. Upon the receipt of the Owner's written authorization for Work to commence prior to completion of the Architect's Contract Documents Phase, the Architect shall provide the services designated in an overlapping manner rather than in the normal chronological sequence in order to expedite the Owner's early occupancy of all or a portion of the Project. The Owner shall furnish to the Architect in a timely manner information obtained from all Contractors and prospective contractors regarding

B163—1993   9

anticipated market conditions and construction cost, availability of labor, materials and equipment, and their proposed methods, sequences and time schedules for construction of the Work. Upon receipt of their proposed Work schedules, the Architect shall prepare a schedule for providing services. In the event of a conflict between the proposed Work schedules and the Architect's proposed schedule, the Architect shall inform the Owner of such conflict.

2.2.9.3 Supplemental Services. Supplemental Services may be provided, however, during a single phase or several phases and may not necessarily follow the normal chronological sequence.

ARTICLE 2.3

DESCRIPTIONS OF DESIGNATED SERVICES

PROJECT ADMINISTRATION AND MANAGEMENT SERVICES

.01   Project Administration services consisting of administrative functions including:

    .01   Consultation

    .02   Research

    .03   Conferences

    .04   Communications

    .05   Travel time

    .06   Progress reports

    .07   Direction of the work of in-house architectural personnel

    .08   Coordination of work by the Owner's forces.

.02   Disciplines Coordination/Document Checking consisting of:

    .01   Coordination between the architectural work and the work of engineering and other disciplines involved in the Project

    .02   Review and checking of documents prepared for the Project by the Architect and the Architect's Consultants.

.03   Agency Consulting/Review/Approval services, including:

    .01   Agency consultations

    .02   Research of critical applicable regulations

    .03   Research of community attitudes

    .04   Preparation of written and graphic explanatory materials

    .05   Appearances on Owner's behalf at agency and community meetings.

    The services below apply to applicable laws, statutes, regulations and codes of regulating entities and to reviews required of user or community groups with limited or no statutory authority but significant influence on approving agencies and individuals, including:

    .06   Local political subdivisions

    .07   Planning boards

    .08   County agencies

    .09   Regional agencies

    .10   Federal agencies

    .11   User organizations

    .12   Community organizations

    .13   Consumer interest organizations

    .14   Environmental interest groups.

.04   Owner-Supplied Data Coordination, including:

    .01   Review and coordination of data furnished for the Project as a responsibility of the Owner

    .02   Assistance in establishing criteria

    .03   Assistance in obtaining data, including, where applicable, documentation of existing conditions.

.05   Schedule Development/Monitoring services, including:

.01   Establishment of initial schedule for Architect's services, decision-making, design, documentation, contracting and construction, based on determination of scope of Architect's services

.02   Review and update of previously established schedules during subsequent phases.

.06   Preliminary Estimate of the Cost of the Work, including:

.01   Preparation of a preliminary estimate of the Cost of the Work

.02   Review and update the preliminary estimate of the Cost of the Work during subsequent phases.

.07   Presentation services consisting of presentations and recommendations by the Architect to the following client representatives:

.01   Owner

.02   Building committee(s)

.03   Staff committee (s)

.04   User group(s)

.05   Board(s) of Directors

.06   Financing entity (entities)

.07   Owner's consultant(s).

PRE-DESIGN SERVICES

.08   Programming services consisting of consultation to establish and document the following detailed requirements for the Project:

.01   Design objectives, limitations and criteria

.02   Development of initial approximate gross facility areas and space requirements

.03   Space relations

.04   Number of functional responsibilities personnel

.05   Flexibility and expandability

.06   Special equipment and systems

.07   Site requirements

.08   Development of a preliminary budget for the Work based on programming and scheduling studies

.09   Operating procedures

.10   Security criteria

.11   Communications relationships

.12   Project schedule.

.09   Space Schematics/Flow Diagrams consisting of diagrammatic studies and pertinent descriptive text for:

.01   Conversion of programmed requirements to net area requirements

.02   Internal functions

.03   Human, vehicular and material flow patterns

.04   General space allocations

.05   Analysis of operating functions

.06   Adjacency

.07   Special facilities and equipment

.08   Flexibility and expandability.

.10   Existing Facilities Surveys consisting of researching, assembling, reviewing and supplementing information for Projects involving alterations and additions to existing facilities or determining new space usage in conjunction with a new building program and including:

.01   Photography

.02   Field measurements

.03   Review of existing design data

B163—1993   11

221

.04 Analysis of existing structural capabilities
.05 Analysis of existing mechanical capabilities
.06 Analysis of existing electrical capabilities
.07 Review of existing drawings for critical inaccuracies, and the development of required measured drawings.

.11 **Marketing Studies** relating to determination of social, economic and political need for and acceptability of the Project and consisting of:
.01 Determination with Owner of the scope, parameters, schedule and budget for marketing studies
.02 Identification, assembly, review and organization of existing pertinent data
.03 Arrangement of clearances for use of existing data
.04 Mail survey studies
.05 Personal survey studies
.06 Analysis of data
.07 Assistance in obtaining computerized analysis and modeling
.08 Computerized analysis and modeling
.09 Preparation of interim reports
.10 Preparation of final report
.11 Assistance in production of final report.

.12 **Economic Feasibility Studies** consisting of the preparation of economic analysis and feasibility evaluation of the Project based on estimates of:
.01 Total Project cost
.02 Operation and ownership cost
.03 Financing requirements
.04 Cash flow for design, construction and operation
.05 Return on investment studies
.06 Equity requirements.

.13 **Project Financing** services as required in connection with:
.01 Assistance to Owner in preparing and submitting data, supplementary drawings and documentation
.02 Research of financing availability
.03 Direct solicitation of financing sources by the Architect.

Project financing services are required for:

.04 Development costs
.05 Site control and/or acquisition
.06 Predesign and site analysis services
.07 Planning, design, documentation and bidding services
.08 Interim or construction financing
.09 Permanent or long-term financing.

SITE DEVELOPMENT SERVICES

.14 **Site Analysis and Selection** consisting of:
.01 Identification of potential site(s)
.02 On-site observations
.03 Movement systems, traffic and parking studies
.04 Topography analysis
.05 Analysis of deed, zoning and other legal restrictions
.06 Studies of availability of labor force to staff Owner's facility
.07 Studies of availability of construction materials, equipment and labor
.08 Studies of construction market
.09 Overall site analysis and evaluation
.10 Comparative site studies.

.15 Site Development Planning consisting of preliminary site analysis, and preparation and comparative evaluation of conceptual site development designs, based on:

.01   Land utilization
.02   Structures placement
.03   Facilities development
.04   Development phasing
.05   Movement systems, circulation and parking
.06   Utilities systems
.07   Surface and subsurface conditions
.08   Ecological requirements
.09   Deeds, zoning and other legal restrictions
.10   Landscape concepts and forms.

.16 Detailed Site Utilization Studies consisting of detailed site analyses, based on the approved conceptual site development design, including:

.01   Land utilization
.02   Structures placement
.03   Facilities development
.04   Development phasing
.05   Movement systems, circulation and parking
.06   Utilities systems
.07   Surface and subsurface conditions
.08   Review of soils report
.09   Vegetation
.10   Slope analysis
.11   Ecological studies
.12   Deeds, zoning and other legal restrictions
.13   Landscape forms and materials.

.17 On-Site Utility Studies consisting of establishing requirements and preparing initial designs for on-site:

.01   Electrical service and distribution
.02   Gas service and distribution
.03   Water supply and distribution
.04   Site drainage
.05   Sanitary sewer collection and disposal
.06   Process waste water treatment
.07   Storm water collection and disposal
.08   Central-plant mechanical systems
.09   Fire systems
.10   Emergency systems
.11   Security
.12   Pollution control
.13   Site illumination
.14   Communications systems.

.18 Off-Site Utility Studies consisting of:

.01   Confirmation of location, size and adequacy of utilities serving the site
.02   Determination of requirements for connections to utilities
.03   Planning for off-site utility extensions and facilities
.04   Design of off-site utility extensions and facilities.

AIA DOCUMENT B163 · OWNER-ARCHITECT AGREEMENT FOR DESIGNATED SERVICES
AIA®· ©1993 · THE AMERICAN INSTITUTE OF ARCHITECTS, 1735 NEW YORK AVENUE,
N.W., WASHINGTON, D.C. 20006-5292 · **WARNING: Unlicensed photocopying
violates U.S. copyright laws and will subject the violator to legal prosecution.**

B163—1993   13

223

.19 **Environmental Studies and Reports** consisting of:

    .01   Determination of need or requirements for environmental monitoring, assessment and/or impact statements

    .02   Ecological studies

    .03   Preparation of environmental assessment reports

    .04   Preparation of environmental impact reports

    .05   Attendance at public meetings and hearings

    .06   Presentations to governing authorities.

.20 **Zoning Processing Assistance** consisting of:

    .01   Assistance in preparing applications

    .02   Development of supporting data

    .03   Preparation of presentation materials

    .04   Attendance at public meetings and hearings.

.21 **Geotechnical Engineering** services, including, but not limited to:

    .01   Test borings, test pits, determinations of soil bearing values, percolation tests, evaluations of hazardous materials, ground corrosion and resistivity tests, including necessary operations for anticipating subsoil conditions

    .02   Reports and appropriate professional recommendations.

.22 **Site Surveying** services, to include:

    .01   Furnishing a survey by a licensed surveyor, describing the physical characteristics, legal limitations and utility locations for the site of the Project, including a written legal description of the site

    .02   Include, as applicable, grades and lines of streets, alleys, pavements and adjoining property and structures; adjacent drainage; rights-of-way, restrictions, easements, encroachments, zoning, deed restrictions, boundaries and contours of the site; locations, dimensions and necessary data pertaining to existing buildings, other improvements and trees; and information concerning available utility services and lines, both public and private, above and below grade, including inverts and depths. All information shall be referenced to a project benchmark.

DESIGN SERVICES

.23 **Architectural Design/Documentation:**

    .01   During the Schematic Design Phase, responding to program requirements and preparing:

        .01   Review of Owner's Program and Budget

        .02   Conceptual site and building plans

        .03   Preliminary sections and elevations

        .04   Preliminary selection of building systems and materials

        .05   Development of approximate dimensions, areas and volumes

        .06   Perspective sketch(es)

        .07   Study model(s).

    .02   During the Design Development Phase consisting of continued development and expansion of architectural Schematic Design Documents to establish the final scope, relationships, forms, size and appearance of the Project through:

        .01   Plans, sections and elevations

        .02   Typical construction details

        .03   Three-dimensional sketch(es)

        .04   Study model(s)

        .05   Final materials selection

        .06   Equipment layouts.

    .03   During the Contract Documents Phase consisting of preparation of Drawings based on approved Design Development Documents setting forth in detail the architectural construction requirements for the Project.

.24 **Structural Design/Documentation:**

.01 During the Schematic Design Phase consisting of recommendations regarding basic structural materials and systems, analyses, and development of conceptual design solutions for:

    .01 A predetermined structural system

    .02 Alternate structural systems.

.02 During the Design Development Phase consisting of continued development of the specific structural system(s) and Schematic Design Documents in sufficient detail to establish:

    .01 Basic structural system and dimensions

    .02 Final structural design criteria

    .03 Foundation design criteria

    .04 Preliminary sizing of major structural components

    .05 Critical coordination clearances

    .06 Outline Specifications or materials lists.

.03 During the Contract Documents Phase consisting of preparation of final structural engineering calculations, Drawings and Specifications based on approved Design Development Documents, setting forth in detail the structural construction requirements for the Project.

.25 **Mechanical Design/Documentation:**

.01 During the Schematic Design Phase consisting of consideration of alternate materials, systems and equipment, and development of conceptual design solutions for:

    .01 Energy source(s)

    .02 Energy conservation

    .03 Heating and ventilating

    .04 Air conditioning

    .05 Plumbing

    .06 Fire protection

    .07 General space requirements.

.02 During the Design Development Phase consisting of continued development and expansion of mechanical Schematic Design Documents and development of outline Specifications or materials lists to establish:

    .01 Approximate equipment sizes and capacities

    .02 Preliminary equipment layouts

    .03 Required space for equipment

    .04 Required chases and clearances

    .05 Acoustical and vibration control

    .06 Visual impacts

    .07 Energy conservation measures.

.03 During the Contract Documents Phase consisting of preparation of final mechanical engineering calculations, Drawings and Specifications based on approved Design Development Documents, setting forth in detail the mechanical construction requirements for the Project.

.26 **Electrical Design/Documentation:**

.01 During the Schematic Design Phase consisting of consideration of alternate systems, recommendations regarding basic electrical materials, systems and equipment, analyses, and development of conceptual solutions for:

    .01 Power service and distribution

    .02 Lighting

    .03 Telephones

    .04 Fire detection and alarms

B163—1993 15

.05   Security systems
.06   Electronic communications
.07   Special electrical systems
.08   General space requirements.

.02   During the Design Development Phase consisting of continued development and expansion of electrical Schematic Design Documents and development of outline Specifications or materials lists to establish:

.01   Criteria for lighting, electrical and communications systems
.02   Approximate sizes and capacities of major components
.03   Preliminary equipment layouts
.04   Required space for equipment
.05   Required chases and clearances.

.03   During the Contract Documents Phase consisting of preparation of final electrical engineering calculations, Drawings and Specifications based on approved Design Development Documents, setting forth in detail the electrical requirements for the Project.

.27 Civil Design/Documentation:

.01   During the Schematic Design Phase consisting of consideration of alternate materials and systems and development of conceptual design solutions for:

.01   On-site utility systems
.02   Fire protection systems
.03   Drainage systems
.04   Paving.

.02   During the Design Development Phase consisting of continued development and expansion of civil Schematic Design Documents and development of outline Specifications or materials lists to establish the final scope of and preliminary details for on-site and off-site civil engineering work

.03   During the Contract Documents Phase consisting of preparation of final civil engineering calculations, Drawings and Specifications based on approved Design Development Documents, setting forth in detail the civil construction requirements for the Project.

.28 Landscape Design/Documentation:

.01   During the Schematic Design Phase consisting of consideration of alternate materials, systems and equipment and development of conceptual design solutions for land forms, lawns and plantings based on program requirements, physical site characteristics, design objectives and environmental determinants

.02   During the Design Development Phase consisting of continued development and expansion of landscape Schematic Design Documents and development of outline Specifications or materials lists to establish final scope and preliminary details for landscape work

.03   During the Contract Documents Phase consisting of preparation of Drawings and Specifications based on approved Design Development Documents, setting forth in detail the landscape requirements for the Project.

.29 Interior Design/Documentation:

.01   During the Schematic Design Phase consisting of space allocation and utilization plans based on functional relationships, consideration of alternate materials, systems and equipment and development of conceptual design solutions for architectural, mechanical, electrical and equipment requirements in order to establish:

.01   Partition locations
.02   Furniture and equipment layouts
.03   Types and qualities of finishes and materials for furniture, furnishings and equipment.

AIA DOCUMENT B163 · OWNER-ARCHITECT AGREEMENT FOR DESIGNATED SERVICES
AIA® · ©1993 · THE AMERICAN INSTITUTE OF ARCHITECTS, 1735 NEW YORK AVENUE, N.W., WASHINGTON, D.C. 20006-5292 · **WARNING: Unlicensed photocopying violates U.S. copyright laws and will subject the violator to legal prosecution.**

.02 During the Design Development Phase consisting of continued development and expansion of interior Schematic Design Documents and development of outline Specifications or materials lists to establish final scope and preliminary details relative to:

    .01 Interior construction of the Project

    .02 Special interior design features

    .03 Furniture, furnishings and equipment selections

    .04 Materials, finishes and colors.

.03 During the Contract Documents Phase consisting of preparation of Drawings, Specifications and other documents based on approved Design Development Documents, setting forth in detail the requirements for interior construction and for furniture, furnishings and equipment for the Project.

.30 Special Design/Documentation, including:

    .01 Preparation and coordination of special Drawings and Specifications for obtaining bids or prices on alternate subdivisions of the Work

    .02 Preparation and coordination of special Drawings and Specifications for obtaining alternate bids or prices on changes in the scope of the Work

    .03 Preparation and coordination of Drawings, Specifications, Bidding Documents and schedules for out-of-sequence bidding or pricing of subdivisions of the Work

    .04 Preparation and coordination of Drawings, Specifications and Bidding Documents for multiple prime contracts for subdivisions of the Work.

.31 Materials Research/Specifications:

    .01 During the Schematic Design Phase consisting of:

        .01 Identification of potential architectural materials, systems and equipment and their criteria and quality standards consistent with the conceptual design

        .02 Investigation of availability and suitability of alternative architectural materials, systems and equipment

        .03 Coordination of similar activities of other disciplines.

    .02 During the Design Development Phase consisting of activities by in-house architectural personnel in:

        .01 Presentation of proposed General and Supplementary Conditions of the Contract for Owner's approval

        .02 Development of architectural outline Specifications or itemized lists and brief form identification of significant architectural materials, systems and equipment, including their criteria and quality standards

        .03 Coordination of similar activities of other disciplines

        .04 Production of design manual including design criteria and outline Specifications or materials lists.

    .03 During the Contract Documents Phase consisting of activities of in-house architectural personnel in:

        .01 Assistance to the Owner in development and preparation of bidding and procurement information which describes the time, place and conditions of bidding, bidding forms, and the form(s) of Agreement between the Owner and Contractor(s)

        .02 Assistance to the Owner in development and preparation of the Conditions of the Contract (General, Supplementary and other Conditions)

        .03 Development and preparation of architectural Specifications describing materials, systems and equipment, workmanship, quality and performance criteria required for the construction of the Project

        .04 Coordination of the development of Specifications by other disciplines

        .05 Compilation of Project Manual including Conditions of the Contract, bidding and procurement information and Specifications.

B163—1993   17

227

BIDDING OR NEGOTIATION SERVICES

.32 **Bidding Materials** services consisting of organizing and handling Bidding Documents for:

    .01   Coordination
    .02   Reproduction
    .03   Completeness review
    .04   Distribution
    .05   Distribution records
    .06   Retrieval
    .07   Receipt and return of document deposits
    .08   Review, repair and reassembly of returned materials.

.33 **Addenda** services consisting of preparation and distribution of Addenda as may be required during bidding or negotiation and including supplementary Drawings, Specifications, instructions and notice(s) of changes in the bidding schedule and procedure.

.34 **Bidding/Negotiation** services consisting of:

    .01   Assistance to Owner in establishing list of Bidders or proposers
    .02   Prequalification of Bidders or proposers
    .03   Participation in pre-bid conferences
    .04   Responses to questions from Bidders or proposers and clarifications or interpretations of the Bidding Documents
    .05   Attendance at bid opening(s)
    .06   Documentation and distribution of bidding results

.35 **Analysis of Alternates/Substitutions** consisting of consideration, analyses, comparisons, and recommendations relative to alternates or substitutions proposed by Bidders or proposers either prior or subsequent to receipt of Bids or proposals.

.36 **Special Bidding** services consisting of:

    .01   Attendance at bid openings, participation in negotiations, and documentation of decisions for multiple contracts or phased Work
    .02   Technical evaluation of proposals for building systems
    .03   Participation in detailed evaluation procedures for building systems proposals.

.37 **Bid Evaluation** services consisting of:

    .01   Validation of bids or proposals
    .02   Participation in reviews of bids or proposals
    .03   Evaluation of bids or proposals
    .04   Recommendation on award of Contract(s)
    .05   Participation in negotiations prior to or following decisions on award of the Contract(s).

.38 **Contract Award** services consisting of:

    .01   Notification of Contract award(s)
    .02   Assistance in preparation of construction contract Agreement forms for approval by Owner
    .03   Preparation and distribution of sets of Contract Documents for execution by parties to the Contract(s)
    .04   Receipt, distribution and processing, for Owner's approval, of required certificates of insurance, bonds and similar documents
    .05   Preparation and distribution to Contractor(s), on behalf of the Owner, of notice(s) to proceed with the Work.

CONTRACT ADMINISTRATION SERVICES

.39 **Submittal Services** consisting of:

   .01 Processing of submittals, including receipt, review of, and appropriate action on Shop Drawings, Product Data, Samples and other submittals required by the Contract Documents

   .02 Distribution of submittals to Owner, Contractor and/or Architect's field representative as required

   .03 Maintenance of master file of submittals

   .04 Related communications.

.40 **Observation Services** consisting of visits to the site at intervals appropriate to the stage of the work or as otherwise agreed by the Owner and Architect in writing to become generally familiar with the progress and quality of the Work completed and to determine in general if the Work when completed will be in accordance with Contract Documents; preparing related reports and communications.

.41 **Project Representation** consisting of selection, employment and direction of:

   .01 Project Representative(s) whose specific duties, responsibilities and limitations of authority shall be as described in the edition of AIA Document B352 current as of the date of this Agreement or as set forth in an exhibit to be incorporated in this Agreement under Article 1.6.

.42 **Testing and Inspection Administration** relating to independent inspection and testing agencies, consisting of:

   .01 Administration and coordination of field testing required by the Contract Documents

   .02 Recommending scope, standards, procedures and frequency of testing and inspections

   .03 Arranging for testing and inspection on Owner's behalf

   .04 Notifying inspection and testing agencies of status of Work requiring testing and inspection

   .05 Evaluating compliance by testing and inspection agencies with required scope, standards, procedures and frequency

   .06 Review of reports on inspection and tests and notifications to Owner and Contractor(s) of observed deficiencies in the Work.

.43 **Supplemental Documentation** services consisting of:

   .01 Preparation, reproduction and distribution of supplemental Drawings, Specifications and interpretations in response to requests for clarification by Contractor(s) or the Owner

   .02 Forwarding Owner's instructions and providing guidance to the Contractor(s) on the Owner's behalf relative to changed requirements and schedule revisions.

.44 **Quotation Requests/Change Orders** consisting of:

   .01 Preparation, reproduction and distribution of Drawings and Specifications to describe Work to be added, deleted or modified

   .02 Review of proposals from Contractor(s) for reasonableness of quantities and costs of labor and materials

   .03 Review and recommendations relative to changes in time for Substantial Completion

   .04 Negotiations with Contractor(s) on Owner's behalf relative to costs of Work proposed to be added, deleted or modified

   .05 Assisting in the preparation of appropriate Modifications of the Contract(s) for Construction

   .06 Coordination of communications, approvals, notifications and record-keeping relative to changes in the Work.

.45 **Contract Cost Accounting** services consisting of:

   .01 Maintenance of records of payments on account of the Contract Sum and all changes thereto

   .02 Evaluation of Applications for Payment and certification thereof

   .03 Review and evaluation of expense data submitted by the Contractor(s) for Work performed under cost-plus-fee arrangements.

AIA DOCUMENT B163 · OWNER-ARCHITECT AGREEMENT FOR DESIGNATED SERVICES
AIA® · ©1993 · THE AMERICAN INSTITUTE OF ARCHITECTS, 1735 NEW YORK AVENUE,
N.W., WASHINGTON, D.C. 20006-5292 · **WARNING: Unlicensed photocopying
violates U.S. copyright laws and will subject the violator to legal prosecution.**

B163 1993 19

229

.46 **Furniture, Furnishings and Equipment Installation Administration** consisting of:

.01 Assistance to the Owner in coordinating schedules for delivery and installation of the Work

.02 Review of final placement and inspection for damage, quality, assembly and function to determine that furniture, furnishings and equipment are in accordance with the requirements of the Contract Documents.

.47 **Interpretations and Decisions** consisting of:

.01 Review of claims, disputes or other matters between the Owner and Contractor relating to the execution or progress of the Work as provided in the Contract Documents

.02 Rendering written decisions within a reasonable time and following the procedures set forth in the General Conditions of the Contract for Construction, AIA Document A201, current as of the date of this Agreeement, or the General Conditions of the Contract for Furniture, Furnishings and Equipment, AIA Document A271, current as of the date of this Agreement, for Resolution of Claims and disputes.

.48 **Project Closeout** services initiated upon notice from the Contractor(s) that the Work, or a designated portion thereof which is acceptable to the Owner, is sufficiently complete, in accordance with the Contract Documents, to permit occupancy or utilization for the use for which it is intended, and consisting of:

.01 A detailed inspection with the Owner's representative for conformity of the Work to the Contract Documents to verify the list submitted by the Contractor(s) of items to be completed or corrected

.02 Determination of the amounts to be withheld until final completion

.03 Securing and receipt of consent of surety or sureties, if any, to reduction in or partial release of retainage or the making of final payment(s)

.04 Issuance of Certificate(s) of Substantial Completion

.05 Inspection(s) upon notice by the Contractor(s) that the Work is ready for final inspection and acceptance

.06 Notification to Owner and Contractor(s) of deficiencies found in follow-up inspection(s), if any

.07 Final inspection with the Owner's representative to verify final completion of the Work

.08 Receipt and transmittal of warranties, affidavits, receipts, releases and waivers of liens or bonds indemnifying the Owner against liens

.09 Securing and receipt of consent of surety or sureties, if any, to the making of final payment(s)

.10 Issuance of final Certificate(s) for Payment.

POST-CONTRACT SERVICES

.49 **Maintenance and Operational Programming** services consisting of:

.01 Assistance in the establishment by the Owner of in-house or contract program(s) of operation and maintenance of the physical plant and equipment

.02 Arranging for and coordinating instructions on operations and maintenance of equipment in conjunction with manufacturer's representatives

.03 Assistance in the preparation of operations and maintenance manual(s) for the Owner's use.

.50 **Start-Up Assistance** consisting of:

.01 On-site assistance in the operation of building systems during initial occupancy

.02 Assistance in the training of the Owner's operation and maintenance personnel in proper operations, schedules and procedures

.03 Administration and coordination of remedial work by the Contractor(s) after final completion.

.51 **Record Drawing** services consisting of:

.01 Making arrangements for obtaining from Contractor(s) information in the form of marked-up prints, drawings and other data certified by them on changes made during performance of the Work

.02 Review of general accuracy of information submitted and certified by the Contractor(s)

.03 Preparation of record drawings based on certified information furnished by the Contractor(s)

.04 Transmittal of record drawings and general data, appropriately identified, to the Owner and others as directed.

.52 **Warranty Review** consisting of:

    .01   Consultation with and recommendation to the Owner during the duration of warranties in connection with inadequate performance of materials, systems and equipment under warranty

    .02   Inspection(s) prior to expiration of the warranty period(s) to ascertain adequacy of performance of materials, systems and equipment

    .03   Documenting defects or deficiencies and assisting the Owner in preparing instructions to the Contractor(s) for correction of noted defects.

.53 **Post-Contract Evaluation** consisting of a Project inspection at least one year after completion of the Work; review with appropriate supervisory, operating and maintenance personnel, and analysis of operating costs and related data for evaluation of:

    .01   The initial Project programming versus actual facility use

    .02   The functional effectiveness of planned spaces and relationships

    .03   The operational effectiveness of systems and materials installed.

ARTICLE 2.4

DESCRIPTIONS OF SUPPLEMENTAL SERVICES

SUPPLEMENTAL SERVICES

.54 **Special Studies** consisting of investigation, research and analysis of the Owner's special requirements for the Project and documentation of findings, conclusions and recommendations for:

    .01   Master planning to provide design services relative to future facilities, systems and equipment which are not intended to be constructed as part of the Project during the Construction Phase

    .02   Providing special studies for the project such as analyzing acoustical or lighting requirements, record retention, communications and security systems.

.55 **Tenant-Related Services** consisting of design and documentation services for tenants or potential tenants relating to:

    .01   Space planning, partition and furnishings locations, and furniture and equipment layouts

    .02   Material and color selections and coordination

    .03   Adaptation of mechanical, electrical and other building systems to meet tenant needs

    .04   Preliminary estimate of Construction Cost.

.56 **Special Furnishings Design** services relating to Architect-designed special furnishings and/or equipment incorporated into or provided for the Project and consisting of:

    .01   Design and documentation

    .02   Specifications or standards

    .03   Management of procurement

    .04   Coordination of installation

    .05   Purchase on the Owner's behalf.

.57 **Furniture, Furnishings and Equipment Services** relating to equipment and furnishings not incorporated into the construction of the Project and consisting of:

    .01   Establishment of needs and criteria

    .02   Preparation of requirements, Specifications and bidding or purchasing procedures

    .03   Management of procurement

    .04   Coordination of delivery and installation.

B163—1993   21

.58 **Special Disciplines Consultation,** which entails retaining, directing and coordinating the work of special disciplines consultants identified from the following list and as more specifically described in Article 1.6, whose specialized training, experience and knowledge relative to specific elements and features of the Project are required for the Project:

.01	Acoustics	.14	Elevators/Escalators	.27	Public Relations
.02	Audio-Visual	.15	Fallout Shelters	.28	Radiation Shielding
.03	CPM Scheduling	.16	Financial	.29	Real Estate
.04	Code Interpretation	.17	Fire Protection	.30	Reprographics
.05	Communications	.18	Food Service	.31	Safety
.06	Computer Technology	.19	Insurance	.32	Sociology
.07	Concrete	.20	Historic Preservation	.33	Soils/Foundations
.08	Cost Estimating	.21	Legal	.34	Space Planning
.09	Demography	.22	Life Safety	.35	Specifications
.10	Display	.23	Lightning	.36	Traffic/Parking
.11	Ecology	.24	Management	.37	Transportation
.12	Economics	.25	Materials Handling	.38	Security
.13	Editorial	.26	Psychology	.39	Record Retention

.59 **Special Building Type Consultation,** which entails retaining, directing and coordinating the work of special building type consultants whose specialized training, experience and knowledge relative to the requirements, planning and design of the Project are required for the Project.

.60 **Fine Arts and Crafts** services relating to acquisition of fine arts or crafts to be a part of the Project and consisting of:

.01 Consultations on selection, commissioning and/or execution
.02 Design integration
.03 Managing procurement
.04 Purchasing fine arts or crafts on the Owner's behalf.

.61 **Graphic Design** services consisting of:

.01 Design and selection of interior and exterior signs and identifying symbols
.02 Material and color selections and coordination
.03 Documentation of requirements for procurement of graphics work
.04 Managing procurement of graphics work
.05 Coordination of delivery and installation.

.62 **Renderings** relating to graphic pictorial representations, as required by the Owner, of the proposed Project and consisting of:

.01 Black and white elevation view(s)
.02 Black and white perspective view(s)
.03 Elevation view(s) in color
.04 Perspective view(s) in color.

.63 **Model Construction** consisting of preparation of:

.01 Small-scale block model(s) showing relationship of structure(s) to site
.02 Moderate-scale block model(s) of structure(s) designed for the Project
.03 Moderate-scale detailed model(s) of structure(s) designed for the Project showing both interior and exterior design
.04 Large-scale models of designated interior or exterior components of the Project.

.64 **Still Photography** consisting of:

.01 Documentation of existing conditions
.02 Aerial site photography
.03 Photographic recording for study purposes of facilities similar to the Project

---

22   B163—1993

.04 Periscopic photography of models for the Project

.05 Presentation photography of renderings(s) and model(s) for the Project

.06 Construction progress photography

.07 Architectural photography of the completed Project.

.65 Motion Picture and Videotape services relating to preparation of promotional or explanatory presentations of the Project during the design and/or construction phases.

.66 Life Cycle Cost Analysis consisting of assessment, on the basis of established relevant economic consequences over a given time period, of:

.01 A given planning and design solution for the Project

.02 Alternative planning and design solutions for the Project

.03 Selected systems, subsystems or building components proposed for the Project.

.67 Value Analysis consisting of the review during design phases of the cost, quality and time influences of proposed building materials, systems and construction methods relative to design objectives in order to identify options for obtaining value for the Owner.

.68 Energy Studies consisting of special analyses of mechanical systems, fuel costs, on-site energy generation and energy conservation options for the Owner's consideration.

.69 Quantity Surveys consisting of:

.01 A detailed determination of the quantities of materials to be used in the Project to establish the basis for price determination by bidding or negotiation.

.02 Making investigations, inventories of materials or furniture, furnishings and equipment, or valuations and detailed appraisals of existing facilities, furniture, furnishings and equipment, and the relocation thereof.

.70 Detailed Cost Estimating services consisting of:

.01 Development, when the Contract Documents are approximately 90% complete, of a Detailed Estimate of the Cost of the Work based on quantity take-offs and unit-cost pricing of materials, labor, tools, equipment and services required for the Work plus estimates for the Contractor's supervision cost, Work required by General and Supplementary Conditions, and an allowance for reasonable Contractor's overhead and profit; or

.02 Continuous development during all phases of design and documentation, of an Estimate of the Cost of the Work for the purpose of greater cost control, culminating in a Detailed Estimate of the Cost of the Work or detailed quantity surveys or inventories of material, equipment and labor.

.71 Environmental Monitoring services consisting of:

.01 Monitoring of air, water and other designated components of the environment to establish existing conditions, and the preparation of related analyses and reports.

.72 Expert Witness services consisting of preparing to serve and/or serving as an expert witness in connection with any public hearing, arbitration proceeding or legal proceeding.

.73 Materials and Systems Testing relating to testing of components of the completed Project for conformance with Contract requirements and consisting of:

.01 Establishment of requirements

.02 Procurement of testing services

.03 Monitoring testing

.04 Review, analysis and reporting of test results.

AIA DOCUMENT B163 • OWNER-ARCHITECT AGREEMENT FOR DESIGNATED SERVICES
AIA• • ©1993 • THE AMERICAN INSTITUTE OF ARCHITECTS, 1735 NEW YORK AVENUE,
N.W., WASHINGTON, D.C. 20006-5292 • **WARNING: Unlicensed photocopying
violates U.S. copyright laws and will subject the violator to legal prosecution.**

B163—1993   23

233

.74 Demolition Services consisting of:

    .01   Preparation of Contract Documents for demolition of existing structures
    .02   Managing the bidding/negotiation/award process
    .03   Providing field observation and general administration services during demolition.

.75 Mock-Up Services relating to the construction of full-size details of components of the Project for study and testing during the design phases and consisting of:

    .01   Design and documentation for the required mock-up(s)
    .02   Management and coordination of pricing and contracting for mock-up services
    .03   Construction administration of mock-up construction activities
    .04   Arrangements for testing and monitoring performance of mock-up(s)
    .05   Administration of testing and monitoring services
    .06   Review, analysis and reporting of results of testing and monitoring services.

.76 Coordination of Designated Services with those of non-design professionals, such as economists, sociologists, attorneys and accountants, consiting of:

    .01   Preparation of economic studies
    .02   Condominium documentation
    .03   Sociological impact studies.

.77 Furniture, Furnishings and Equipment Purchasing/Installation, consisting of:

    .01   Purchasing furniture, furnishings and equipment on behalf of the Owner with funds provided by the Owner
    .02   Receipt, inspection and acceptance on behalf of the Owner of furniture, furnishings and equipment at the time of their delivery to the premises and installation
    .03   Providing services including travel for the purpose of evaluating materials, furniture, furnishings and equipment proposed for the Project

.78 Computer Applications consisting of computer program development and/or computer program search and acquisition, plus on-line computer time charges, for:

.01 Programming	.06 Detailed Project scheduling	.10 Mechanical analysis and design
.02 Economic feasibility	.07 Market analysis	.11 Electrical analysis and design
.03 Financial analysis	.08 Architectural analysis and design	.12 Production of Drawings
.04 Site analysis	.09 Structural analysis and design	.13 Construction cost accounting
.05 Construction cost estimating		

.79 Project Promotion/Public Relations relating to presentation of the Project to the public or identified groups and consisting of:

    .01   Preparation of press releases
    .02   Preparation of special brochures and/or promotional pieces
    .03   Assistance in production and distribution of promotional materials
    .04   Presentations at public relations and/or promotional meetings.

.80 Leasing Brochures, including preparation of special materials to assist the Owner in leasing the Project and consisting of:

    .01   Design
    .02   Preparation of illustrations and text
    .03   Arranging for and managing production.

.81 Pre-Contract Administration/Management, consisting of:

    .01   Evaluating feasibility of Owner's program, schedule and budget for the Work, each in terms of the other
    .02   Preparing, updating and monitoring Detailed Project Schedule, including services and contract Work, identifying critical and long-lead items

AIA DOCUMENT B163 · OWNER-ARCHITECT AGREEMENT FOR DESIGNATED SERVICES AIA® · ©1993 · THE AMERICAN INSTITUTE OF ARCHITECTS, 1735 NEW YORK AVENUE, N.W., WASHINGTON, D.C. 20006-5292 · **WARNING: Unlicensed photocopying violates U.S. copyright laws and will subject the violator to legal prosecution.**

.03   Preparing, updating and monitoring Detailed Estimates of the Cost of the Work prior to completion of each design phase

.04   Assisting the Owner in selecting, retaining and coordinating the professional services of surveyors, testing labs and other special consultants as designated

.05   Assisting the Owner in evaluating relative feasibility of methods of executing the Work, methods of project delivery, availability of materials and labor, time requirements for procurement, installation and delivery, and utilization of the site for mobilization and staging

.06   Assisting the Owner in determining the method of contracting for the Work; evaluating single versus multiple contracts; advising on categories of separate contracts and provisions for coordinating responsibilities.

.82   Extended Bidding services, consisting of:

.01   Developing Bidders' interest in the Project and establishing bidding schedules

.02   Receiving and analyzing bids and providing recommendations as to the Owner's acceptance or rejection of bids

.03   Advising the Owner on acceptance of Contractors

.04   Conducting pre-award conferences.

.83   Extended Contract Administration/Management, consisting of:

.01   Assisting Owner in obtaining building permits

.02   Updating and monitoring actual costs against estimates of final cost; assisting Owner in monitoring cash flow

.03   Providing a detailed schedule showing time periods for each Contractor, including long-lead items and Owner's occupancy requirements; updating and monitoring periodically; recommending corrective action when required

.04   Endeavoring to achieve satisfactory performance of Contractors through development and implementation of a quality control program; assisting Owner in determining compliance with schedule, cost and Contract Documents

.05   Scheduling and conducting periodic project meetings with the Owner, Contractor and Subcontractors

.06   Assisting Owner in maintaining cost accounting records

.07   Maintaining a daily log including conditions at site and job progress, periodically indicating percentage of completion of each contract

.08   Assisting the Owner in coordinating and scheduling activities of the separate Contractors.

.09   Maintaining and periodically updating a record of all significant changes made during construction; maintaining record copies of Contract Documents; maintaining samples and lay-out drawings at the job site.

B163—1993   25

TERMS AND CONDITIONS
of the Agreement Between Owner and Architect
for Designated Services

ARTICLE 3.1

ARCHITECT'S RESPONSIBILITIES

3.1.1 Designated Services. Unless otherwise provided, the Architect's designated services consist of those services identified in the Schedule of Designated Services as being performed by the Architect, Architect's employees and Architect's consultants, and as described in the Descriptions of Designated Services.

3.1.2 Contingent Additional Services. Contingent Additional Services described in Subparagraphs 3.1.2.1 through 3.1.2.7 are not included in the Architect's Designated Services, but may be required due to circumstances beyond the Architect's control. The Architect shall notify the Owner prior to commencing such services. If the Owner deems that such services are not required, the Owner shall give prompt written notice to the Architect. If the Owner indicates in writing that all or part of such Contingent Additional Services are not required, the Architect shall have no obligation to provide those services.

3.1.2.1 Document Revisions. Services required to revise Drawings, Specifications or other documents when such revisions are:

  .1 inconsistent with approvals or instructions previously given by the Owner, including revisions made necessary by adjustments in the Owner's program or Project budget;

  .2 required by the enactment or revision of codes, laws or regulations subsequent to the preparation of such documents; or

  .3 due to changes required as a result of the Owner's failure to render decisions in a timely manner.

3.1.2.2 Changes in Project Scope. Services required because of significant changes in the Project including, but not limited to, size, quality, complexity, the Owner's schedule, or the method of bidding or negotiating and contracting for construction, except for services required under Subparagraph 1.6.

3.1.2.3 Replacement of Damaged Work. Consultation concerning replacement of Work damaged by fire or other cause during construction, and furnishing services required in connection with the replacement of such Work.

3.1.2.4 Default by Others. Services made necessary by the default of the Owner's consultants or the Contractor, by major defects or deficiencies in their services or the Work, or by failure of performance of any of them under their respective contracts.

3.1.2.5 Correction Period. Advice and consultation to the Owner during the correction period described in the Contracts for Construction or for Furniture, Furnishings and Equipment.

3.1.2.6 Purchasing of Furniture, Furnishings and Equipment by the Architect. If the Owner and Architect agree that the Architect will purchase furniture, furnishings and equipment on behalf of the Owner with funds provided by the Owner, the duties relating to such services shall be set forth in Article 1.6 of this Agreement. The Owner shall provide and maintain working funds with the Architect, if required, to pay invoices charged to the Project for materials and furnishings, to secure cash discounts and for required deposits.

3.1.2.7 Services Related to Separate Consultants. The Architect shall provide information to and incorporate information received in a timely manner from those separate consultants retained by the Owner and identified in this Agreement whose activities directly relate to the Project.

ARTICLE 3.2

OWNER'S RESPONSIBILITIES

3.2.1 Representative. The Owner shall designate a representative authorized to act on the Owner's behalf with respect to the Project. The Owner or such authorized representative shall render decisions in a timely manner pertaining to documents submitted by the Architect in order to avoid unreasonable delay in the orderly and sequential progress of the Architect's services.

3.2.2 Notice. Prompt written notice shall be given by the Owner to the Architect if the Owner becomes aware of any fault or defect in the Project or nonconformance with the Contract Documents.

3.2.3 Designated Services. The Owner's responsibilities consist of those services identified in the Schedule of Designated Services as being performed by the Owner, Owner's employees and Owner's consultants.

3.2.4 Information. The Owner shall provide full information regarding requirements for the Project.

3.2.5 Owner's Financial Arrangements. If requested by the Architect, the Owner shall furnish evidence that financial arrangements have been made to fulfill the Owner's obligations to the Architect under this Agreement.

3.2.6 Tests, Inspections and Reports Furnished by Owner. The Owner shall furnish structural, mechanical, chemical, air and water pollution tests, tests for hazardous materials, and other laboratory and environmental tests, inspections and reports required by law or the Contract Documents, or unless otherwise provided in this Agreement.

3.2.7 Legal, Accounting and Insurance Services Furnished by Owner. The Owner shall furnish all legal, accounting and insurance counseling services required for the Project, including auditing services the Owner may require to verify the Contractor's Applications for Payment or to ascertain how or for what purposes the Contractor has used the money paid by or on behalf of the Owner.

3.2.8 Space Arrangements. The Owner shall provide suitable space for the receipt, inspection and storage of materials, furniture, furnishings and equipment.

3.2.9 Removal of Existing Facilities. The Owner shall be responsible for the relocation or removal of existing facilities, furniture, furnishings and equipment, and the contents thereof, unless otherwise provided by this Agreement.

3.2.10 Responsibility for Services. The drawings, specifications, services, information, surveys and reports required of the Owner under the Agreement shall be furnished at the Owner's expense, and the Architect shall be entitled to rely upon the accuracy and completeness thereof.

3.2.11 Certificates and Certifications. The proposed language of certificates or certifications requested of the Architect or Architect's consultants shall be submitted to the Architect for review and approval at least 14 days prior to execution. The Owner shall not request certifications that would require knowledge or services of the Architect or the Architect's Consultants beyond the scope of this Agreement.

3.2.12 Communications and Security Systems. The Owner shall contract for all temporary and permanent telephone, communications and security systems required for the Project so as not to delay the performance of the Architect's services.

ARTICLE 3.3

CONTRACT ADMINISTRATION

3.3.1 General. The following terms and conditions shall apply to the relevant Contract Administration Phase services, if any, as may be included in the Schedule of Designated Services.

3.3.1.1 Interpretations and Decisions: Timing. To the extent that the following services of the Architect have been designated in the Schedule of Designated Services, the Architect shall interpret and decide matters concerning performance of the Owner and Contractor under the requirements of the Contract Documents on written request of either the Owner or Contractor. The Architect's response to such requests shall be made with reasonable promptness and within any time limits agreed upon.

3.3.1.2 Interpretations and Decisions: Form and Intent. Interpretations and decisions of the Architect shall be consistent with the intent of and reasonably inferable from the Contract Documents and shall be in writing or in the form of drawings. When making such interpretations and initial decisions, the Architect shall endeavor to secure faithful performance by both Owner and Contractor, shall not show partiality to either, and shall not be liable for the results of interpretations or decisions so rendered in good faith.

3.3.1.3 Decisions on Aesthetic Effect. The Architect's decisions on matters relating to aesthetic effect shall be final if consistent with the intent expressed in the Contract Documents.

3.3.1.4 Architect's Decisions Subject to Arbitration. The Architect's decisions on claims, disputes or other matters, including those in question between the Owner and Contractor, except for those relating to aesthetic effect as provided in Clause 3.3.1.3, shall be subject to arbitration as provided in this Agreement and in the Contract Documents.

3.3.2 Duration of Contract Administration Phase. The Architect's responsibility to provide services for the Contract Administration Phase under this Agreement commences with the award of the initial Contract for Construction or for Furniture, Furnishings and Equipment, and terminates at the earlier of the issuance to the Owner of the final Certificate for Payment or 60 days after the date of Substantial Completion of the Work.

3.3.3 Contract(s) for the Work. The Architect shall provide administration of Contract(s) for Construction or Furniture, Furnishings and Equipment as set forth below and in the edition of AIA Document A201, General Conditions of the Contract for Construction, or AIA Document A271, General Conditions of the Contract for Furniture, Furnishings and Equipment, current as of the date of this Agreement.

3.3.4 Modification of Responsibilities. Duties, responsibilities, and limitations of authority of the Architect shall not be restricted, modified or extended without written agreement of the Owner and Architect with the consent of the Contractor; which consent shall not be unreasonably withheld.

3.3.5 Authority of Architect. The Architect shall be a representative of and shall advise and consult with the Owner (1) during the Contract Administration Phase, and (2) by an amendment to this Agreement, from time to time during the correction period described in the Contract for Construction. The Architect shall have authority to act on behalf of the Owner only to the extent provided in this Agreement unless otherwise modified by written instrument.

3.3.6 CONSTRUCTION OBSERVATION SERVICES

3.3.6.1 Architect's Responsibility for Observation. On the basis of on-site observations as an architect, the Architect shall keep the Owner informed of the progress and quality of the Work, and shall endeavor to guard the Owner against defects and deficiencies in the Work. The Architect shall not be required to make exhaustive or continuous on-site inspections to check the quality or quantity of the Work.

3.3.6.2 Project Representation. The furnishing of Project representation services shall not modify the rights, responsibilities or obligations of the Architect as described elsewhere in this Agreement.

3.3.6.3 Means and Methods. The Architect shall not have control over or charge of and shall not be responsible for construction means, methods, techniques, sequences or procedures, or for safety precautions and programs in connection with the Work, since these are solely the Contractor's responsibility under the Contract for Construction and the Contract for Furniture, Furnishings and Equipment. The Architect shall not be responsible for the Contractor's schedules or failure to carry out the Work in accordance with the Contract Documents. The Architect shall not have control over or charge of acts or omissions of the Contractor, Subcontractors, or their agents or employees, or of any other persons performing portions of the Work.

3.3.6.4 Access to Work. The Architect shall at all times have access to the Work wherever it is in preparation or progress.

3.3.6.5 Communications. Except as may otherwise be provided in the Contract Documents or when direct communications have been specially authorized, the Owner and Contractor shall communicate through the Architect. Communications by and with the Architect's consultants shall be through the Architect.

3.3.6.6 Minor Changes. The Architect may authorize minor changes in the Work not involving an adjustment in Contract Sum or an extension of the Contract Time which are not inconsistent with the intent of the Contract Documents.

3.3.6.7 Coordination of Furniture, Furnishings and Equipment Delivery and Installation. When the Architect assists the Owner in coordinating schedules for delivery and installation of furniture, furnishings and equipment, the Architect shall not be responsible for malfeasance, neglect or failure of a Contractor, Subcontractor, Sub-subcontractor or material supplier to meet their schedules for completion or to perform their respective duties and responsibilities.

3.3.7 COST ACCOUNTING SERVICES

3.3.7.1 Certificates for Payment. If certification of the Contractor's Applications for Payment is required by this Agreement, the Architect's certification for payment shall constitute a representation to the Owner, based on the Architect's observations at the site as provided in Subparagraph 3.3.6.1 and on the data comprising the Contractor's Application for Payment, that the Work has progressed to the point indicated and that, to the best of the Architect's knowledge, information and belief, the quality of the Work is in accordance with the Contract Documents. The foregoing representations are subject to an evaluation of the Work for conformance with the Contract Documents upon Substantial Completion, to results of subsequent tests and inspections, to minor deviations from the Contract Documents correctable prior to completion and to specific qualifications expressed by the Architect.

3.3.7.2 Limitations. The issuance of a Certificate for Payment shall not be a representation that the Architect has (1) made exhaustive or continuous on-site inspections to check the quality or quantity of the Work, (2) reviewed means, methods, techniques, sequences or procedures, (3) reviewed copies of requisitions received from Subcontractors and material suppliers and other data requested by the Owner to substantiate the Contractor's right to payment or (4) ascertained how or for what purpose the Contractor has used money previously paid on account of the Contract Sum.

3.3.8 INSPECTION AND TESTING ADMINISTRATION SERVICES

3.3.8.1 Rejection of Work. Except as provided in Subparagraph 3.3.8.3, the Architect shall have authority to reject Work which does not conform to the Contract Documents. Whenever the Architect considers it necessary or advisable for implementation of the intent of the Contract Documents, the Architect will have authority to require additional inspection or testing of the Work in accordance with the provisions of the Contract Documents, whether or not such Work is fabricated, installed or completed. However, neither this authority of the Architect nor a decision made in good faith either to exercise or not to exercise such authority shall give rise to a duty or responsibility of the Architect to the Contractor, Subcontractors, material and equipment suppliers, their agents or employees or other persons performing portions of the Work.

3.3.8.2 Review and Inspection of Work. The Architect shall review final placement and inspect for damage, quality, assembly and function in order to determine that furniture, furnishings and equipment are in accordance with the requirements of the Contract Documents.

3.3.8.3 Rejection of Work Involving Furniture, Furnishings and Equipment. Unless otherwise designated, the Architect's duties shall not extend to the receipt, inspection and acceptance on behalf of the Owner of furniture, furnishings and equipment at the time of their delivery to the premises and installation. The Architect is not authorized to reject nonconforming furniture, furnishings and equipment, sign Change Orders on behalf of the Owner, stop the Work, or terminate a Contract on behalf of the Owner. However, the Architect shall recommend to the Owner rejection of furniture, furnishings and equipment which does not conform to the Contract Documents. Whenever the Architect considers it necessary or advisable for implementation of the intent of the Contract Documents, the Architect will have authority to require additional inspection or testing of furniture, furnishings and equipment in accordance with the provisions of the Contract Documents, whether or not such furniture, furnishings and equipment is fabricated, installed or completed.

3.3.9 SUBMITTAL SERVICES

3.3.9.1 Submittal Review. To the extent required by this Agreement, the Architect shall review and approve or take other appropriate action upon Contractor's submittals such as Shop Drawings, Product Data and Samples, but only for the limited purpose of checking for conformance with information given and the design concept expressed in the Contract Documents. The Architect's action shall be taken with such reasonable promptness as to cause no delay in the Work or in the construction of the Owner or of separate contractors, while allowing sufficient time in the Architect's professional judgment to permit adequate review.

3.3.9.2 Limitations. Review of such submittals is not conducted for the purpose of determining the accuracy and completeness of other details such as dimensions and quantities or for substantiating instructions for installation or performance of equipment or systems designed by the Contractor, all of which remain the responsibility of the Contractor to the extent required by the Contract Documents. The Architect's review shall not constitute approval of safety precautions or, unless otherwise specifically stated by the Architect, of construction means, methods, techniques, sequences or procedures. The Architect's approval of a specific item shall not indicate approval of an assembly of which the item is a component.

3.3.10 Reliance on Professional Certification. When professional certification of performance characteristics of materials, systems or equipment is required by the Contract Documents, the Architect shall be entitled to rely upon such certification to establish that the materials, systems or equipment will meet the performance criteria required by the Contract Documents.

ARTICLE 3.4

USE OF PROJECT DRAWINGS, SPECIFICATIONS AND OTHER DOCUMENTS

3.4.1 Architect's Reserved Rights. The Drawings, Specifications and other documents prepared by the Architect for this Project are instruments of the Architect's service for use solely with respect to this Project and, unless otherwise provided, the Architect shall be deemed the author of these documents and shall retain all common law, statutory and other reserved rights, including the copyright.

3.4.2 Limitations on Use. The Owner shall be permitted to retain copies, including reproducible copies, of the Project Drawings, Specifications and other documents for information and reference in connection with the Owner's use and occupancy of the Project. The Project Drawings, Specifications or other documents shall not be used by the Owner or others on other projects, for additions to this Project or for completion of this Project by others, unless the Architect is adjudged to be in default under this Agreement, except by agreement in writing and with appropriate compensation to the Architect.

3.4.3 Unpublished Works. Submission or distribution of documents to meet official regulatory requirements or for similar purposes in connection with the Project is not to be construed as publication in derogation of the Architect's reserved rights.

ARTICLE 3.5

COST OF THE WORK

3.5.1 DEFINITION

3.5.1.1 Total Cost. The Cost of the Work shall be the total cost or estimated cost to the Owner of all elements of the Project to be included in the Contract Documents.

3.5.1.2 Items Included. The Cost of the Work shall include the cost at current market rates of labor and materials furnished by the Owner and equipment designated, specified, selected or specially provided for by the Architect in the Contract Documents, including the cost of the Contractor's management or supervision of construction or installation, plus a reasonable allowance for the Contractor's overhead and profit. In addition, a reasonable allowance for contingencies shall be included for market conditions at the time of bidding and for changes in the Work during construction.

3.5.1.3 Items Excluded. The Cost of the Work does not include the compensation of the Architect and the Owner's or Architect's consultants, the costs of the land, rights-of-way, financing or other costs which are the responsibility of the Owner as provided in Article 3.2.

3.5.2 RESPONSIBILITY FOR COST OF THE WORK

3.5.2.1 Limitation of Responsibility. Evaluations of the Owner's Project budget, preliminary estimates of the Cost of the Work and detailed estimates of the Cost of the Work, if any, prepared by the Architect, represent the Architect's best judgment as a design professional familiar with the construction industry. It is recognized, however, that neither the Architect nor the Owner has control over the cost of labor, materials or equipment, over the Contractor's methods of determining bid prices, or over competitive bidding, market or negotiating conditions. Accordingly, the Architect cannot and does not warrant or represent that bids or negotiated prices will not vary from the Owner's Project budget or from any estimate of the Cost of the Work or evaluation prepared or agreed to by the Architect.

3.5.2.2 Fixed Limit of the Cost of the Work. If a fixed limit on the Cost of the Work has been established, the Architect shall be permitted to include contingencies for design, bidding and price escalation, to determine what materials, furniture, furnishings and equipment, component systems and types of construction are to be included in the Contract Documents, to make reasonable adjustments in the scope of the Project and to include in the Contract Documents alternate bids to adjust the Cost of the Work to the fixed limit. Fixed limits, if any, shall be increased in the amount of an increase in the Contract Sum occurring after execution of the Contract for Construction.

3.5.2.3 Adjustments. If the Bidding or Negotiation Phase has not commenced within 90 days after the Contract Documents are submitted to the Owner, the Project budget or fixed limit of the Cost of the Work shall be adjusted to reflect changes in the general level of prices in the construction industry between the date of submission of the Contract Documents to the Owner and the date on which bids or negotiated proposals are sought.

3.5.2.4 Owner's Responsibility to Meet Fixed Limit. If a fixed limit of the Cost of the Work (adjusted as provided in Subparagraph 3.5.2.3) is exceeded by the lowest bona fide bid or negotiated proposal, the Owner shall:

  .1 give written approval of an increase in such fixed limit;

  .2 authorize rebidding or renegotiation of the Project within a reasonable time;

  .3 if the Project is abandoned, terminate in accordance with Paragraph 3.9; or

  .4 cooperate in revising the Project scope and quality as required to reduce the Construction Cost.

3.5.2.5 Architect's Responsibility to Meet Fixed Limit. If the Owner chooses to proceed under Clause 3.5.2.4.4, the Architect, without additional compensation, shall modify the documents that the Architect is responsible for preparing under the Designated Services portion of this Agreement as necessary to comply with the fixed limit. The modification of such documents shall be the limit of the Architect's responsibility arising out of the establishment of a fixed limit. The Architect shall be entitled to compensation in accordance with this Agreement for all services performed whether or not the Construction Phase is commenced.

ARTICLE 3.6

PAYMENTS TO THE ARCHITECT

3.6.1 Direct Personnel Expense. Direct Personnel Expense is defined as the direct salaries of the Architect's personnel engaged on the Project and the portion of the cost of their mandatory and customary contributions and benefits related thereto, such as employment taxes and other statutory employee benefits, insurance, sick leave, holidays, vacations, pensions and similar contributions and benefits.

3.6.2 Reimbursable Expenses. Reimbursable Expenses are in addition to compensation for the Architect's services and include expenses incurred by the Architect and Architect's employees and consultants in the interest of the Project, as identified in the following Clauses:

.1 transportation in connection with the Project, authorized out-of-town travel, long-distance communications, and fees paid for securing approval of authorities having jurisdiction over the Project;

.2 reproductions, postage and handling of Drawings, Specifications and other documents;

.3 facsimile services, courier services, overnight deliveries or other similar project-related expenditures;

.4 if authorized in advance by the Owner, expense of overtime work requiring higher than regular rates;

.5 renderings, models and mock-ups requested by the Owner;

.6 additional insurance coverage or limits, including professional liability insurance, requested by the Owner in excess of that normally carried by the Architect and Architect's consultants; and

.7 Expense of computer-aided design and drafting equipment time when used in connection with the Project.

3.6.3 Payments for Contingent Additional Services and Reimbursable Expenses. Payments on account of the Architect's Contingent Additional Services and for Reimbursable Expenses shall be made monthly upon presentation of the Architect's statement of services rendered or expenses incurred.

3.6.4 Extended Time. If and to the extent that the time initially established in this Agreement is exceeded or extended through no fault of the Architect, compensation for any services rendered during the additional period of time shall be computed in the manner set forth in Article 1.6.

3.6.5 Changes Affecting Percentage Compensation Method. When compensation is based on a percentage of Construction Cost and any portions of the Project are deleted or otherwise not constructed, compensation for those portions of the Project shall be payable to the extent services are

performed on those portions, in accordance with the schedule set forth in Part 1, Subparagraph 1.3.2, based on (1) the lowest bona fide bid or negotiated proposal, or (2) if no such bid or proposal is received, the most recent preliminary estimate of Construction Cost or detailed estimate of Construction Cost for such portions of the Project.

3.6.6 Payments Withheld. No deductions shall be made from the Architect's compensation on account of penalty, liquidated damages or other sums withheld from payments to contractors, or on account of the cost of changes in the Work other than those for which the Architect has been found to be liable.

3.6.7 Architect's Accounting Records. Records of Reimbursable Expenses, of expenses pertaining to Contingent Additional Services, and of services performed on the basis of a multiple of Direct Personnel Expense shall be available to the Owner or the Owner's authorized representative at mutually convenient times.

ARTICLE 3.7

DISPUTE RESOLUTION

3.7.1 Claims and Disputes. Claims, disputes or other matters in question between the parties to this Agreement arising out of or relating to this Agreement or breach thereof shall be subject to and decided by mediation and arbitration in accordance with the Construction Industry Mediation and Arbitration Rules of the American Arbitration Association currently in effect.

3.7.2 Mediation. In addition to and prior to arbitration, the parties shall endeavor to settle disputes by mediation in accordance with the Construction Industry Mediation Rules of the American Arbitration Association currently in effect. Demand for mediation shall be filed in writing with the other party to this Agreement and with the American Arbitration Association. A demand for mediation shall be made within a reasonable time after the claim, dispute or other matter in question has arisen. In no event shall the demand for mediation be made after the date when institution of legal or equitable proceedings based on such claim, dispute or other matter in question would be barred by the applicable statute of repose or limitations.

3.7.3 Arbitration. Demand for arbitration shall be filed in writing with the other party to this Agreement and with the American Arbitration Association. A demand for arbitration shall be made within a reasonable time after the claim, dispute or other matter in question has arisen. In no event shall the demand for arbitration be made after the date when institution of legal or equitable proceedings based on such claim, dispute or other matter in question would be barred by the applicable statutes of repose or limitations.

3.7.4 Consolidation and Joinder. An arbitration pursuant to this paragraph may be joined with an arbitration involving common issues of law or fact between the Architect and any person or entity with whom the Architect has a contractual obligation to arbitrate disputes. No other arbitration arising out of or relating to this Agreement shall include, by consolidation, joinder or in any other manner, an additional person or entity not a party to this Agreement, except by written consent containing a specific reference to this Agreement signed by the Owner, Architect, and any other person or entity sought to be joined. Consent to arbitration involving an additional person or entity shall not constitute consent to arbitration of any claim, dispute or other matter in question not described in the written consent or with a person or entity not named or described therein. The foregoing agreement to arbitrate and other agreements to arbitrate with an additional person or entity duly consented to by the parties to this Agreement shall be specifically enforceable in accordance with applicable law in any court having jurisdiction thereof.

3.7.5 Award. The award rendered by the arbitrator or arbitrators shall be final, and judgment may be entered upon it in accordance with applicable law in any court having jurisdiction thereof.

ARTICLE 3.8

MISCELLANEOUS PROVISIONS

3.8.1 Governing Law. This Agreement shall be governed by the law of the place of the Project.

3.8.2 Definitions. Terms in this Agreement shall have the same meaning as those in AIA Document A201, General Conditions of the Contract for Construction, and AIA Document A271, General Conditions of the Contract for Furniture, Furnishings and Equipment, current as of the date of this Agreement.

3.8.3 Statutes of Repose or Limitations. Causes of action between the parties to this Agreement pertaining to acts or failures to act shall be deemed to have accrued and the applicable statutes of repose or limitations shall commence to run not later than either the Date of Substantial Completion for acts or failures occurring prior to Substantial Completion, or the date of issuance of the final Certificate for Payment for acts or failures to act occurring after Substantial Completion.

3.8.4 Waivers of Subrogation. The Owner and the Architect waive all rights against each other and against the contractors, consultants, agents and employees of the other for damages, but only to the extent covered by property insurance during construction, except such rights as they may have to the proceeds of such insurance as set forth in the editions of AIA Document A201, General Conditions of the Contract for Construction, and AIA Document A271, General Conditions of the Contract for Furniture, Furnishings and Equipment, current as of the date of this Agreement. The Owner and Architect shall each require similar waivers from their contractors, consultants and agents.

3.8.5 Successors and Assigns. The Owner and Architect, respectively, bind themselves, their partners, successors, assigns and legal representatives to the other party to this Agreement and to the partners, successors, assigns and legal representatives of such other party with respect to all covenants of this Agreement. Neither Owner nor Architect shall assign this Agreement without the written consent of the other.

3.8.6 Titles and Headings. The titles and headings in this Agreement are for convenience and shall not be interpreted as

supplementing or superseding the intent of the parties as expressed in the body of this Agreement.

3.8.7 Third Parties. Nothing contained in this Agreement shall create a contractual relationship with or a cause of action in favor of a third party against either the Owner or Architect.

3.8.8 Hazardous Materials. Unless otherwise provided in this Agreement, the Architect and Architect's consultants shall have no responsibility for the discovery, presence, handling, removal or disposal of or exposure of persons to hazardous materials or toxic substances in any form at the Project site. If the Architect is required to perform services related to hazardous materials, the Owner agrees to indemnify and hold harmless the Architect, the Architect's consultants and their agents and employees from and against any and all claims, damages, losses and expenses, including but not limited to attorneys' fees, arising out of or resulting from performance of services by the Architect, the Architect's consultants or their agents or employees related to such services, except where such liability arises from the sole negligence or willful misconduct of the person or entity seeking indemnification.

3.8.9 Publicity. The Architect shall have the right to include representations of the design of the Project, including photographs of the exterior and interior, among the Architect's promotional and professional materials. The Architect's materials shall not include the Owner's confidential or proprietary information if the Owner has previously advised the Architect in writing of the specific information considered by the Owner to be confidential or proprietary. The Owner shall provide professional credit for the Architect on the construction sign and in the promotional materials for the Project.

3.8.10 Conflict of Interest. Except with the Owner's knowledge and consent, the Architect shall not (1) accept trade discounts, (2) have a substantial direct or indirect financial interest in the Project, or (3) undertake any activity or employment or accept any contribution, if it would reasonably appear that such activity, employment, interest or contribution could compromise the Architect's professional judgment or prevent the Architect from serving the best interest of the Owner

ARTICLE 3.9

TERMINATION, SUSPENSION OR ABANDONMENT

3.9.1 Termination for Breach. This Agreement may be terminated by either party upon not less than seven days' written notice should the other party fail substantially to perform in accordance with the terms of this Agreement, through no fault of the party initiating the termination. Failure of the Owner to make payments to the Architect in accordance with this Agreement shall be considered substantial nonperformance and cause for termination.

3.9.2 Suspension. If the Project is suspended by the Owner for more than 30 consecutive days, the Architect shall be compensated for services performed prior to notice of such suspension. When the Project is resumed, the Architect's compensation shall be equitably adjusted to provide for expenses incurred in the interruption and resumption of the Architect's services.

B163—1993   31

241

3.9.3 Termination on Abandonment. This Agreement may be terminated by the Owner upon not less than seven days' written notice to the Architect in the event that the Project is permanently abandoned. If the Project is abandoned by the Owner for more than 90 consecutive days, the Architect may terminate this Agreement by giving written notice to the Owner.

3.9.4 Failure of the Owner to make payments to the Architect in accordance with this Agreement shall be considered substantial nonperformance and cause for termination.

3.9.5 Suspension by Architect. If the Owner fails to make payment when due the Architect for services and expenses, the Architect may, upon seven days' written notice to the Owner, suspend performance of services under this Agreement. Unless payment in full is received by the Architect within seven days of the date of the notice, the suspension shall take effect without further notice. In the event of a suspension of services, the Architect shall have no liability to the Owner for delay or damage caused the Owner because of such suspension of services.

3.9.6 Compensation of Architect. In the event of termination not the fault of the Architect, the Architect shall be compensated for services performed prior to termination, together with Reimbursable Expenses then due and all Termination Expenses as defined in Subparagraph 3.9.7.

3.9.7 Termination Expenses. Termination expenses are in addition to compensation for the Architect's services, and include expenses which are directly attributable to termination. Termination Expenses shall be computed as a percentage of the total compensation for all services earned to the time of termination, as follows:

.1 Twenty percent of the total compensation for all services earned to date if termination occurs before or during the Predesign, Site Analysis or Schematic Design Phases; or

.2 Ten percent of the total compensation for all services earned to date if termination occurs during the Design Development Phase; or

.3 Five percent of the total compensation for all services earned to date if termination occurs during any subsequent phase.

AIA DOCUMENT B163 • OWNER-ARCHITECT AGREEMENT FOR DESIGNATED SERVICES
AIA® • ©1993 • THE AMERICAN INSTITUTE OF ARCHITECTS, 1735 NEW YORK AVENUE,
N.W., WASHINGTON, D.C. 20006-5292 • **WARNING: Unlicensed photocopying
violates U.S. copyright laws and will subject the violator to legal prosecution.**

Appendix II

AIA Document B727, *Standard Form of Agreement Between owner and Architect for Special Services,* 1988.

SAMPLE

1/88

AIA Document B163

Standard Form of Agreement Between Owner and Architect with Descriptions of Designated Services and Terms and Conditions

THIS DOCUMENT HAS IMPORTANT LEGAL CONSEQUENCES; CONSULTATION WITH AN ATTORNEY IS ENCOURAGED WITH RESPECT TO ITS COMPLETION OR MODIFICATION.

1993 EDITION

TABLE OF ARTICLES

PART 1—FORM OF AGREEMENT

ARTICLE 1.1   SCHEDULE OF DESIGNATED SERVICES
ARTICLE 1.2   COMPENSATION
ARTICLE 1.3   PAYMENTS
ARTICLE 1.4   TIME AND COST
ARTICLE 1.5   ENUMERATION OF DOCUMENTS
ARTICLE 1.6   OTHER CONDITIONS OR SERVICES

PART 2—DESCRIPTIONS OF DESIGNATED SERVICES

ARTICLE 2.1   DESIGNATED SERVICES
ARTICLE 2.2   PHASES OF DESIGNATED SERVICES
ARTICLE 2.3   DESCRIPTIONS OF DESIGNATED SERVICES
ARTICLE 2.4   DESCRIPTIONS OF SUPPLEMENTAL SERVICES

PART 3—TERMS AND CONDITIONS

ARTICLE 3.1   ARCHITECT'S RESPONSIBILITIES
ARTICLE 3.2   OWNER'S RESPONSIBILITIES
ARTICLE 3.3   CONTRACT ADMINISTRATION
ARTICLE 3.4   USE OF PROJECT DRAWINGS, SPECIFICATIONS AND OTHER DOCUMENTS
ARTICLE 3.5   COST OF THE WORK
ARTICLE 3.6   PAYMENTS TO THE ARCHITECT
ARTICLE 3.7   DISPUTE RESOLUTION
ARTICLE 3.8   MISCELLANEOUS PROVISIONS
ARTICLE 3.9   TERMINATION, SUSPENSION OR ABANDONMENT

B163—1993   1

Copies of the current edition of this AIA document may be purchased from The American Institute of Architects or its local distributors. The text of this document is not "model language" and is not intended for use in other documents without permission of the AIA.

AIA Document B727

Standard Form of Agreement Between Owner and Architect

for Special Services

1988 EDITION

THIS DOCUMENT HAS IMPORTANT LEGAL CONSEQUENCES; CONSULTATION WITH AN ATTORNEY IS ENCOURAGED WITH RESPECT TO ITS COMPLETION OR MODIFICATION.

AGREEMENT

made as of the   day of   in the year of
Nineteen Hundred and

BETWEEN the Owner:
(Name and address)

and the Architect:
(Name and address)

For the following Project:
(Include detailed description of Project, location, address and scope.)

The Owner and the Architect agree as set forth below.

AIA DOCUMENT B727 • OWNER-ARCHITECT AGREEMENT • 1988 EDITION • AIA® • ©1988 • THE AMERICAN INSTITUTE OF ARCHITECTS, 1735 NEW YORK AVENUE, N.W., WASHINGTON, D.C. 20006

B727-1988 1

ARTICLE 1
ARCHITECT'S SERVICES

(Here list those services to be provided by the Architect under the Terms and Conditions of this Agreement. Note under each service listed the method and means of compensation to be used, if applicable, as provided in Article 8.)

TERMS AND CONDITIONS OF AGREEMENT BETWEEN OWNER AND ARCHITECT

ARTICLE 2
OWNER'S RESPONSIBILITIES

2.1 The Owner shall provide full information regarding requirements for the Project. The Owner shall furnish required information as expeditiously as necessary for the orderly progress of the Work, and the Architect shall be entitled to rely on the accuracy and completeness thereof.

2.2 The Owner shall designate a representative authorized to act on the Owner's behalf with respect to the Project. The Owner or such authorized representative shall render decisions in a timely manner pertaining to documents submitted by the Architect in order to avoid unreasonable delay in the orderly and sequential progress of the Architect's services.

ARTICLE 3
USE OF ARCHITECT'S DOCUMENTS

3.1 The documents prepared by the Architect for this Project are instruments of the Architect's service for use solely with respect to this Project and, unless otherwise provided, the Architect shall be deemed the author of these documents and shall retain all common law, statutory and other reserved rights, including the copyright. The Owner shall be permitted to retain copies, including reproducible copies, of the Architect's documents for the Owner's information, reference and use in connection with the Project. The Architect's documents shall not be used by the Owner or others on other projects, for additions to this Project or for completion of this Project by others, unless the Architect is adjudged to be in default under this Agreement, except by agreement in writing and with appropriate compensation to the Architect.

ARTICLE 4
ARBITRATION

4.1 Claims, disputes or other matters in question between the parties to this Agreement arising out of or relating to this Agreement or breach thereof shall be subject to and decided by arbitration in accordance with the Construction Industry Arbitration Rules of the American Arbitration Association currently in effect unless the parties mutually agree otherwise.

4.2 A demand for arbitration shall be made within a reasonable time after the claim, dispute or other matter in question has arisen. In no event shall the demand for arbitration be made after the date when institution of legal or equitable proceedings based on such claim, dispute or other matter in question would be barred by the applicable statutes of limitations.

4.3 No arbitration arising out of or relating to this Agreement shall include, by consolidation, joinder or in any other manner, an additional person or entity not a party to this Agreement, except by written consent containing a specific reference to this Agreement signed by the Owner, Architect and any other person or entity sought to be joined. Consent to arbitration involving an additional person or entity shall not constitute consent to arbitration of any claim, dispute or other

matter in question not described in the written consent or with a person or entity not named or described therein. The foregoing agreement to arbitrate and other agreements to arbitrate with an additional person or entity duly consented to by the parties to this Agreement shall be specifically enforceable in accordance with applicable law in any court having jurisdiction thereof.

4.4 The award rendered by the arbitrator or arbitrators shall be final, and judgment may be entered upon it in accordance with applicable law in any court having jurisdiction thereof.

ARTICLE 5
TERMINATION OR SUSPENSION

5.1 This Agreement may be terminated by either party upon not less than seven days' written notice should the other party fail substantially to perform in accordance with the terms of this Agreement through no fault of the party initiating the termination.

5.2 If the Owner fails to make payment when due the Architect for services and expenses, the Architect may, upon seven days' written notice to the Owner, suspend performance of services under this Agreement. Unless payment in full is received by the Architect within seven days of the date of the notice, the suspension shall take effect without further notice. In the event of a suspension of services, the Architect shall have no liability to the Owner for delay or damage caused the Owner because of such suspension of services.

5.3 In the event of termination not the fault of the Architect, the Architect shall be compensated for services performed prior to termination, together with Reimbursable Expenses then due and all Termination Expenses as defined in Paragraph 5.4.

5.4 Termination Expenses shall be computed as a percentage of the compensation earned to the time of termination, as follows:

   .1 For services provided on the basis of a multiple of Direct Personnel Expense, 20 percent of the total Direct Personnel Expense incurred to the time of termination; and

   .2 For services provided on the basis of a stipulated sum, 10 percent of the stipulated sum earned to the time of termination.

ARTICLE 6
MISCELLANEOUS PROVISIONS

6.1 Unless otherwise provided, this Agreement shall be governed by the law of the principal place of business of the Architect.

6.2 Causes of action between the parties to this Agreement pertaining to acts or failures to act shall be deemed to have accrued and the applicable statute of limitations shall commence to run not later than the date payment is due the Architect pursuant to Paragraph 8.4.

AIA DOCUMENT B727 • OWNER-ARCHITECT AGREEMENT • 1988 EDITION • AIA® • ©1988 • THE AMERICAN INSTITUTE OF ARCHITECTS, 1735 NEW YORK AVENUE, N.W., WASHINGTON, D.C. 20006

B727-1988   3

6.3 The Owner and Architect, respectively, bind themselves, their partners, successors, assigns and legal representatives to the other party to this Agreement and to the partners, successors, assigns and legal representatives of such other party with respect to all covenants of this Agreement. Neither Owner nor Architect shall assign this Agreement without the written consent of the other.

6.4 This Agreement represents the entire and integrated agreement between the Owner and Architect and supersedes all prior negotiations, representations or agreements, either written or oral. This Agreement may be amended only by written instrument signed by both Owner and Architect.

6.5 Nothing contained in this Agreement shall create a contractual relationship with or a cause of action in favor of a third party against either the Owner or Architect.

6.6 Unless otherwise provided in this Agreement, the Architect and Architect's consultants shall have no responsibility for the discovery, presence, handling, removal or disposal of or exposure of persons to hazardous materials in any form at the Project site, including but not limited to asbestos, asbestos products, polychlorinated biphenyl (PCB) or other toxic substances.

ARTICLE 7
PAYMENTS TO THE ARCHITECT

7.1 DIRECT PERSONNEL EXPENSE

7.1.1 Direct Personnel Expense is defined as the direct salaries of the Architect's personnel engaged on the Project and the portion of the cost of their mandatory and customary contributions and benefits related thereto, such as employment taxes and other statutory employee benefits, insurance, sick leave, holidays, vacations, pensions, and similar contributions and benefits.

7.2 REIMBURSABLE EXPENSES

7.2.1 Reimbursable Expenses are in addition to the Architect's compensation and include expenses incurred by the Architect and Architect's employees and consultants in the interest of the Project for:

.1 expense of transportation and living expenses in connection with out-of-town travel authorized by the Owner;

.2 long-distance communications;

.3 fees paid for securing approval of authorities having jurisdiction over the Project;

.4 reproductions;

.5 postage and handling of documents;

.6 expense of overtime work requiring higher than regular rates, if authorized by the Owner;

.7 renderings and models requested by the Owner;

.8 expense of additional coverage or limits, including professional liability insurance, requested by the Owner in excess of that normally carried by the Architect and the Architect's consultants; and

.9 Expense of computer-aided design and drafting equipment time when used in connection with the Project.

7.3 PAYMENTS ON ACCOUNT OF THE ARCHITECT'S SERVICES

7.3.1 Payments on account of the Architect's services and for Reimbursable Expenses shall be made monthly upon presentation of the Architect's statement of services rendered or as otherwise provided in this Agreement.

7.3.2 An initial payment as set forth in Paragraph 8.1 is the minimum payment under this Agreement.

7.4 ARCHITECT'S ACCOUNTING RECORDS

7.4.1 Records of Reimbursable Expenses and expenses pertaining to services performed on the basis of a multiple of Direct Personnel Expense shall be available to the Owner or the Owner's authorized representative at mutually convenient times.

ARTICLE 8
BASIS OF COMPENSATION

The Owner shall compensate the Architect as follows:

8.1 AN INITIAL PAYMENT OF   Dollars ($) shall be made upon execution of this Agreement and credited to the Owner's account at final payment.

8.2 COMPENSATION FOR THE ARCHITECT'S SERVICES, as described in Article 1, Architect's Services, shall be computed as follows:

(Insert basis of compensation, including stipulated sums, multiples or percentages, and identify the services to which particular methods of compensation apply, if necessary.)

AIA DOCUMENT B727 • OWNER-ARCHITECT AGREEMENT • 1988 EDITION • AIA® • ©1988 • THE AMERICAN INSTITUTE OF ARCHITECTS, 1735 NEW YORK AVENUE, N.W. WASHINGTON, D.C. 20006

8.3 FOR REIMBURSABLE EXPENSES, as described in Article 7, and any other items included in Article 9 as Reimbursable Expenses, a multiple of (   ) times the expenses incurred by the Architect, the Architect's employees and consultants in the interest of the Project.

8.4 Payments are due and payable (   ) days from the date of the Architect's invoice. Amounts unpaid (   ) days after the invoice date shall bear interest at the rate entered below, or in the absence thereof, at the legal rate prevailing from time to time at the principal place of business of the Architect.

(Insert rate of interest agreed upon.)

(Usury laws and requirements under the Federal Truth in Lending Act, similar state and local consumer credit laws and other regulations at the Owner's and Architect's principal places of business, the location of the Project and elsewhere may affect the validity of this provision. Specific legal advice should be obtained with respect to deletions or modifications, and also regarding other requirements such as written disclosures or waivers.)

8.5 IF THE SCOPE of the Project or of the Architect's services is changed materially, the amounts of compensation shall be equitably adjusted.

ARTICLE 9
OTHER CONDITIONS

This Agreement entered into as of the day and year first written above.

OWNER   ARCHITECT

_____   _____
(Signature)   *(Signature)*

_____   _____
(Printed name and title)   *(Printed name and title)*

■ BIBLIOGRAPHY

I. Ethics in Business

American Society of Landscape Architects. *1993 Member Handbook*. Washington: ASLA, 1992.

Beauchamp, T. L., and N. E. Bowie. *Ethical Theory and Business*. Englewood Cliffs, N.J.: Prentice-Hall, 1979.

Beets, S. Douglas. "Personal Morals and Professional Ethics: A Review and an Empirical Examination of Public Accounting." *Business and Professional Ethics Journal*, 10, 2 (Summer 1991): 63–84.

Berney, Karen. "Finding the Ethical Edge." *Nation's Business*, 75 (August 1987): 18–19.

Caropreso, Frank. *Communications Strategies or Changing Times*. New York: Conference Board, 1991.

Dreilinger, Craig, and Dan Rice. "Office Ethics: Five Common Ethical Dilemmas and How to Resolve Them." *Working Woman*, 16 (December 1991): 35–38.

Drucker, Peter F. "Corporate Takeovers: What Is to Be Done?" *The Public Interest*, 82 (Winter 1986): 3–24.

Freeman, R. Edward, and Daniel R. Gilbert Jr. *Corporate Strategy and the Search for Ethics*. Englewood Cliffs, N.J.: Prentice-Hall, 1988.

Kelly, Charles M. *The Destructive Achiever: Power and Ethics in the American Corporation*. Reading, Mass.: Addison-Wesley, 1988.

Kuhn, James W., and Donald W. Shriver. *Beyond Success: Corporations and Their Critics in the 1990s*. New York: Oxford University Press, 1991.

March, James G., and Michael D. Cohen. *Leadership and Ambiguity: The American College President*, 2nd ed. Boston, Mass.: Harvard Business School Press, 1986.

MacIntyre, Alastair. *After Virtue: A Study in Moral Theory*, 2nd ed. Notre Dame, Ind.: University of Notre Dame Press, 1984.

Paul, Karen, ed. *Business Environment and Business Ethics: The Social Moral, and Political Dimensions of Management*. Cambridge, Mass.: Ballinger, 1987.

Sandroff, Ronni. "How Ethical is American Business?" *Working Woman*, 15 (September 1990): 113–114.

Smith, T.V. *The Ethics of Compromise and the Art of Containment*. Boston: Starr King Press, 1956.

Tuleja, Tad. *Beyond the Bottom Line: How Business Leaders Are Turning Principles into Profits*. New York: Facts on File, 1985.

II. Legal Considerations and Contracts

American Institute of Architects. "Construction Documents." In *Architect's Handbook of Professional Practice*, Vol. 2, Sec. 2.6. Washington: AIA, 1987.

——. *General Conditions of the Contract for Construction*, Document A201. Washington: AIA, 1987.

251

————. *Standard Form of Agreement Between Owner and Architect for Designated Services.* Document B163. Washington: AIA, 1993.

————. *Standard Form of Agreement Between Owner and Architect for Special Services.* Document B727. Washington: AIA, 1988.

Bennett, Bruce E. *Professional Liability and Risk Management.* Washington: American Psychological Association, 1990.

Brown, John Prather. "Toward an Economic Theory of Liability." *Journal of Legal Studies,* II, 2 (1973): 323–349.

Cable, Carole. *The Architect, Liability Law, and Insurance: A Bibliography of Articles Published 1971–1981.* Monticello, Ill.: Vance Bibliographies, 1987.

Carroll, Stephen J., with Nicholas Pace. *Assessing the Effects of Tort Reform.* Santa Monica, Calif.: Rand, Institute of Civil Justice, 1987.

Cecil, Ray. *Professional Liability.* London: Architectural Press, 1986.

Coplan, Norman. "Waiving Liens." *Progressive Architecture* (August 1989): Vol. LXX, No. 8 43–46.

David, Leon Thomas. *The Tort Liability of Public Officers.* Chicago, Ill.: Public Administration Service, 1940.

Duke University School of Law. *Home Financing.* Durham, N.C.: School of Law, Duke University, 1938.

Fordham, Jefferson B., and William T. Pegues. *Local Government Responsibility in Tort in Louisiana.* Baton Rouge, La.: Louisiana State University Press, 1941.

Gertz, Frederick A. *Construction Mechanics' and Materialmen's Lien: The Law in South Carolina.* Norcross, Ga.: Harrison, 1983.

Glazer, Steven A. "Dealing With Clients' Unpaid Bills: Mechanics' Lien Statutes." *Architectural Record,* 39 (March 1987).

Greenstreet, Bob and Karen. *The Architect's Guide to Law and Practice.* New York: Van Nostrand Reinhold, 1984.

Harrington, Scott E. "Fact versus Fiction on Advisory Rates." *Best's Review Property/Casualty Insurance Edition,* 90, 6 (October 1989): 56–60, 119.

Harrington, Scott, and Robert E. Litan. "Causes of the Liability Insurance Crisis." *Science,* 239, 4841 (February 12, 1988): 737–741.

Henderson, J., and T. Eisenberg. "The Quiet Revolution in Products Liability: An Empirical Study of Legal Change." *UCLA Law Review,* 37 (1990).

Hiltner, Arthur A., and John W. Gillett. *Professional Liability Insurance and the North Dakota CPA.* Grand Forks, N.D.: Bureau of Business and Economic Research, University of North Dakota, 1987.

Hinkel, Daniel F. *Construction Mechanics' and Materialmen's Lien: The Law in Georgia.* Norcross, Ga.: Harrison, 1978.

Huber, Peter W. *Liability: The Legal Revolution and Its Consequences.* New York: Basic Books, 1988.

Kornblut, Arthur. "Approving Payments for Off-Site Materials, Risky." *Architectural Record,* 39 (January 1984).

————. "Mechanics' Liens for Unpaid Architectural Fees." *Architectural Record,* 69 (November 1981).

Levinson, Daniel R. *Personal Liability of Managers and Supervisors for Corporate EEO Policies and Decisions.* Washington: Equal Employment Advisory Council, 1982.

McHarg, Ian L. *Design with Nature.* Garden City, N.Y.: Natural History Press, 1969. Republished New York: Wiley, 1992.

Ontario Association of Architects. *Legal Aspects of Architectural Practice.* Toronto: Ontario Association of Architects, 1963.

Pierce, R. "Institutional Aspects of Tort Reform." *California Law Review,* 78 (1985).

Priest, G. L. "The Continuing Crisis in Liability." *Products Liability Law Journal,* (October 1989).

Rose-Ackerman, Susan. "Market Share Allocations in Tort Law: Strength and Weaknesses." *Journal of Legal Studies,* 19, 2 (1990): 739–746.

Schuck, Peter H., ed. *Tort Law and the Public Interest: Competition, Innovation, and Consumer Welfare.* New York: Norton, 1991.

Shubert, Gustave H. *Some Observations on the Need for Tort Reform.* Santa Monica, Calf.: Institute for Civil Justice, 1986.

Streeter, Harrison. *Professional Liability of Architects and Engineers.* New York: Wiley, 1988.

United States. An act to provide for a uniform national three-year statute of limitations in actions to recover damages for personal injury of death, arising out of a maritime tort, and for other purposes. Washington: GPO, 1980.

———. Cong. House. Committee in the Judiciary. Subcommittee in Administrative Law and Governmental Relations. *Hearings on Legislation to Amend the Federal Tort Claims Act.* 100th Cong., 2nd. sess. H. Res. 4358, 3872, and 3083. Washington: GPO, 1988.

———. Department of the Treasury. Internal Revenue Service. *Handbook on Determining Statute of Limitations.* Washington: IRS, 1986.

III. Corporations

Baratz, Morton S. "Corporate Giants and the Power Structure." *Western Political Quarterly,* 9, 2, (June 1956): 406–415.

Encyclopedia of Corporate Meetings, Minutes, and Resolutions. Englewood Cliffs, N.J.: Prentice-Hall, 1978.

Green, Mark, ed., with Michael Waldman and Robert Massie Jr., eds. *The Big Business Reader: On Corporate America.* New York: Pilgrim Press, 1983.

Harper, John D. *A View of the Corporate Role in Society.* New York: Carnegie-Mellon University Press, 1977.

Krainin, Harold L. *What You Should Know About Operating Your Business as a Corporation.* Dobbs Ferry, N.Y.: Oceana Publications, 1967.

Read, William E. *Corporate Officer's and Director's Desk Book, with Model Documents, Agreements, and Forms.* Englewood Cliffs, N.J.: Prentice-Hall, 1980.

Rogers, David, and Zimet Nelvin. "The Corporation and the Community: Perspective and Recent Developments." In Ivar Berg, ed., *The Business of America.* New York: Harcourt, Brace and World, 1968.

Ross, Christopher, ed. *The Urban System and Networks of Corporate Control.* Greenwich, Conn.: JAI Press, 1991.

Rumelt, Richard P. *Strategy, Structure, and Economic Performance.* Boston: Harvard Business School Press, 1986.

Schwartz, Michael, ed. *The Structure of Power in America: The Corporate Elite as a Ruling Class.* New York: Holmes and Meier, 1987.

IV. Technical Specifications

Adams, Myron Whitlock. *A62 Guide for Modular Coordination: A Guide to Assist Architects and Engineers in Applying Modular Coordination to Building Plans and Details.* Boston: Modular Service Association, 1946.

Architectural Specifications. Berkeley, Calif.: Guidelines Publications, 1969.

Dyer, Ben H. *Specification Work Sheets.* Washington: American Institute of Architects, 1951.

Edwards, H. Griffith. *Specifications.* Princeton, N.J.: Van Nostrand, 1961.

Emerick, Robert H. *Handbook of Mechanical Specifications for Building and Plants: A Checklist for Engineers and Architects.* New York: McGraw-Hill, 1966.

Goldsmith, Goldwin. *Architects' Specifications: How to Write Them.* Washington: American Institute of Architects, 1948.

Joint Venture Architects. *Architectural Specifications and Related Documents: Block 258 Venture.* Houston: 1971.

Purdy, David. *A Guide to Writing Successful Engineering Specifications.* New York: McGraw-Hill, 1991.

Rosen, Harold J. *Specifications Guide: A Pertinent Compilation of Specification Information, Arranged in the CSI Format for Convenience.* Stamford, Conn.: Reinhold, 1970.

V. Personnel Compensation and Benefits

Balkin, David B., and Luis R. Gomez-Mejia, eds. *New Perspectives on Compensation.* Englewood Cliffs, N.J.: Prentice-Hall, 1987.

Bartley, Douglas L. *Job Evaluation: Wage and Salary Administration.* Reading, Mass.: Addison-Wesley, 1981.

Bullock, R. J., and E. E. Lawler. "Gainsharing: A Few Questions and Fewer Answers." *Human Resource Management,* 5 (1984): 197–212.

Caropreso, Frank, and Charles Peck, eds. *New Strategies and Innovations in Compensation.* New York: Conference Board, 1989.

Jahnston, R., and P. R. Lawrence. "Beyond Vertical Integration: The Rise of the Value-Adding Partnership." *Harvard Business Review,* 66, 4 (1988): 94–101.

Knetsch, Jack L. *Property Rights and Compensation: CompulsoryAcquisition and Other Losses.* Toronto: Butterworths, 1983.

Lawler, Edward E. Ill. *Strategic Pay: Aligning Organizational Strategies and Pay Systems.* San Francisco: Jossey-Bass, 1990.

McCaffery, Robert M. *Employee Benefit Programs: A Total Compensation Perspective.* Boston: PWS-Kent, 1988.

Mirvis, P. H., and E. E. Lawler. "Measuring the Financial Impact of Employee Attitudes." *Journal of Applied Psychology,* 62, 1 (1977): 1–8.

Smith, Ian G. *The Management of Remuneration: Paying for Effectiveness.* London: Institute of Personnel Management, and Aldershot, Hants/Gower, 1983.

VI. Office and Project Management

American Institute of Architects. *Architect's Handbook of Professional Practice.* David Haviland, ed. Washington: AIA, 1987.

Balderston, Jack. *Improving Office Operations: A Primer for Professionals.* New York: Van Nostrand Reinhold, 1985.

Ballast, David K. *Creative Records Management: A Guidebook for Architects, Engineers, and Interior Designers.* Newton, Mass.: Practice Management Institute, 1987.

Birchall, D. W., and V. J. Hammond. *Tomorrow's Office Today: Managing Technological Change.* New York: Wiley, 1981.

Burstein, David, and Frank Slasiowski. *Project Management for the Design Professional.* New York: Whitney Library of Design, 1982.

Coxe, W. "Charting Your Course: Master Strategies for Organizing and Managing Architectural Firms." *Architectural Technology* (May/June 1986).

Coxe, W. "Where Is the Practice Going?" In Fred A. Stitt, ed., *Design Office Management Handbook*. Santa Monica, Calif.: Arts and Architecture Press, 1986.

Foote, Rosslynn F. *Running an Office for Fun and Profit: Business Techniques for Small Design Firms*. Stroudsburg, Pa.: Dowden Hutchinson and Ross, 1978.

Getz, L. *Business Management in the Smaller Design Firm*. Newton, Mass.: Practice Management Associates, 1986.

Getz, Lowell, and Frank Stasiowski. *Financial Management for the Design Professional: A Handbook for Architects, Engineers and Interior Designers*. New York: Whitney Library of Design, 1984.

Herman Miller Research Corporation. *Everybody's Business: A Fund of Retrievable Ideas for Humanizing Life in the Office*. Zeeland, Mich.: Herman Miller Research Corporation, 1985.

Karner, Gary. *Contracting Design Services*. Washington: American Society of Landscape Architects, 1989.

Kish, Joseph L., Jr., with Keith Costello, Joel Culmone, and Margo Corson. *Office Management Problem Solver*. Radnor, Pa.: Chilton Book Company, 1983.

Long, Richard J. *New Office Information Technology: Human and Managerial Implications*. New York: Croom Helm, 1987.

Marshall, Lane L. *Landscape Architecture: Guidelines to Professional Practice*. Washington: American Society of Landscape Architects, 1981.

Ranney, J. M., and C. E. Carder. "Socio-Technical Design Methods in Office Settings: Two Cases." *Office: Technology and People,* 2 (1984): 169–186.

Rausch, Edward N. *Profitable Office Management for the Growing Business*. New York: American Management Association, 1984.

Schuck, Gloria. "Intelligent Technology, Intelligent Workers: A New Pedagogy for the High-Tech Work Place." *Organizational Dynamics,* 14, 2 (Autumn 1985): 66–79.

Scott, W. *Organizations: Rational, Natural and Open Systems,* 2nd ed. Englewood Cliffs, N.J.: Prentice-Hall, 1987.

Stasiowski, Frank. *Project Management Forms II*. Newton, Mass.: Practice Management Association, 1986.

Stitt, Fred A., ed. *Design Office Management Handbook*. Santa Monica, Calif.: Arts and Architecture Press, 1986.

Taylor, J. R. "Office Communications: Reshaping Our Society?" *Computer Communications,* 5 (1982): 174–180.

VII. Bookkeeping Systems

Alley, Brian. *Keeping Track of What You Spend: The Librarian's Guide to Simple Bookkeeping*. Phoenix, Ariz.: Oryx Press, 1982.

Cotton, John. *Keeping Records in Small Business*. Washington: U.S. Small Business Administration, Office of Business Development, 1988.

Eldridge, Herbert James. *The Evolution of the Science of Bookkeeping*. London: Gee, 1954.

Forkner, Hamden Landon. *The Teaching of Bookkeeping*. Cincinnati, Ohio: South-Western Publishing, 1960.

Hammer, Hy. *Bookkeeper, Account Clerk: The Complete Study Guide for Scoring High*. New York: Arco Press, 1983.

Ijiri, Yuji. *Momentum Accounting and Triple-Entry Bookkeeping: Exploring the Dynamic Structure of Accounting Measurements*. Sarasota, Fla.: American Accounting Association, 1989.

Mitchell, William. *A New and Complete System of Bookkeeping by an Improved Method of Double Entry.* New York: Arco Press, 1978.

VIII. Cash Flow Management

Cash Flow/Cash Management. San Francisco: Bank of America, 1984.

Glau, Gregory R. *Controlling Your Cash Flow with Jazz and the Macintosh.* Homewood, Ill.: Dow Jones-Irwin, 1986.

Hill, Roger W. *Cash Management Techniques.* New York: American Management Association, 1970.

Kelly, John M. *Cash Management.* New York: F. Watts, 1986.

Loscalzo, William. *Cash Flow Forecasting.* New York: McGraw-Hill, 1982.

Milling, Bryan E. *Business Survival: Strategies for an Uncertain Economy.* Radnor, Pa.: Chilton Book Company, 1983.

———. *Cash Flow Problem Solver, Procedures and Rationale for the Independent Business.* Radnor, Pa.: Chilton Book Company, 1984.

Nunes, Morris A. *Operational Cash Flow Management and Control.* Englewood Cliffs, N.J.: Prentice-Hall, 1982.

Peterson, Edward D. *Cash Management: A Guide to Increasing Profits.* Belmont, Calif.: Lifetime Learning, 1984.

Wilson, Frank C. *Managing Costs and Improving Cash Flow.* Homewood, Ill.: Dow Jones-Irwin, 1984.

IX. Marketing

Burden, E. *Design Presentation: Techniques for Marketing and Project Proposals.* New York: McGraw-Hill, 1984.

Comiskey, James C. *How to Start, Expand, and Sell a Business.* San Jose, Calif.: Venture Perspective Press, 1985.

Connor, R., and Davidson, J. *Marketing Your Consulting and Professional Services.* New York: Wiley, 1985.

Jones, G. *How to Market Professional Design Services.* New York: Wiley, 1985.

Kotler, Philip. *Marketing Management,* 6th ed. Englewood Cliffs, N.J.: PrenticeHall, 1988.

Kuriloff, Arthur H., and John M. Hemphill Jr. *How to Start Your Own Business and Succeed.* New York: McGraw-Hill, 1981.

Porter, Michael E. *Competitive Advantage: Creating and Sustaining Superior Performance.* New York: Free Press, 1985.

Rachman, David J. *Marketing Today.* New York: Dryden Press, 1985.

Sulzinger, Richard A., and C. Robert Clements. *Marketing Design Services: Principles, Management and Strategies for Landscape Architectural Practices.* Washington: Professional Practice Institute of the American Society of Landscape Architects, 1983.

X. General Interest

American Society of Landscape Architects. "State of the Profession: Education and Practice." *L.A. Letter,* 91, 1, (March 1991).

Cetron, Marvin, and Owen Davies. *The Gardening of America.* Radnor, Pa.: Chilton Press, 1991.

Cowan, S. W. *Job Search Manual for Students of the Design Professions.* Washington: American Society of Landscape Architects, 1986.

Laurie, Michael. *An Introduction to Landscape Architecture.* New York: American Elsevier, 1975.

Laudon, Kenneth C., and Jane Price Laudon. *Business Information Systems* Chicago, Ill.: Dryden Press, 1991.

Newton, Norman T. *Design on the Land: The Development of Lands cape Architecture.* Cambridge, Mass.: Belknap Press of Harvard University, 1971.

Tishler, William H, ed. *American Landscape Architecture: Designers and Places.* Washington: Preservation Press, 1988.

Tobey, G. B. *A History of Landscape Architecture: The Relationship of People to the Environment.* New York: American Elsevier, 1973.

White, Leslie A. *The Concept of Cultural Systems: A Key to Understanding Tribes and Nations.* New York: Columbia University Press, 1975.

A/E Services (Architectural-Engineering Services), 121
Academic:
  practice, 36–38
  preparation, 42
Accounting system, 107–108
Accredited degree, 19
Additional services, 174
Additive alternative, 184
Administrative and managerial plan, 106–111
Administrative law(s), 153, 156–157, 160
Advanced academic studies, 45
Altruistic endeavors, 46
American National Standards Institute (ANSI), 181
American Society of Landscape Architects (ASLA), 10, 47–50
American Society for Testing and Materials (ASTM), 181
Americans with Disabilities Act of 1991 (ADA), 161
Apprenticeship, 41, 44
Arbitration, 175
Areas of professional practice, 25–27, 31–39
As-built or record drawings, 150
As indicated, 185
Assessing the job market, 61
Assistant, 69
Associate, 69
Associated General Contractors, 173
Associates, ASLA, 50

Bachelor of Landscape Architecture, 43–44
Basic services, 142–143, 174, 186
Benefit package, 70
Benefits, 69, 110
Bid bonds, 166
Bid forms, 166
Bidding, 146–147, 162
Board of Trustees, ASLA, 48
Bond amount(s), 166
Bonding requirements, 166

Breach of contract, 152
Bridge Conference, ASLA, 83
Building codes, 161
Building permits, 161
Business law, 153–154
Business management records, 126
Business marketing, 114–121
Business plan, 99, 111–112
Business structure, 88

Career, 40
Central Park, 13
Certified payroll, 165
Chains of command, 168
Church, Thomas, 11
Civil law, 156
Client, 137, 140
  satisfaction, 28–29
Code of Conduct, 16
Codes, 153, 158
Commerce Business Daily, 106, 121
Competition, 101–102
Competitive advantage, 72
Concept(s), 81
Conditions and terms, 173
Confidentiality, 163
Constitution, 158
Construction:
  administration, 147
  contract, 187–188
  contract administration, 147–149
  documents, 146
  drawings, 178
  package, 136
  startup, 137
Construction Specification Institute (CSI), 181
Consultant, 78
Consultation, 78
Continuing education, 19, 52
Contract administration, 163
Contract(s), 171–176
  conditions, 187

Contract(s) (*Continued*)
  construction, 173, 187–188
  design services, 173
  negotiations, 187
  sample construction, 187
Contractor's performance, 164
Corporate laws, 91
Corporation, 91–92
Council of Education (COE), ASLA, 47
Council of Landscape Architectural
    Boards (CLARB), 51, 52
  CLARB certification, 51
Covenants, 162
Cross-referenced specification sections, 184
CSI Format, 182

Damages, 155
Deductive alternate, 184
Defective work, 167
Delegation of authority, 87
Deliverables, 115, 139
Descriptive specifications, 179
Design, 80–81
  development, 145–146
  intent, 164
  services contracts, 173
  solutions, 29
  standards, 161
Design-build, 10, 82
Designated services, 142
Disagreements, 155
Downing, Andrew Jackson, 8–9

Easements, 162
Eckbo, Garrett, 11
Eco-tourism, 31
Economic feasibility, 144
Effective date, 175
Emerging forms of practice, 38–39
Employee:
  recruitment, 109
  selection criteria, 58–59
Employer contacts, 67
English system, civil law, 156
Entry-level position, 44
Equal opportunity policy, 109
Errors and omissions insurance, 159
Estimate of probable construction costs,
    145
Ethics, 16–24
  code of, 17, 21
Executive Committee, ASLA, 48
Expert witness, 79

Farrand, Beatrix Jones, 10
Fees, 174
Fellows, ASLA, 50
Filing system(s), 131
Final payment, 149
Financial:
  accountability, 86
  management, 107–108
  plan, 104–105
  records, 126–127
Firm concept, 99
Fixed-fee basis, fees, 174
Flextime, 70
Foreign Associates, ASLA, 50

General business liability insurance, 159
General warranty, 162
Geographic market, 101
Government procurement regulations, 163
Green industry, 38

Halprin, Lawrence, 11–12
Hard copy documents, 123
Harvard University, 10, 19
Hiring criteria, 109
Historic preservation, 30–31

Incentive pay structure, 110
Industry standards, 182
Instruments:
  of practice, 28
  of service, 27, 123

Jefferson, Thomas, 8
Jensen, Jens, 10
Job:
  description, 68–69, 108–109
  market, 61
  offer, 68
  search, 55–68
    market-oriented approach, 55
    preparing for, 63–68
    process, 56–58
    solicited approach, 62
    unsolicited approach, 62–63
Joint venture, 92
Judicial jurisdiction, 175
Jurisdictional hierarchy, 157

Kiley, Dan, 11

Labor and materials payment bond, 167
Land-use controls, 160–161

Landscape Architect Registration
    Examination (LARE), 51–53
Landscape Architectural Accreditation
    Board (LAAB), 19, 47
Landscape architecture:
  coining of the term, 6
  collaboration with other disciplines, 29
  competition with other disciplines, 29–30
  education, 19–20
  practice in the U.S., 13–15
  professional practice terms, 4
  services, 77–78
Laws, 158
Legal competency, 172
Legal exposure, limiting, 158
Legal issues, 152–170
Liability, 153
  limitations, 175
  for materials, 165
  for workmen, 164–165
License examination, 41
Licensure, 41, 50–53
Life-cycle cost, 150

Management and administration, 45
Market niches, 102
Market-driven criteria, landscape
    architectural services, 115
Marketing, 114–121
  documents, 127
  plan, 106
Master of Landscape Architecture,
    43–44
Master Spec, 181
Materials lien, 165
McHarg, Ian, 12
Medical insurance, 70
Members, ASLA, 49
Moonlighting, 110–111
Multiplier basis, fees, 174
Mutual consent, 172

Name recognition, 120
National Environmental Policy Act, 13
National Environmental Protection Act
    (1970), 35
Needs assessment, 144
Negligence, 153
Negotiation, 146–147
Nontraditional forms of practice, 38–39

Occupational Safety and Health
    Administration (OSHA), 161

Office:
  hours, 70
  location and setting, 102–104
  log, 132–133
  management:
    autocratic style, 94–95
    facilitative style, 94
    future of, 95–96
    pyramidal management structure, 94
    team-building style, 94
    top-down chain of command, 95
    vertical management structure, 94
  manual, 108
  records, 130
Olmsted, Frederick Law, 6, 9–10, 13
Or equal clause, 183–184
Ordinances, 153, 158
Outline specifications, 146
Overtime, 70
Ownership opportunities, 110

Paper trail, 167–168
Park planning and design, 9
Parmentier, Andre, 8
Partnership, 89–91
Percentage basis, fees, 174
Percentage of work completed, 175
Performance, 153
  bond(s), 159, 167
  review, 110
  specifications, 179–180
  stipulations, 154
Personal interview, 110
Personal journal, 128, 208
Personnel:
  management, 108
  records, 127
Plan Coordination, 184
Planning, 79–80
Planning process, 79
Portfolio, 64, 67
Postconstruction:
  evaluation, 150
  services, 149
Practice act, 50–51
Predesign services, 143–144
Preinterview preparations, 67–68
Preproposal meeting, 121
Prime consultant, 172
Principal, 69
Private practice, 35–36
Problem:
  definition, 80

Problem (*Continued*)
 solving, 27–28
Professional:
 behavior, 18–19, 21–22
 conduct, 16
  ASLA Code of, 22–23
  code of, 17, 21
  guidelines for, 23
 development, 40
  continuum of, 40–54
 license, 44–45
 organizations, 47–50
 practice liability, 87
 registration, 50–53
 services, 27
Profit-sharing, 70
Programming, 143
 of functional elements, 145
Project:
 budgeting, 144
 closeout, 137
 feasibility, 145
 landscape architect, 187
 management, 45, 111
 manager, 69
 process, 137–138
 scope, 136
Project-related documents, 127
Proprietary specifications, 180
Public:
 law(s), 153, 156–157, 160
 practice, 32–35
 safety and welfare, 153
Punchlist, 137, 203

Quality Assurance, 184
Quitclaim, 162

Raises, 69
Record-keeping taxonomies,
 131–132
Records management, 107
Reference(s), 109–110
 documents, 127
 specifications, 180–181
Referrals, 120
Regulations, 153, 158
Request for Proposals (RFP), 121
Request for Services, 121
Responsibility, 153, 173–174
Resume, 64–66

Roman law, 156
Rose, James, 11

Salary, 69, 110
Schematic design, 144–145
Scope of work, 174
Scott, Geraldine Knight, 11
Sesoned practitioner, 46
Services permits, 161
Site:
 analysis, 144
 selection, 144
Skill requirements, 83
Societal imperative, 20
Sole proprietorship, 88–89
Sole source basis, 121
Solicited proposals, 120–121
Space schematics, 143
Special warranty, 162
Standard Form of Agreement between
  Owner and Architect for Special
  Services, 176
Standards of care, 18, 159, 160, 184
State license(s), 50–51
Statute, 152
 of limitations, 125, 159
Subconsultant, 172
Submittal(s), 140
 packages, 130
Supervisor(s), 71
Supplemental services, 150
Surety:
 bonds, 166
 company, 167
Sweet's Catalogue, 181

Tangible products, 123
Target customer groups, 100
Targeted firms, 64
Tax:
 law, 153–154
 liability, 87
Technical specifications, 177–185
Termination, 175
Terms of employment, 68–71
Third-party claims, 148, 166
Title law, 50
Tort law, 153
Trial period, 70–71

Uniform Building Code, 181

Unsolicited proposals, 121
Utilities permits, 161

Vested interest clause, 70

Warranty items, 149
Washington, George, 8

Wild and Scenic Rivers Act, 13
Wilderness Act, 13
Work in progress, 161

Yosemite National Park, 9

Zoning, 160–161